Researching Language and Literacy in Social Context

Language and Literacy in Social Context

This Reader is part of an Open University Course (E825) forming one module in the MA in Education Programme. The selection is related to other material available to students. Opinions expressed in individual articles are not necessarily those of the course team or of the University.

Other volumes published as part of this course by Multilingual Matters Ltd in association with The Open University:

Language and Literacy in Social Practice
    JANET MAYBIN (ed.)
Language, Literacy and Learning in Educational Practice
    BARRY STIERER and JANET MAYBIN (eds)
Media Texts: Authors and Readers
    DAVID GRADDOL and OLIVER BOYD-BARRETT (eds)

Other books of related interest, published by Multilingual Matters Ltd:

Critical Theory and Classroom Talk
    ROBERT YOUNG
Language Policy Across the Curriculum
    DAVID CORSON
Language, Minority Education and Gender
    DAVID CORSON
School to Work Transition in Japan
    KAORI OKANO
Reading Acquisition Processes
    G. B. THOMPSON, W. E. TUNMER and T. NICHOLSON (eds)
Worlds of Literacy
    D. BARTON, M. HAMILTON and R. IVANIC (eds)

Please contact us for the latest book information:
Multilingual Matters Ltd,
Frankfurt Lodge, Clevedon Hall, Victoria Road,
Clevedon, Avon BS21 7SJ, England.

Language and Literacy in Social Context

Researching Language and Literacy in Social Context

A Reader edited by

David Graddol, Janet Maybin and Barry Stierer

at The Open University

MULTILINGUAL MATTERS LTD
Clevedon • Philadelphia • Adelaide
in association with
THE OPEN UNIVERSITY

Library of Congress Cataloging in Publication Data

Researching Language and Literacy in Social Practice: A Reader/Edited by
David Graddol, Janet Maybin and Barry Stierer
p. cm.
'Language and Literacy in Social Context'.
Includes bibliographical references and index.
1. Sociolinguistics. 2. Language and education. 3. Literacy.
I. Graddol, David. II. Maybin, Janet, 1950- . III. Stierer, Barry.
P40.R47   1993   93-23198
306.4'4–dc20   CIP

British Library Cataloguing in Publication Data

A CIP catalogue record for this book is available from the British Library.

ISBN 1-85359-222-6 (hbk)
ISBN 1-85359-221-8 (pbk)

Multilingual Matters Ltd

UK: Frankfurt Lodge, Clevedon Hall, Victoria Road, Clevedon, Avon BS21 7SJ.
USA: 1900 Frost Road, Suite 101, Bristol, PA 19007, USA.
Australia: P.O. Box 6025, 83 Gilles Street, Adelaide, SA 5000, Australia.

Cover design by Bob Jones Associates.
Index compiled by Meg Davies (Society of Indexers).
Printed and bound in Great Britain by WBC Ltd, Bridgend.

Contents

Preface

This is one of four volumes of readings compiled as a part of an Open University MA course called *Language and Literacy in Social Context* (E825). The course draws on a variety of work in sociolinguistics, grammar, semiotics, media studies, anthropology, psychology and education and the interdisciplinary nature of the course is reflected in the articles collected together in this series. Each volume contains a mix of classic and newly published material which will be of interest to a wide audience.

Anyone who studies these papers will inevitably be drawn in to some of the most exciting intellectual debates of the closing years of the 20th century. The authors deal with many of the 'big issues' relating to life in the postmodern world — identity, social relations, social control, ideology, freedom, democracy, power, aesthetics, pleasure — but always with a concern for the way these very abstract notions manifest themselves in individual lives.

I would like to take the opportunity of thanking all those who, in various ways, supported, encouraged (and sometimes cautioned), the course team during the production process. In particular, I should mention Myra Barrs, Rebecca Bunting, Jane Cooper, Norman Fairclough, Gordon Gibson, Gunther Kress, Gemma Moss, Brian Street, Terry Threadgold, Gill Watson, many students and tutors of a predecessor course on language and literacy (E815), and colleagues in the School of Education at The Open University.

David Graddol
Course Chair

Sources

We would like to thank the authors and publishers concerned for kindly granting permission to reproduce copyright material in this reader. Every effort has been made to trace the correct copyright owners, both authors and publishers, as listed in the Contents and by chapter below.

1. Based on Chapter 1 of *Reading Ethnographic Research* by M. Hammersley. Harlow: Longman, 1990.
2. From the Introduction to *Researching Language: Issues of Power and Method* by D. Cameron *et al.* London: Routledge, 1992.
3. Commissioned article.
4. From *Language and Education* 4 (2), 103-115. Clevedon: Multilingual Matters, 1990.
5. Commissioned article.
6. From *Language and Education* 5 (3), 161-176. Clevedon: Multilingual Matters, 1991.
7. From *Literacy and Schooling* by D. Bloome. Norwood: Ablex Publishing Co., 1992.
8. First published this volume, © Author.
9. From *English in Education* 22, 48-65. Sheffield: NATE, 50 Broadfield Road, Broadfield Business Centre, Sheffield S8 0XS, UK.
10. From Open University Study Pack *Talk and Learning, 5-16* (P535). Milton Keynes: The Open University.
11. First published this volume, © Author.
12. First published this volume, © Author.
13. From *Writing in the Community* by D. Barton and R. Ivanic. Newbury Park: Sage, 1991.

Introduction

The papers included in this volume are all concerned with empirical investigations of language and literacy in social context and provide models of a kind useful to individual researchers contemplating small scale studies. The articles demonstrate aspects of method, analysis, and the use of empirical data in presentation and argument. Much of the research reported here took place in an educational context, but the methods and techniques exemplified are ones which can easily be extended to non educational settings and, indeed, anywhere that people talk, read or write in the course of leisure or work activities.

Chapters 5, 8, 11 and 12 appear here for the first time. Chapters 1 and 3 have been specially revised by their authors for this volume.

Part 1: Principles and Approaches

1. Martyn Hammersley

For those researching language within the field of education, ethnographic methods hold a particular appeal because of their attention to contextual detail within small naturalistic settings and to insider interpretations and meanings. Martyn Hammersley outlines the various research strategies which make up ethnography and briefly traces their history. He examines arguments about ethnography's lack of scientific method, and also criticisms from other directions of its failure to break away more sharply from the natural science model. In particular he discusses problems concerning generalisation, bias, precision and control of variables, and he also explores issues raised more recently within critical theory and feminism concerning the politics of social research and particularly the relationship between researcher and researched.

2. Deborah Cameron *et al.*

This chapter is concerned with the politics of the research process and in particular with the relationship between researcher and researched. The authors explore whether, and how, social research can be empowering for its subjects. They discuss the consequences of three possible positions which researchers can take up: ethics, advocacy and empowerment. They argue that the first two, which aim for scientific objectivity, are not empowering. Empowering research, they suggest, moves outside the traditional scientific paradigm in its use of interactive methods, respect for subjects' own agendas and the practice of providing feedback and sharing knowledge.

3. Joan Swann

Joan Swann discusses some of the practical techniques involved in observing and recording language interaction in natural settings. Starting with the question of what to observe and finishing with a discussion of quantitative and qualitative analyses of transcript data, she leads the reader through many of the practical stages which face any researcher: resolving ethical issues, techniques of systematic observation, taking field notes, making audio and video recordings, laying out a transcript, how to record nonverbal behaviour. Swann provides some useful illustrations from the unpublished materials of experienced researchers.

Part 2: Research in Practice

4. Eve Gregory

Eve Gregory presents a close analysis of spoken exchanges between Tajul, a five year old Bengali-speaking child, and his teacher as they share stories during the first few months following Tajul's start at school. Gregory's interpretation of these exchanges suggests that, through skilful intervention by the teacher, a number of culturally-embedded 'reading lessons' are being learned. Gregory's research casts the classroom activity of shared story reading as a cultural event rather than as an opportunity for certain specific cognitive skills to be taught and learned. In this sense, her overriding research question was not 'How is reading learned and how should it be taught?' but instead 'What counts as reading in the classroom, and how do children acquire the knowledge needed in order to display what counts as reading?'. She uses the concept of 'negotiation' to show that, through repeated shared story reading events, Tajul gradually becomes initiated into 'a cultural practice and the uses of language relevant to it as they are performed in school'. In this sense Tajul's acquisition of reading competence is inseparable from his acquisition of broader knowledge about dominant British cultural norms.

5. Beverley Naidoo

Beverley Naidoo examines the attitudes towards racism shown by 13–14 year olds in an all-white school. She studies their responses to selected books, all of them written from a perspective strongly indicting racism. Quite apart from the interesting issues raised in her research about the nature of racism, the project was informed by a theoretical perspective on the relationship between readers, writers and texts which contributes to an understanding of reading and writing activities in the classroom. Naidoo's project is 'action research', underpinned by a strong, personal and explicit commitment to antiracism and cultural change through the use of literature. She rejects the idea that there was a 'message' she wished the pupils to understand which was invested unproblematically in the texts. Rather, she saw the texts as catalysts for discussion and thought. She acknowledges explicitly that each pupil's response to the texts, and the degree to which they were challenged by the ideas within them, were filtered through the context in which they were read, with the context including such elements as the pupil's past experience (or lack of it, in this case) their cultural and political attitudes, and the way in which the texts were introduced in the classroom.

6. A.P. Biggs and Viv Edwards

A.P. Biggs and Viv Edwards examine the interactions of five different teachers working with multi-ethnic classes of five and six year olds in the UK. Through a systematic statistical analysis of significant features of the talk, Biggs and Edwards found that teachers interacted less frequently with black children than with white, that they had fewer exchanges lasting more than thirty seconds with black children, and that they spent less time with black children discussing the particular task which had been set. Their quantitative evidence was extended with qualitative data through observations and interviews, and these revealed some of the underlying assumptions and attitudes on the part of the teachers in the study which, the researchers assert, were communicated to pupils through the talk. Such an analysis exemplifies the way in which discourse is determined by and at the same time perpetuates dominant ideologies, through its capacity to position participants.

7. David Bloome

Through a detailed micro-ethnographic analysis of reading events video-taped in an American classroom of fourteen year olds, David Bloome argues that the social interactional processes involved in teaching reading strongly influence what students learn. He uses his analysis to suggest that students' experience of interacting with texts is mediated by a frame constructed partly through the patterns of teacher–student interaction and partly by the tasks presented. He claims that this frame involves students reproducing pieces of text rather than engaging with their content, interacting with the teacher to produce an essentially vacuous 'procedural display' of learning and adopting a passive, alienated attitude towards extended text.

8. Janet Maybin

Janet Maybin argues that children's informal talk provides an important site for the collaborative construction of knowledge and understanding. In order to research this talk, however, she suggests that we need to move away from the individualistic models of speaker and listener underlying traditional views of communication towards the more dialogic model emerging from the writings of Vygotsky, Bakhtin and Volosinov. She uses radio microphones, observation and interviews to collect data about 10–12 year olds' informal talk throughout the school day. She analyses the structure and contents of this talk focusing particularly on how collaboration is accomplished and on how children's reporting and taking on of other people's voices contributes both to individual development and to their induction into particular cultural practices.

9. Joan Swann and David Graddol

The departure point of this study is the common research finding that women say less than men in mixed sex interactions. In the classroom, a similar inequality is often to be found between girls and boys and this gives rise to specific educational concerns given the important role played by talk in learning. Joan Swann and David Graddol compare mechanisms of turn-taking during interactions between teacher and pupils in two classrooms. How do individual pupils get to speak? What part is played by the teacher and other pupils? The authors analyse transactions recorded by video camera, and show the importance of the teacher's gaze in regulating pupil's turns. They conclude, however, that girls, boys and the teacher all play an important role in managing turn taking.

10. Julie Fisher

Julie Fisher examines the quality and quantity of boys' and girls' contributions to mixed and single-sex small group discussions. Fisher's article represents an interesting example of a small-scale classroom-based research project, which combined a carefully-structured and partly quantitative approach with a close focus on a small number of children in a single classroom. Her findings suggest that there is no direct relationship between the quantity of an individual's contribution to a group discussion and the actual degree of collaboration achieved. In particular, Fisher shows that boys can dominate small group discussions even when the volume of their contributions is smaller than that of some girls. Fisher concludes by arguing for a principled intervention by teachers to ensure that both the content and quality of group discussions provides genuine equality of opportunity. The assessment implications here are clear: 'This study suggests that, if teachers do not intervene in peer discussion, the voices of the girls and no doubt quieter boys may not be heard and the assessment of their performance may be a very unequal affair indeed'.

11. Jennifer Coates

Jennifer Coates critically examines the model of turn-taking in conversation which has dominated research in this area for over two decades: that presented by Sacks, Schegloff and Jefferson (1974) (SSJ). This model assumes that speakers behave as autonomous subjects, each making their own contribution to a conversation according to accepted norms of turn-taking behaviour. Coates argues that the model fails to describe and explain her own conversational data, taken from women's friendship groups. Here, turns are often jointly constructed by more than one participant and 'two speakers can function as a single voice'. She concludes that the SSJ turn-taking mechanism does not apply to all social contexts. The article demonstrates techniques of presenting complex conversational data, and shows how fragments of data can be used to illustrate and develop theoretical argument.

12. Meeri Hellsten

Meeri Hellsten is concerned with issues of language and culture, of minority language rights, and processes of socialisation in bilingual communities. Her approach is an empirical one: a corpus linguistic analysis of the textbooks created for beginning readers in Australia and in the Samish community of Northern Scandinavia. She concludes that very different representations of the world are offered to young children in the two communities and are revealed by careful textual scrutiny. She examines gender bias, for example, in the verbs which have boys and girls as subjects, and in the authority relations implied in the way intellectual activities are described. One important cultural difference between the Australian and Samish texts lies in the adult constructions of childhood. Why, asks Hellsten, do the children's books of minority indigenous peoples not display the same preoccupation with fantasy worlds as those characteristic of western societies?

13. David Barton and Sarah Padmore

This study contributes to a growing body of research documenting the social and cultural role of literacy within people's everyday lives. David Barton and Sarah Padmore carried out ethnographic research into the literacy practices of people in a North of England local community. They used interviews and participant observation to collect data about their reading and writing, and about their attitudes to literacy. The authors discuss the ways in which peoples' literacy practices are related to their social networks, and to the roles they take on in different areas of their lives.

Their chapter focuses on writing, and demonstrates the wide range of practices of a number of individuals, most of the whom have expressed problems with reading or writing at some point in their adult lives.

1 Introducing Ethnography

MARTYN HAMMERSLEY

The term 'ethnography' is not clearly defined in common usage, and there is some disagreement about what count and do not count as examples of it. Furthermore, the meaning of the term overlaps with that of several others—such as 'qualitative method', 'interpretative research', 'case study', 'participant observation', 'life history method', 'discourse analysis', etc.; and none of these terms is used in a very precisely defined way either.[1] This diversity and looseness of terminology reflects some dissensus even on fundamental issues among advocates of these approaches. It also sometimes results from a certain vagueness in thinking about methodological issues that arises from a widespread emphasis among ethnographers on the primacy of research practice over 'theory' about how to do it. Sometimes this amounts to an anti-methodological and anti-theoretical prejudice. Many ethnographers tend to distrust general formulations, whether about human social life or about how to do research, in favour of a concern with particulars. But however much one distrusts theory, one cannot escape it. As we shall see, the practice of ethnography is surrounded by a host of philosophical ideas. And while we must recognise the limits of abstract reasoning, we should press it as far as it will go in seeking to provide useful understanding.

I will examine some of the philosophical ideas associated with ethnography later in this chapter. First, though, I want to look briefly at the forms of research design, data collection and analysis that are characteristic of it, and to sketch something of ethnography's history.

Ethnography as Method

In terms of method, generally speaking, the term 'ethnography' refers to social research that has most of the following features:

(a) It is concerned with analysis of empirical data that are systematically selected for the purpose.

(b) Those data come from 'real world' contexts, rather than being produced under experimental conditions created by the researcher.

1

(c) Data are gathered from a *range* of sources, but observation and/or relatively informal conversations are usually the main ones.

(d) The approach to data collection is 'unstructured', in the sense that it does not involve following through a detailed plan set up at the beginning; nor are the categories used for interpreting what people say and do pre-given or fixed.

(e) The focus is a single setting or group, of relatively small scale; or a small number of these. In life history research the focus may even be a single individual.

(f) The analysis of the data involves interpretation of the meanings and functions of human actions and mainly takes the form of verbal descriptions and explanations, with quantification and statistical analysis playing a subordinate role at most.

Looking at the contents of this volume in these terms, it would not be unreasonable to characterise as ethnographic the work of Janet Maybin on children's talk or David Bloome's study of reading events, for instance. But there is no hard and fast line between these and other work that does not share all of the features listed, such as Biggs and Edwards' quantitative analysis of teacher–pupil talk.

As a set of methods, ethnography is not far removed from the sort of approach that we all use in everyday life to make sense of our surroundings. It is less specialised and technically sophisticated than approaches like the experiment or the social survey; though all research methods have their historical origins in the ways in which human beings gain information about their world in everyday life. The more specific origins of ethnography lie in the writings of travellers concerned to inform their fellows about other societies, whether it is Herodotus exploring the western provinces of the Persian Empire (Rowe, 1965) or Hans Stade reporting on his captivity by the 'wild tribes of Eastern Brazil' (Pratt, 1986). And the societies explored were not always so geographically or culturally distant: thus, in the nineteenth century we have the French aristocrat Toqueville reporting on *Democracy in America*, Friedrich Engels, the son of a German industrialist, investigating the lives of Lancashire factory workers, and Henry Mayhew writing newspaper articles about the working class underlife of London (Toqueville, 1835; Engels, 1892 and 1840; Mayhew, 1861–2 and 1971).

The writings of such people form the early history of what we would today call social or cultural anthropology and sociology.[2] However, the data on which these reports were based were usually unsystematic and sometimes misleading; and the analysis was frequently speculative and evaluative (though often valuable for all that). One of the most important features of the development of the social science disciplines in the nineteenth and early twentieth centuries was the attempt to overcome such deficiencies of earlier accounts. The influence of the natural sciences was particularly important here. Even in the nineteenth century many anthropologists relied on the reports of travellers and missionaries for their data, but from the turn of the century onwards it became widely accepted that it was necessary for them to collect their own data, and to do so in a systematic and rigorous manner. Initially, this tended to take the form of expeditions that were primarily concerned with collecting artefacts, both material and non-material (such as myths). Later, particularly through the influence of Bronislaw Malinowski, it came to be required that the anthropologist live among the people being studied, learn their language, and observe their lives firsthand.[3] In addition, anthropologists became much more concerned with avoiding the speculative excesses of their predecessors and with adopting a scientific approach to the handling of evidence. Since the early decades of the century, ethnography has been the staple research method employed by social and cultural anthropologists, though they have sometimes combined it with social survey work and even with the use of psychological tests.

Sociologists have also employed ethnographic methods since early in the twentieth century, though it has not occupied as central a place in their discipline as in anthropology. One of the earliest developments here arose in what is sometimes referred to as the 'Chicago School of Sociology'. Sociologists working at the University of Chicago became increasingly preoccupied with the character of their city. They saw it as a kind of natural laboratory in which the diversity and processes of change characteristic of human behaviour could be studied. Some of the work carried out was statistical in character, but much of it took the form of what was then called 'case study'. This involved detailed investigation of a single case, or a small number of cases, such as areas of the city, city organisations, or even individual people. These studies used methods that approximated the ethnography of today, though they tended to place greater emphasis on written documents.[4]

Methodological Debates about Ethnography

Debates about ethnography can be broadly divided into two categories, with the first being pre-eminent in discussions in the 1960s and 70s, the second becoming more salient in the 1980s:

(1) Debates centring on criticisms of ethnography for not meeting the criteria of science, as represented by the work of natural scientists.

(2) Arguments that ethnography has not broken sharply enough with, or moved far enough away from, quantitative research and the model of natural science.

I shall look at each of these two sorts of criticism in turn.

Criticism of ethnography for not being 'scientific'

Competition with quantitative approaches to research, and especially with experimental and survey research, has long shaped the way in which ethnographers have thought about their work, raising the question: Is ethnography scientific? By the 1960s, across several disciplines and areas, quantitative research in the form of experimentalism and social surveys had become highly developed, and sophisticated methodological literatures had grown up around them which took it for granted that they were implementing scientific method. While there was disagreement about some points, there was considerable agreement on the basics; and in large part this was framed in terms of the positivist outlook that had dominated the philosophy of science in the 1940s and early 50s. Central here was the idea that what was required in empirical research was clear and operational specification of hypotheses; the selection of a research design that allowed those hypotheses to be tested, either by the physical manipulation of variables (as in experiments) or through statistical analysis of large samples of cases (as in survey research); along with the assessment of measurement error by means of reliability (and, more rarely, validity) tests.

Ethnographers responded in several ways to this influential view of the nature of social science methodology:

> Some claimed that ethnography is *more* scientific (that is, closer in character to natural science) than quantitative research. In the early decades of the century this was argued on the grounds that case study can produce universal laws not just the probabilistic findings characteristic of statistical method (Znaniecki, 1934). This argument is rarely used today, both because of the statistical character of some parts of more recent work in physics (notably quantum theory), and because most ethnographers have lost faith in the possibility of discovering laws. In recent times, it is more common to find the scientific character of ethnography being justified on the grounds that it is more suited than are experimental and survey research to the nature of human behaviour, in particular its processual and meaning-laden character (Bruyn, 1966; Blumer 1969; Harré & Secord, 1973).

> A second sort of response involves broadly accepting the view of sociological method characteristic of quantitative research, but treating ethnography as distinctive in its suitability to particular phases of the research process or to particular research problems. For example, it might be regarded as especially appropriate in the pilot stages of social surveys or the debriefing phases of experiments; and/or it might be seen as well-suited to the study of groups whose small size or secrecy make them inaccessible to survey research.

On this view, also, ethnography may be usefully combined with other methods, which are assumed to have complementary strengths and weaknesses.

A third position is that ethnography represents a different kind of science to that characteristic of the natural sciences. Here quantitative methods may be criticised for aping the natural sciences. Often associated with this is the claim that ethnography is idiographic rather than nomothetic (that it focuses on the unique as much as the general), and/or interpretative rather than observational (that the understanding of human behaviour always involves interpretation not mere physical description).

In their methodological writings ethnographers often combine these three positions in various ways. The first and third are typically given the most emphasis, with ethnography viewed as based on assumptions about human society and how it can be best understood that diverge from those implicit in most quantitative research. These assumptions may also be found in milder versions among advocates of the second position. They can be summarised under the headings of naturalism, understanding and discovery:

(1) *Naturalism*. This is the view that the aim of social research is to capture the character of naturally occurring human behaviour, and that this can only be achieved by first-hand contact with it, not by theoretical speculation or by inferences from what people do in artificial settings like experiments or from what they say in interviews about what they do in other settings. In the study of language a similar concern with naturalism lay behind the shift from the study of invented examples of language-use, which was characteristic of influential approaches to linguistics like transformational grammar, or examples elicited in psychological laboratories, to the collection and analysis of naturally occurring talk in everyday situations or informal interviews, as for example in the 'ethnography of communication' (Gumperz & Hymes, 1972).

So, on the basis of naturalism, ethnographers insist on grounding their analyses in actual data and carrying out research in 'natural' settings, settings that exist independently of the research process, rather than in those set up specifically for the purposes of research. Furthermore, in studying those settings the researcher seeks to minimise her or his effects on the behaviour of the people being studied. The aim of this is to increase the chances that what is discovered in the setting will be generalisable to other similar settings that have not been researched. Finally, the notion of naturalism implies that social events and processes must be explained in terms of their relationship to the context in which they occur. What is involved here is an appeal to what is sometimes called the 'pattern model of explanation' as against the covering law model characteristic of positivist philosophy of science.[5]

(2) *Understanding*. Central here is the argument that human actions differ from the behaviour of physical objects, and even from that of other animals: they do not consist simply of fixed responses or even of learned responses to stimuli, but involve *interpretation* of stimuli and the *construction* of responses. Sometimes this argument reflects a complete rejection of the concept of causality as inapplicable to the social world, and an insistence on the freely constructed character of human actions and institutions. But it may equally be argued that causal relations *are* to be found in the social world, but that they differ from the 'mechanical' causality typical of physical phenomena. From this point of view, if we are to be able to explain human actions effectively we must gain an understanding of the cultural perspectives on which they are based. That this is necessary is obvious when we are studying a society that is alien to us, since we will find much of what we see and hear puzzling. However, ethnographers argue that it is just as important when we are studying more familiar settings. Indeed, when a setting is familiar the danger of misunderstanding is especially great. It is argued that we cannot assume that we already know others' perspectives, even in our own society, because particular groups and individuals develop distinctive worldviews. This is especially true in large complex societies. Ethnic, occupational, and small informal groups (even individual families or school classes) develop distinctive ways of orienting to the world, often signalled in the use of distinctive argot, that may need to be understood if their behaviour is to be explained.

Ethnographers argue, then, that it is necessary to learn the culture of the group one is studying, and experience their way of life, before one can produce valid explanations for their behaviour. This is the reason for the centrality of participant observation and unstructured interviewing to ethnographic method. This sort of argument also lies behind advocacy of practitioner research, for example of teachers carrying out research in their own classrooms and schools.[6]

(3) *Discovery*. Another feature of ethnographic thinking is a conception of the research process as inductive or discovery-based; rather than as being limited to the testing of explicit hypotheses. It is argued that if one approaches a phenomenon with a set of hypotheses one may fail to discover the true nature of that phenomenon, being blinded by the assumptions built into the hypotheses. Instead, one should begin research with minimal assumptions so as to maximise one's capacity for learning. It is for this reason that ethnographers

rarely begin their research with specific hypotheses. Rather, they have a general interest in some type of social phenomena and/or in some theoretical issue or practical problem. The focus of the research is narrowed and sharpened, and perhaps even changed substantially, as it proceeds. Similarly, and in parallel, theoretical ideas that frame descriptions and explanations of what is observed are developed over the course of the research. Such ideas are regarded as a valuable outcome of, not a precondition for, research.

These methodological principles are closely related, indeed they overlap; and, as I have indicated, they provide the rationale for the specific features of ethnographic method that I outlined earlier. They are also the basis for much ethnographic criticism of quantitative research for failing to capture the true nature of human social behaviour: because it relies on the study of artificial settings and/or on what people say rather than what they do; because it seeks to reduce meanings to what is 'observable'; and because it reifies social phenomena by treating them as more clearly defined and stable than they are, and as mechanical products of social and psychological factors.

In turn, of course, quantitative researchers have questioned the scientific status of ethnography. Let us look briefly at the sort of debate there has been on this issue. Here are some of the criticisms that have been made of ethnographic research, along with the sort of answers given to them by ethnographers.[7]

Criticism: Ethnographic research suffers from a lack of precision as a result of the absence of quantification. For example, words like 'often' and 'frequently' are used instead of more precise numerical specifications. In this way it is impressionistic.

Answer: There is nothing intrinsic to ethnography which rejects quantification, and indeed ethnographic studies do sometimes employ it. However, precision is not always important. Where differences are large and obvious it may be that they can be reported in relatively imprecise ways without loss. Furthermore, there is the danger of overprecision: by insisting on precise quantitative measures we may produce figures that are more precise than we can justify given the nature of the data available, and which are therefore misleading.

Criticism: Ethnographic observation and interviewing are subjective in the sense that they are not guided by a structure (in the form of a questionnaire or observational schedule) that would maximise the chances that another observer or interviewer would produce the same data. As a result, ethnographic data are peculiarly subject to bias.

Answer: It is true that in ethnographic research what data are collected depends on the researcher, and to one degree or another reflects her or his personal characteristics. But all knowledge is personal and cultural in some sense. At the same time, ethnographers use techniques designed to ensure that their findings are not idiosyncratic, for example by comparing data from different sources, a technique sometimes referred to as 'triangulation'. Conversely, the structuring of data that quantitative research employs to overcome subjectivity has reactive effects. In other words, people react to the structure itself, thereby increasing the chances that the behaviour studied is an artifact of the research process and not representative of the phenomena purportedly being studied. Nor does the use of schedules solve the problem of subjectivity because the same structure can be interpreted differently by different people. For example, the same question asked by an interviewer at the same point in an interview may mean different things to different people if they have different perspectives.

Criticism: By studying very small samples ethnographers produce findings that are of little value because they are not generalisable.

Answer: The choice of small samples represents a trade-off between studying cases in depth or in breadth. Ethnography usually sacrifices the latter for the former; survey research does the reverse. And in sacrificing depth, survey researchers both lose relevant information and run the risk of misunderstanding key features of the cases they study. Moreover, one can make claims about the representativeness of findings without relying on statistical sampling, for example by comparing the features of the cases studied with aggregate data about the population. Equally, one may study a small selection of cases that are designed to represent key dimensions in terms of which the population is assumed to be structured. (It is worth pointing out that social surveys rarely employ pure random sampling, they too rely on assumptions about the 'stratification' of the population.) Ethnographers also sometimes argue that what they are concerned with is not empirical generalisation but rather with making theoretical inferences, and that this does not require the case studied to be representative.

Criticism: By studying natural settings and only small samples ethnographers rule out the possibility of physical or statistical control of variables, and as a result they are not able to identify causal relationships.

Answer: Even if they exist in the social world, causal relationships are not of the same kind as those to be found in the physical world. Thus, they are not accessible to techniques modelled on investigations in physics. By documenting processes occurring over time and/or by means of comparative analysis of cases, ethnography is able to trace patterns of relationships among social phenomena in their natural context in a way that neither experiments nor social surveys can do.

Criticism: A key feature of science is the possibility of replication, of other scientists checking the findings of an experiment by repeating it. Since ethnography does not follow a well-designed and explicit procedure that is replicable, its findings cannot be checked by others and are therefore unscientific.

Answer: Replication is not always possible in natural science, and it is not always carried out even when it is possible. This indicates that replication is not the only means by which scientists assess one another's work, and is therefore not an essential feature of science. The fact that it may not be possible in ethnography does not therefore detract from the validity of ethnographic findings.

Such debate, not always so politely expressed, has gone on for many years; but in some fields in recent times it has largely subsided in favour of a spirit of detente (Rist, 1970; Smith & Heshusius, 1986). One reason is probably that each side has become much more heterogeneous, so that other targets for criticism and issues for debate have emerged. Since the 1960s and 70s, though, when debate about the scientific status of ethnography was at its height in educational research, there has been a trend toward increased adoption of ethnography, and qualitative method generally.

Up to now, I have discussed criticisms of ethnography for not being scientific that have come from quantitative researchers. While that has been the most influential source it has not been the only one. Another is an approach to sociology called ethnomethodology. Ethnomethodologists' conception of science is influenced by the phenomenological movement in philosophy, a movement preoccupied with rigorous explication of the processes by which our perceptions and interpretations of the world are produced. Ethnomethodologists have been very critical of quantitative research, on the grounds that it has not lived up to its own scientific ideal of producing accounts of social phenomena that are rigorously grounded in the analysis of data. Thus, ethnomethodologists have pointed out that although quantitative researchers typically reject commonsense knowledge as unscientific, they nevertheless implicitly depend on it and on the practical forms of reasoning associated with it. This is because all interpretation of human actions relies on background knowledge and involves practical judgment. Of course, this argument applies equally to qualitative research, and ethnomethodologists have therefore extended their criticism to conventional qualitative work as well (Cicourel, 1964; Bittner, 1979). They argue that detailed analysis of the role of commonsense reasoning and knowledge in the way people make sense of the world is at the very least an essential first step if social and educational research is to be rigorous. More than this, though, some of them suggest that because of the context-dependent character of practical reasoning, it can never provide a foundation for a rigorous scientific analysis of social phenomena. Only the study of practical reasoning itself is open to rigorous analysis, since such research is in effect self-explicating. One of the most productive consequences of ethnomethodology has been the development of the field of conversation analysis, and of approaches to discourse analysis deriving from it.[8] The article by Coates in this volume, dealing with turn-taking in talk amongst women, draws on and illustrates this work.

Much of the methodological thinking of ethnographers has been shaped, then, by a concern to place their work in relation to natural science and quantitative method. This has often involved attempts to draw a sharp line between ethnography on the one hand and journalism and fiction on the other, despite (or perhaps because of) the similarities. In recent years, however, there has been a noticeable downplaying, if not rejection, of the scientific model among some ethnographers and increased emphasis on the parallels with literature and the humanities. This probably reflects the growth of questioning about the nature and value of science generally, on the one hand, and the rise of widespread interest in literary theory on the other. It has led to criticism of ethnographic work, from inside and outside, for not making a sharp enough break with the model of natural science and with quantitative method.

Criticisms of ethnography for being too 'scientific'

It is not always easy to tell the difference between criticisms of ethnography for being insufficiently scientific from criticisms of it for being too scientific. Much depends, of course, on the model of science that is being presupposed by the critics. And the past 30 or so years have seen increasing disagreement about the nature of scientific method, along with a trend towards de-emphasising the differences between science and other forms of inquiry and knowledge.

Until the middle of this century, nineteenth century confidence in scientific method as *the* source of knowledge remained predominant. But, partly as a result of major reconstructions in physics and the demonstration of its terrible potential for destruction, this confidence began to be undermined. The philosophy of science in the 1950s experienced the collapse of what had previously been a substantial consensus about the nature of science, founded on logical positivism: that it involved the induction of knowledge from a base of observations that were themselves certain, the process of induction transmitting certainty to the knowledge produced. Doubts about the idea of observational certainties and of the possibility of logical induction were not new, but they and their implications came to be taken seriously much more widely.

Growing doubts about the nature of scientific methodology were symbolised by the impact of Thomas Kuhn's book *The Structure of Scientific Revolutions*, first published in 1962 (Kuhn, 1970). Kuhn argued against views of the history of natural science that portrayed it as a process of cumulative development, achieved by rational investigation founded on evidence. He showed that the work of the scientists involved in many of the major developments of scientific knowledge of the past were shaped by theoretical assumptions about the world that were not themselves based on empirical research; and many of which are now judged to be false. Kuhn further claimed that the history of science, rather than displaying the gradual build-up of knowledge, is punctuated by periods of revolution when the theoretical assumptions underlying the 'paradigm' in terms of which scientists in a particular field have previously operated are challenged and replaced. (An example is the shift from Newtonian physics to relativity and quantum theory in the early part of the twentieth century.) The replacement of one paradigm by another, according to Kuhn, does not occur on the basis simply of rational assessment of evidence. Paradigms are incommensurable: they picture the world in incompatible ways, so that data themselves are interpreted differently by those working within different paradigms. Paradigm shifts occur more through representatives of the old paradigm retiring or dying and those of the new one replacing them than by rational persuasion.[9]

Others have taken these ideas further, for example rejecting the notion of scientific method and the claims of science to produce knowledge (even of the physical world) that is superior to that from other sources, such as religious views (see Feyerabend, 1975 and 1978). And today there remains considerable dissensus among philosophers of science; with disagreement, for example, about whether science provides knowledge of an independent reality or simply a record of successful predictions of experience.[10] None of the various attempts to provide an alternative basis for the claim that science is the distinctive source of soundly based knowledge has created a new consensus. One of the effects of this has been to undermine the capacity of natural science to offer a clear model for the social sciences.

In this new climate, criticism of conventional ethnography has taken a variety of forms. One target has been the separation of research from practice that it inherits from the scientific model, a criticism reflecting an increased concern with the practical value and consequences of knowledge. Critical Theory has been particularly important here, advancing as an alternative what I will call the 'emancipatory' model. This model derives to a large extent from Marxism, and particularly from the early work of Jurgen Habermas. Habermas argues that the cognitive interest motivating natural science is that of instrumental control; and that while this is legitimate in the investigation of physical phenomena, it is inappropriate for the study of human behaviour. He claims that this instrumental interest lies behind quantitative social science, and he criticises it accordingly. Habermas regards interpretive research, in which ethnographic work would be included, as more appropriate in social science, and believes it to be founded on a concern with overcoming inter-cultural misunderstanding. However, he argues that even this approach is inadequate in the study of advanced capitalist societies because it fails to address the need to emancipate people from ideology, one element of which is the overextension of ideas about knowledge and reality deriving from the natural sciences to our understanding of human social life.[11]

From this perspective, conventional ethnography may be criticised for simply representing things as they are; or, perhaps even worse, representing them as the *appear* to the people studied. There are two arguments involved here: that ethnography only captures surface appearances not the underlying reality; and that it is concerned only with documenting how things *are*, not with discovering how they might be *changed for the better*. Critical theory, by contrast, is concerned with dispelling ideology and thereby promoting emancipation. This critical approach has been advocated in proposals for critical ethnography (see for example Anderson, 1989 and Gitlin *et al.*, 1989) and for critical discourse analysis (see for example Fairclough, 1989 and 1992).

A related development has been the tremendous growth in the influence of feminism, and in particular the attempt to identify aspects of Western thinking, including philosophy and methodology, that betray masculinist bias. The model of the natural sciences and the use of quantitative method have sometimes been criticised as representing such a bias (Graham, 1983). There is considerable diversity in feminist thinking about methodology, but an important theme has been criticism of conventional ethnographic work on similar grounds to critical theorists: that it has been content with mere description rather than being directed towards bringing about emancipation, in this case of women.[12]

An area of special concern for feminists, and for others as well, has been the relationship between researcher and researched, viewed as an aspect of the politics of social research. It has been argued that in more traditional forms of ethnography, as in experimental and survey research, a power relationship is involved. The research is very often focused on relatively powerless groups with the researcher, it is claimed, exploiting their powerlessness to carry out the research. Moreover, it is suggested that the research often serves the powerful, perhaps enabling them to exercise more effective control. In both these respects research itself may be a form of domination. And even where researcher and researched are social equals, power is still involved because it is the researcher who makes the decisions about what is to be studied, how, for what purpose, etc. It is argued that not only is this unacceptable in itself, but it distorts the knowledge produced: the findings are often irrelevant to the people being studied, since they are geared to problems defined by social science disciplines not to those that face the people themselves. Furthermore, research reports are written in language that is not comprehensible to those studied. And such research is often invalid because the ethnographer remains an outsider and fails truly to understand the world from a participant point of view. Such arguments have been developed in several fields. They are to be found not only among feminists, but also in educational research in the form of advocacy of 'the teacher as researcher' (see for example Stenhouse, 1975 and Carr & Kemmis, 1986). The remedy advocated is participatory research, research by and for participants, with professional researchers playing no more than a facilitative role.[13]

Another way in which the relevance of the scientific model to ethnography has been challenged focuses on ethnographers' claims that their accounts represent reality. As we saw, a central element of the rationale for ethnography has often been that it can capture the nature of human social life more accurately than quantitative methods. This is a key element of the ethnographic commitment to both 'naturalism' and 'discovery'. However, some critics (including some ethnographers) argue that any such appeal to the representation of reality is ill-founded. Such questioning of the representational capacity of ethnography can arise simply from applying the concept of understanding to the research process itself. If it is true that people construct interpretations of the world, and that different groups and individuals construct different perspectives, then we may be led to conclude that the accounts produced by ethnographers are simply versions of the world that are no more valid than others. This tendency towards rejection of the possibility of representation (what we might call anti-realism) has been reinforced by the influence of a wide range of philosophical ideas, including phenomenology, hermeneutics, structuralism, post-structuralism, and Wittgensteinian language philosophy.[14]

One of the most recent products of this anti-realism has been scrutiny of ethnographic and other accounts as texts, looking at the rhetorical devices that are used to 'create' the world portrayed. The suggestion is that conventional ethnographic work is wedded to a spurious realism. It claims to represent the setting studied 'as it is'. However, the critics argue that this is not possible because we have no access to an independent reality; all we have are interpretations, and the ethnographer's account is just as much an interpretation as are those of the people that he or she is studying. The critics claim that, in order to establish that their accounts represent reality, ethnographers rely on rhetorical devices that are analogous to those employed by travel writers and realist novelists such as Dickens or Zola. For example, anthropologists sometimes include in their accounts a description of their first sight of the setting they were to study, thereby 'proving' in a narrative way that they have 'really' been there. Similarly, one finds superfluous details in ethnographic accounts, information that is not necessary to support the analysis. This is included, it is suggested, to give an added sense of realism to the account, just as novelists like Dickens spend much time describing the details of the settings in which events take place as well as of the appearance and manner of the people involved.[15]

These critics do not reject the use of rhetorical devices. Indeed, they argue that rhetoric cannot be avoided. But some of them argue that what is required is more honest rhetoric, rhetoric that does not pretend to an unattainable realism. These arguments have motived some novel kinds of ethnographic writing, for example texts that incorporate the voices of the people studied in a more substantial and less controlled way than is common in conventional ethnographic accounts, for example through the adoption of dialogical formats.[16]

From a variety of points of view, then, conventional ethnographic research has come under criticism in recent times not so much for failing to be scientific as for staying too close to the model of science, or a particular version of it. Its commitment to describing and explaining the social world, rather than seeking to change it, has been rejected by some. The relationship between ethnography and the people studied has been attacked as exploitative. Furthermore, ethnography's very capacity to represent social reality 'in its own terms' has been challenged.

Conclusion

In this chapter I have outlined the character of ethnography as a set of research strategies as well as the more philosophical ideas that support those strategies. In addition, I have looked at methodological debates about ethnography, both those concerned with criticism that it is not scientific enough and those centred on arguments that the model of natural science is inappropriate for ethnography.

If what I have said makes it sound as if ethnography is currently in crisis, that is not far from the truth. Most obvious is the crisis of fragmentation: there is no single ethnographic paradigm or community, but a diversity of approaches claiming to be ethnographic (and often disagreeing with one another). More fundamentally, though, the crisis stems from deep, unresolved questions about the nature of our knowledge of the social world and about the purposes which that knowledge can and should serve. These questions face all social and educational researchers, not just ethnographers. Ethnographers are beginning to address them, but there is little agreement about answers.

Notes

1. I shall use some of these terms as synonyms for 'ethnography' in this chapter.
2. For a brief overview of the history of ethnography in the context of social and cultural anthropology, see Wax (1971).
3. Malinowski was not the only figure in this movement, nor did his research practice conform very closely to the ethnographic ideal that he recommended. See Kaberry (1957) and Wax (1972).
4. For detailed discussion of the Chicago School, see Bulmer (1984), Harvey (1987), and Hammersley (1989).
5. The use of the term 'naturalism' is ambiguous in the methodological literature. It is sometimes used to refer to the adoption of the natural science model, sometimes (as here) to indicate a concern with capturing the nature of the phenomena studied (which may well imply using different methods to those characteristic of the natural sciences). See Matza (1969) for a discussion of the term and references to its diversity of usage. For a clear account of the covering law model, see Lessnoff (1974) or Keat & Urry (1975). On the pattern model of explanation, see the discussion and references in Hammersley (1989: chaps 7 and 8).
6. It should be said, though, that many ethnographers do not believe that understanding requires that they become full members of the group(s) being studied. Indeed, most believe that this must not occur if a valid and useful account is to be produced. The ethnographer must try to be both outsider and insider, staying on the margins of the group both socially and intellectually. This is because what is required is *both* an outside *and* an inside view. For this reason it is sometimes emphasised that the ethnographer must try to see familiar settings as 'anthropologically strange', as they would be seen by someone from another society, adopting what we might call the Martian perspective.
7. I cannot cover the full range of criticism and response, the aim is simply to give a flavour of the sort of argument and counter-argument that has taken place. I am also not intending to endorse the credibility of either criticisms or defences. The issues involved are often more complex and difficult than such exchanges suggest.
8. On ethnomethodology, see Heritage (1984). For good accounts of conversation analysis and discourse analysis, see Speier (1973) and Potter & Wetherell (1987) respectively.
9. Kuhn did not deny the role of rational judgment entirely, simply that it provided the sole and certain basis for paradigm shift (See, especially, the postscript to the second edition of his book: Kuhn, 1970).
10. For reviews of these arguments, and references: see Siegel (1987), Tiles (1988) and Newton-Smith (1981).
11. For an overview of Habermas's work, see McCarthy (1978).
12. For references and my own assessment of feminist methodology, see

Hammersley (1992b). For critical responses, see Ramazanoglu (1992) and Gelsthorpe (1992).
13. For references and an assessment of the arguments for practitioner research, see Hammersley (1992a: chap 8).
14. While these ideas differ in many ways and are by no means all straightforwardly anti-realist, collectively their influence has encouraged anti-realism. For a useful introductory discussion of these intellectual movements, see Anderson, Hughes & Sharrock (1986).
15. For examples of this sort of analysis, see Geertz (1988), van Maanen (1988) and Atkinson (1990).
16. See for example Krieger (1983), Shostak (1981) and Crapanzano (1980). For a cautious approach to such developments and an argument against some of the ideas on which they are based, see Hammersley (1993).

Bibliography

Anderson, G. (1989) Critical ethnography in education: Origins, current status and new directions. *Review of Educational Research* 59 (3), 249–70.
Anderson, R., Hughes, J. and Sharrock, W. (1986) *Philosophy and the Human Sciences*. London: Croom Helm.
Atkinson, P. (1990) *The Ethnographic Imagination*. London: Routledge.
Bittner, E. (1979) Objectivity and realism in sociology. In G. Psathas (ed.) *Phenomenological Sociology*. New York: Wiley.
Blumer, H. (1969) *Symbolic Interactionism*. Englewood Cliffs, NJ: Prentice-Hall.
Bruyn, S. (1966) *The Human Perspective in Sociology: The Methodology of Participant Observation*. Englewood Cliffs: Prentice Hall.
Bulmer, M. (1984) *The Chicago School of Sociology*. Chicago: University of Chicago Press.
Carr, W. and Kemmis, S. (1986) *Becoming Critical: Education, Knowledge and Action Research*. London: Falmer Press.
Cicourel, A.V. (1964) *Method and Measurement in Sociology*.
Crapanzano, V. (1980) *Tuhami: Portrait of a Moroccan*. Chicago: University of Chicago Press.
Engels, F. (1892) *The Condition of the Working Class in England*. London: Allen and Unwin.
Fairclough, N. (1989) *Language and Power*. London: Longman.
—— (1992) *Discourse and Social Change*. Cambridge: Polity.
Feyerabend, P. (1975) *Against Method*. London: Verso.
—— (1978) *Science in a Free Society*. London: Verso.
Geertz, C. (1988) *Works and Lives: The Anthropologist as Author*. Stanford: Stanford University Press.
Gelsthorpe, L. (1992) Response to Martyn Hammersley's paper 'On feminist methodology'. *Sociology*, 26, 213–8.
Gitlin, A.D., Siefel, M. and Boru, K. (1989) The politics of method: From leftist ethnography to educative research. *Qualitative Studies in Education* 2 (3), 237–53.
Graham, H. (1983) Do her answers fit his questions? Women and the survey method. In E. Gamarnikow, D. Morgan, J. Purvis and D. Taylorson (eds) *The Public and the Private*. London: Heinemann.
Gumperz, J.J. and Hymes, D.H. (eds) (1972) *Directions in Sociolinguistics: The Ethnography of Communication*. New York: Holt, Rinehart and Winston.
Hammersley, M. (1989) *The Dilemma of Qualitative Method: Herbert Blumer and the Chicago Tradition*. London: Routledge.

—— (1992a) *What's Wrong with Ethnography?* London: Routledge.

—— (1992b) On feminist methodology. *Sociology* 26, 187–206.

—— (1993) The rhetorical turn in ethnography, *Social Science Information* 33 (1), 23–37.

Harré, R. and Secord P. (1973) *The Explanation of Social Behaviour*. Oxford: Blackwell.

Harvey, L. (1987) *Myths of the Chicago School*. Aldershot: Gower.

Heritage, J. (1984) *Garfinkel and Ethnomethodology*. Cambridge: Polity.

Kaberry, P. (1957) Malinowski's contribution to field-work methods and the writing of ethnography. In R. Firth (ed.) *Man and Culture*. London: Routledge and Kegan Paul.

Keat, R. and Urry, J. (1975) *Social Theory as Science*. London: Routledge and Kegan Paul.

Krieger, S. (1983) *The Mirror Dance*. Philadelphia: Temple University Press.

Kuhn, T. (1970) (2nd edition) *The Structure of Scientific Revolutions*. Chicago: University of Chicago Press.

Lessnoff, M. (1974) *The Structure of Social Science*. London: Allen and Unwin.

van Maanen, J. (1988) *Tales of the Field*. Chicago: University of Chicago Press.

McCall, G. and Simmons, J. (1969) *Issues in Participant Observation*. Reading, MA: Addison-Wesley.

McCarthy, T. (1978) *The Critical Theory of Jurgen Habermas*. London, Hutchinson.

Matza, D. (1969) *Becoming Deviant*. Englewood Cliffs: Prentice Hall.

Mayhew, H. (1861–2) *London Labour and the London Poor*. London: Cass.

—— (1971) *The Unknown Mayhew*. Edited by E.P. Thompson and E. Yeo. London: Merlin Press.

Newton-Smith, W.H. (1981) *The Rationality of Science*. London: Routledge and Kegan Paul.

Potter, J. and Wetherell, M. (1987) *Discourse and Social Psychology*. London: Sage.

Pratt, M.L. (1986) Fieldwork in common places. In Clifford and Marcus (eds).

Ramazanoglu, C. (1992) On feminist methodology: male reason versus female empowerment. *Sociology*, 26, 207–12.

Rist, R. (1970) Student social class and teacher expectations. *Harvard Educational Review* 40 (3), 411–51.

Rowe, J.H. (1965) The renaissance foundations of anthropology. *American Anthropologists*, 67, 1–20.

Shostak, M. (1981) *Nisa: The Life and Words of a !Kung Woman*. Cambridge, MA: Harvard University Press.

Siegel, H. (1987) *Relativism Refuted*. Dordrecht: Reidel.

Smith, J.K. and Heshusius, L. (1986) Closing down the conversation: The end of the quantitative–qualitative debate among educational inquirers. *Educational Researcher* 15 (1), 4–12.

Speier, M. (1973) *How to Observe Face to Face Communication: A Sociological Introduction*. Goodyear.

Stenhouse, L. (1975) *An Introduction to Curriculum Research and Development*. London, Heinemann.

Tiles, M. (1988) Science and the world. In G. Parkinson (ed.) *An Encyclopedia of Philosophy*. London: Routledge.

Tocqueville, A. (1966) *Democracy in America* (two volumes). New York: Harper and Row. (First published, in French, in 1835 and 1840).

Wax, M. (1972) Tenting with Malinowski. *American Sociological Review* 37 (1), 1–13.

Wax, R. (1971) *Doing Fieldwork: Warnings and Advice*. Chicago: University of Chicago Press.

Znaniecki, F. (1934) *The Method of Sociology*. New York: Farrer and Rinehart.

2 The Relations Between Researcher and Researched: Ethics, Advocacy and Empowerment

D. CAMERON, E. FRAZER, P. HARVEY, M.B.H. RAMPTON
and K. RICHARDSON

Ethics

The potentially exploitative and damaging effects of being researched on have long been recognised by social scientists. Social science is not and has never been a neutral enquiry into human behaviour and institutions. It is strongly implicated in the project of social control, whether by the state or by other agencies that ultimately serve the interests of a dominant group. Even when you do not work for a government agency, and whatever your own political views, it is always necessary to think long and hard about the uses to which findings might be put, or the effects they might have contrary to the interests of subjects. If a researcher observes, for example, that the average attainment of some group of schoolchildren is less than might be anticipated, that can colour the expectations of teachers and contribute to the repetition of underachievement by the same group in future. That might be very far from what the researcher intended, but an ethically aware social scientist will see the possible dangers and perhaps try to forestall them.

A second worry is that the researcher might exploit subjects during the research process. One controversy here concerns the acceptability of covert research, in which subjects cannot give full informed consent because the researcher is deliberately misleading them as to the nature and purpose of the research, or perhaps concealing the fact that research is going on at all. For instance, a great deal of research in social psychology relies on subjects thinking the experimenter is looking for one thing when she is really looking for something else. Some sociological studies have involved the researcher 'passing' as a community member;

18

and some sociolinguists have used the technique of getting subjects to recount traumatic experiences because the surge of powerful emotions stops them from being self-conscious about their pronunciation, circumventing the observer's paradox—the problem of how to observe how people behave when they are not being observed. In cases like these one wonders how far the end justifies the means. Even when the deception is on the face of it innocuous, it raises ethical problems because it is a deception.

A famous example where researchers misled their subjects is provided by the Milgram (1974) experiments on obedience to authority: subjects were ordered to give other people severe electric shocks, but in fact the people who appeared to suffer pain were the experimenter's accomplices, and the shock equipment was bogus. Comments on ethics with regard to this particular study tend to focus on the moral standards of the subjects, who revealed themselves in most cases willing to inflict severe pain because they were ordered to do so. It is less often asked how ethical the researcher was in lying to his subjects, subjecting them to severe stress and in all likelihood undermining their self-esteem when they discovered what the real point of the experiment was.

Most disciplines, government and other research agencies (including universities), do indeed have a strong concern with ethical standards, manifested by published codes of conduct, professional oaths, ethics committees, and so on. These work on the basis of balancing as fairly as possible the needs of a discipline in its pursuit of knowledge and truth with the interests of the people on whom research is conducted. The interests of the researched are a negative force limiting what researchers can do. Apart from preventing the abuse of subjects, an ethical researcher will be advised to ensure that their privacy is protected (e.g. by the use of pseudonyms when the findings are published) and where appropriate to compensate them for inconvenience or discomfort (whether in cash, as commonly happens in psychology, or in gifts, as from anthropologists to a community, or in services rendered, as with many sociolinguistic studies).

In ethical research, then, there is a wholly proper concern to minimise damage and offset inconvenience to the researched, and to acknowledge their contribution (even where they are unpaid, they will probably be thanked in the researcher's book or article). But the underlying model is one of 'research *on*' social subjects. Human subjects deserve special ethical consideration, but they no more set the researcher's agenda than the bottle of sulphuric acid sets the chemist's agenda. This position follows, of course, from the positivist emphasis on distance to avoid interference or bias. Positivism is strongly committed to the idea that observations procured in a scientific manner have the status of value-free facts. However, it is also open to positivistically inclined researchers to go beyond this idea of ethics and make themselves more directly accountable to the researched. They may move, in other words, to an *advocacy* position.

Advocacy

What we are calling the 'advocacy position' is characterised by a commitment on the part of the researcher not just to do research on subjects but research *on and for* subjects. Such a commitment formalises what is actually a rather common development in field situations, where a researcher is asked to use her skills or her authority as an 'expert' to defend subjects' interests, getting involved in their campaigns for healthcare or education, cultural autonomy or political and land rights, and speaking on their behalf.

A notable and relevant example of this kind of accountability in linguistic research is the case of the Ann Arbor 'Black English' trial in 1979. A group of African American parents in Ann Arbor, Michigan, brought a suit against the city schools for their failure to acknowledge and address the specific educational needs of children whose first language was American Vernacular Black English (AVBE). Children were being tracked into slow or learning disabled groups when their problem was in fact linguistic, a mismatch between standard English and the highly divergent AVBE which teachers had not understood.

It was crucial in pursuing the case that AVBE could be shown to be a recognisable, systematic and highly divergent (from Standard English) variety common to African American communities throughout the USA and resulting from the community's history of slavery and segregation. In order to show this, the community sought the help of sociolinguists who had studied AVBE and other Black Englishes. Linguists such as Geneva Smitherman played an important part in organising the campaign and recruiting other experts to it.

One of those who acted as an expert witness in the case was the (white) sociolinguist William Labov. In 1982 Labov published a retrospective account of the Ann Arbor affair, 'Objectivity and commitment in linguistic science', which has become a canonical statement on the social responsibility of linguistic researchers.

Labov suggests two principles. One is the principle of 'error correction': if we as researchers know that people hold erroneous views on something, AVBE for example, we have a responsibility to attempt to correct those views. (This, incidentally, is a clear example of 'commitment' and 'objectivity' serving the exact same ends; Labov believes in or is committed to putting truth in place of error.) The second principle is that of 'the debt incurred'. When a community has enabled linguists to gain important knowledge, the linguist incurs a debt which must be repaid by using the said knowledge on the community's behalf when they need it. This is clearly an advocacy position.

Labov further stresses that the advocate serves the community, and that political direction is the community's responsibility. As an outsider, Labov accepts—and counsels others to accept—an auxiliary role. 'They [linguists] don't claim for themselves the right to speak for the community or make the decision on what forms of language should be used' (Labov, 1982: 27).

The important point we want to make is that while Labov's position is in some ways extremely radical, it is so *within a positivist framework*. That framework sets limits on Labov's advocacy, and without underestimating the usefulness and sincerity of what he says and what he has done, we have to add that in our view the limits of positivism are severe and restrictive.

Labov's positivism is clearly visible in his uneasy juxtaposition of 'objectivity' and 'commitment'. Obviously he is worried that a researcher's advocacy might undermine the validity of her findings (the 'bias' or 'pseudoscience' problem). He gets around the problem by claiming that in this instance, the one reinforced or enhanced the other. It was the work of African American linguists, many motivated at least partly by social and political considerations, that resolved the disagreements, anomalies, distortions and errors of previous work on AVBE. The field became better, more objective and more scientific as a result of these linguists' commitment.

This is a powerful and effective argument if one is inclined to place emphasis on notions of factual truth, error, bias, etc.—in other words, it is a positivistic argument. For a non-positivist it concedes too much— the absolute fact/value distinction for example, and the notion that there is one true account that we will ultimately be able to agree on. It is not the political sensitivity but the more detailed knowledge of the African American linguists, not their values but their facts that Labov implicitly credits here. The argument that there is some intrinsic connection between one's facts and one's values would presumably fail to impress him.

In the course of his argument, Labov also begs some vital questions: for instance, does a shared racial origin reduce the division between researcher and researched to the point of insignificance? What is the researcher, African American or not, to do if the community contains differing interests and opinions within itself (as is actually the case, if not in Ann Arbor then certainly in the African American community as a whole on the question of AVBE)?

The point here is that Labov's account advises advocate researchers to take an auxiliary role, but in practice it leaves them with some very significant powers: the power to identify the 'community' whose interests they will speak for, and the power to decide on an objective truth which they will speak. By alluding to the African American linguists' insider knowledge rather than their political interests, Labov, as we have noted, glosses over the anti-positivist argument that observation is theory-laden and observers bring their values and interests to it. Yet taken seriously, that argument would threaten the basis for Labov's idea of advocacy: that advocates pay their debt to the community by countering error and bias with the objective factual truth to which their expert status gives them privileged access.

In this connection we also have questions about the idea of 'expert testimony', since it accepts a radical, qualitative distinction between 'our' expert knowledge and 'their' lay knowledge (with the African American linguists standing rather uneasily on the border between us and them) that may in fact be a mystification. If expert knowledge depends on the knowledge of the researched (albeit expressed more technically and systematically) then there is something wrong with presenting it as more different and special than it is (though we do not want to imply here that there is *nothing* special about expert knowledge: technicality and systematicity have important virtues. It is mystification of what makes knowledge 'expert' that we argue against).

We are also, of course, aware that it would be stupid and damaging for experts to stop giving evidence tomorrow on the grounds that their knowledge is no more authentic than the knowledge of those on whose behalf they are speaking. Nevertheless we do not think it naïve to put to such experts the following question: is speaking for people enough? For one could ask why, if experts are under an obligation to defend the powerless, they should not be under the further obligation to empower them to defend themselves.

Empowering Research

We have characterised 'ethical research' as *research on* and 'advocacy research' as *research on and for*. We understand 'empowering research' as *research on, for and with*. One of the things we take that additional 'with' to imply is the use of interactive or dialogic research methods, as opposed to the distancing or objectifying strategies positivists are constrained to use. It is the centrality of interaction 'with' the researched that enables research to be empowering in our sense; though we understand this as a necessary rather than a sufficient condition.

We should also point out that we do not think of empowerment as an absolute requirement on all research projects. (There are instances where one would not wish to empower research subjects: though arguably there is political value in researching on powerful groups, such an enterprise might well be one instance where 'research on' would be the more appropriate model.) But if we are going to raise the possibility of 'research on, for and with' as an appropriate goal in some contexts, we must also acknowledge that the standards and constraints of positivist 'research on'—objectivity, disinterestedness, non-interaction—will not be appropriate in those contexts. This raises the question: what alternative standards would be appropriate?

Whatever standards we propose at this stage can only be provisional: much more discussion is needed. We will simply raise—without saying too much about the difficulties—a number of points that strike us as key issues.

The three main issues we will take up in this provisional way are (a) the use of interactive methods; (b) the importance of subjects' own agendas; and (c) the question of 'feedback' and sharing knowledge. On each of these points we will begin with a programmatic statement and then pose various questions in relation to it. Throughout the discussion we will bear in mind our working definition of empowering research as 'research on, for and with'.

(a) 'Persons are not objects and should not be treated as objects.'

The point of this statement is not one that needs to be laboured, since we believe most researchers would find it wholly uncontentious that persons are not objects, and are entitled to respectful treatment. What is more contentious is how strictly we define 'treating persons as objects', and whether if we make the definition a strict one we can avoid objectification and still do good ('valid') research.

We have raised the question of whether 'ethical research' permits methods (e.g. concealment of the researcher's purpose) that might be regarded as objectifying. Indeed, we have asked whether non-interactive methods are by definition objectifying, and thus inappropriate for empowering research. If empowering research is research done 'with' subjects as well as 'on' them it must seek their active co-operation which requires disclosure of the researcher's goals, assumptions and procedures.

On the question of whether this kind of openness undermines the quality or validity of the research, it will already be clear what we are suggesting. We want to argue that interaction *enhances* our understanding of what we observe, while the claims made for non-interaction as a guarantee of objectivity and validity are philosophically naïve.

The question before us, then, is how we can make our research methods more open, interactive and dialogic. This is not a simple matter, particularly in situations of inequality.

(b) 'Subjects have their own agendas and research should try to address them.'

One of the ways in which researchers are powerful is that they set the agenda for any given project: what it will be about, what activities it will involve, and so on. But from our insistence that 'persons are not objects' it obviously follows that researched persons may have agendas of their own, things they would like the researcher to address. If we are researching 'with' them as well as 'on and for' them, do we have a responsibility to acknowledge their agendas and deal with them in addition to our own?

This might involve only fairly minor adjustments to research procedures: making it clear, for instance, that asking questions and introducing topics is not the sole prerogative of the researcher. While traditional handbooks for positivist research warn against addressing questions subjects might ask, interactive methods oblige the researcher not only to listen but also, if called upon, to respond. But making space for subjects' agendas might mean rather more than this. It might mean allowing the researched to select a focus for joint work, or serving as a resource or facilitator for research they undertake themselves. There are obvious similarities here with the tradition of 'action research'.

(c) 'If knowledge is worth having, it is worth sharing.'

This is perhaps the most complicated of the issues we are raising here. Is it, or should it be, part of the researcher's brief to 'empower' people in an educational sense, by giving them access to expert knowledge, including the knowledge a research project itself has generated?

First, let us backtrack: what is this 'expert knowledge'? For, to a very substantial degree, social researchers' knowledge is and must be constructed out of subjects' own knowledge; if this is made explicit (as arguably it should be) the effect might be to demystify 'expert knowledge' as a category. Such a blurring of the boundary between what 'we' know and what 'they' know, brought about by making explicit the processes whereby knowledge acquires its authority and prestige, might itself be empowering. But it does complicate the picture of 'sharing knowledge', suggesting that there are different sorts of knowledge to be shared and different ways of sharing.

Needless to say, we are not greatly upset if our practice separates us from positivist researchers. But it might also seem to separate us from the many researchers who, sincerely and properly concerned about the imbalance of power between themselves and their subjects, follow the apparently very different practice of 'letting subjects speak for themselves'. There is a convention in some contemporary research of reproducing subjects' own words on the page unmediated by authorial comment, in order to give the subject a voice of her own and validate her opinions. This *non*-intervention might also be claimed as an empowering move.

In assessing these two strategies, intervention versus 'giving a voice' one might want to distinguish between what is empowering in the context of *representing* subjects (that is, in a text such as an article, a book or a film) and what is empowering in the context of *interacting* with them. In the former context we see that there may be value in non-intervention. But in the latter context we have our doubts whether subjects are most empowered by a principled refusal to intervene in their discourse. Discourse after all is a historical construct: whether or not intervention changes someone's opinions, it is arguable that they gain by knowing where those opinions have 'come from' and how they might be challenged or more powerfully formulated. Clearly, it is a principle we use when we teach: not only do we engage with students' views, we engage with them *critically*. The question we are raising, then, is whether there is some merit in extending that practice from the context of the classroom to the context of research.

Even if we decide to answer this question in the affirmative, other questions remain as to how knowledge can be shared, and what the effects might be. There is also the question of how to integrate educational or knowledge-sharing aims into the broader scope of a research project.

Reference

Labov, W. (1982) Objectivity and commitment in linguistic science: The case of the Black English trial in Ann Arbor. *Language in Society* 11, 165–201.
Milgram, S. (1974) *Obedience to Authority*. New York: Harper and Row.

3 Observing and Recording Talk in Educational Settings

JOAN SWANN

Introduction

This article provides guidance for those who wish to carry out an investigation into aspects of spoken language. It is designed mainly for use in educational settings, and will probably be particularly appropriate for teachers and other educationists engaged on small-scale research projects. Many of the techniques and principles it discusses, however, apply equally well to investigations of spoken language in non-educational contexts.

I shall discuss factors to take into account when planning observations of spoken language, then look at different ways of making and recording observations. The article does not provide detailed guidance on analysis, but I shall refer to other articles in this volume that serve as examples of different ways of analysing talk.

Deciding What to Observe and How to Make Observations

I am assuming that, as a reader of this article, you will already have in mind a clear purpose for observing spoken language—that you will have identified certain issues to focus on, perhaps specified, in the case of a formal project, as a set of research questions. These questions will affect the contexts in which you decide to observe and the particular observations you make. In drawing up more detailed plans for your work there are several specific points to consider: what people and events you wish to observe; to what extent you wish, or need to, participate in these events; ethical issues related to making observations; and what types of observation you wish to make.

Selecting people and events

Since you cannot, and will not wish to observe everything that is going on you will need to select people and events to focus on. If your interest is in aspects of classroom talk, you may wish to focus on talk between the teacher (yourself or a colleague) and pupils, or between different pupils, or both. You may be interested in whole-class discussion or small-group talk. You may wish to compare contributions from a small number of pupils in different contexts, or to monitor one child closely in a range of activities.

You will also need to think about the representativeness of the types of talk you wish to examine. For instance, how are you selecting the types of activity in which to observe children? Do these cover the full range of activities normally encountered? Or are you contrasting contexts you think are distinctive in some way?

If you are carrying out a small-scale investigation focusing on talk in one or two contexts, there are two important points to bear in mind about the samples of talk you eventually come up with:

- Your observations may provide great insights into peoples' conversational strategies, the way they manage certain activities or their understanding of certain concepts—but you cannot make broad generalizations on the basis of a small number of observations. For instance, observations of peoples' behaviour in one set of contexts do not provide evidence of how they 'generally' behave.
- A related point is that there are problems in making inferences about people's abilities or understanding on the basis of what they happen to do when you are observing them. For instance, just because young pupils do not produce certain types of talk doesn't mean they cannot. On the other hand, pupils may develop coping strategies that make it appear they understand more than they do.

Observing and participating in talk

A distinction is commonly made in research between *participant* and *non-participant* observation. A participant observer is someone who takes part in the event she or he is observing; a non-participant observer does not take part. In practice, this distinction is not so straightforward: by virtue of being in a classroom (or meeting, etc.) and watching what is going on you are, to some extent, a participant—and you are likely to have an effect on the interaction that takes place. The linguist Labov identified what he termed 'the observer's paradox' (Labov, 1970)—that, although there are various ways of minimising the intrusion, the mere act of observing people's language behaviour (or, for that matter, other aspects of their behaviour) is inclined to change that behaviour. Different effects are likely to be produced by different observers (it may matter whether an observer is female or male, or perceived as relatively senior or junior).

There are specific issues to consider if you are observing in your own institution: it is probably impossible to maintain a strict separation between your role as observer and your usual role (e.g. as teacher or colleague). When interpreting the talk you collect you will need to take into account the effect your own presence, and the way you carried out the observations, may have had on your data.

The ethics of observation

As the previous article in this volume argues, watching people, and writing down what they do, has certain ethical implications. If you are observing adults—say in a staff meeting—it may seem obvious that you need to get their permission first. But it is equally important to consider the ethical implications of observing young children in a classroom. Such issues need to be considered as part of planning an observation, because they will have an impact on what you observe, how you carry out the observation, and how you interpret the results of the observation. Some points to consider are:

- *Is any kind of talk available for inspection?* For instance, is it legitimate to observe casual or 'private' conversations—particularly in the case of pupils in school, who may find it difficult to withold consent?
- *Should you ask people's permission to observe them?* This must depend on the context and purpose of the observation. For instance, if the observation were being carried out entirely for the observer's benefit, it might seem necessary to ask permission (perhaps from parents in the case of very young children). At the other end of the spectrum, you probably feel it is a normal part of teaching to keep a note of how pupils are progressing, not something that would require special permission.
- *Should you tell people they are being observed?* Bound up with this question is the notion of the observer's paradox: it is likely that the more you tell people about your observation, the more their behaviour will be affected. Some researchers compromise: they tell people they are being observed, but are rather vague about the object of the observation. They may say more about this after the event. You may feel that you can afford to be more open; or, if you are observing as a colleague or teacher (rather than a researcher from outside), that it is important to retain an atmosphere of trust between yourself and those you work with.
- *Should you discuss the results of your observation with those you have observed?* This is partly an ethical question of whether people have a right to know what you're saying about them. But discussing observations with others also lets you check your interpretations against theirs. It may give you a different understanding of something you have observed.

- *Should you identify those you have observed?* In writing reports, researchers often give pseudonyms to people they have observed or institutions in which they have carried out observations. If you are observing in your own institution you may find it more difficult to maintain confidentiality in this way—the identity of those you refer to may still be apparent to other colleagues, for instance. One solution may be to discuss with colleagues or pupils how much confidentiality they feel is necessary, and how this may be maintained.
- *Should you consult those you have observed about the dissemination and further use of your work?* People may give permission to be observed for a particular purpose, but what if your purposes change? E.g. you may wish to disseminate your work to a wider audience; or to use a video obtained for your research in an INSET session. Bound up with this is the degree of anonymity you are able to ensure those you have observed.

Several handbooks for educational researchers discuss broader ethical issues—see for instance Hitchcock & Hughes (1989) and Walker (1989). Many professional associations also produce guidelines covering various aspects of research. At the time of writing BAAL (the British Association for Applied Linguistics) are producing guidelines that are particularly relevant to those whose primary concern is with language. You might also be interested in the fuller discussion of ethical issues in sociolinguistic research and the researchers' case studies included in Cameron *et al* (1992), from which article 2 in this volume was abstracted.

Types of observation

There are several ways in which observations of spoken language may be recorded. In the sections that follow I shall consider recording observations on the spot using field notes or an observation schedule; making audio and video recordings; and transcribing talk for more detailed analysis.

Throughout all these sections I shall make a broad distinction between *qualitative* and *quantitative* approaches. Coolican (1990) describes this distinction as follows:

> 'Quantification' means to measure on some numerical basis. . . . Whenever we count or categorise we quantify. . . . A qualitative approach, by contrast, emphasises meanings, experiences . . . descriptions and so on. Raw data will be exactly what people have said (in interview or recorded conversation) or a description of what has been observed. (Coolican, 1990: 36–7)

Quantitative approaches allow a numerical comparison to be made between talk produced by different speakers or in different contexts. They would be used if you wanted to know how much speakers talked, the extent to which they produced certain categories of talk, how frequently certain events occurred, etc.

A qualitative approach would tend to be used if the questions you wished to investigate were more open-ended—if you wanted to identify what happened during a meeting, or how pupils worked together in certain learning activities.

In practice the distinction is not always so clear-cut: a qualitative approach may lead you to identify certain categories of talk which you then wish to quantify; a quantitative analysis may suggest something is going on that you wish to explore in more detail using a qualitative approach.

The sections that follow contain examples of different types of observation. Other articles in this volume provide further illustrations, and may suggest ideas for your own research.

'On the Spot' Observation

If you are teaching a class, you will necessarily be observing what is going on. These observations can be focused on the research question(s) you are investigating. If you have sole responsibility for the class, however, it will be difficult to take notes while teaching. *How* difficult this is depends on a variety of factors: the pupils themselves, the type of lesson you are interested in, how work is organized, and so on. If the class is working independently (for instance, in groups) this time can be used to jot down observations about one particular group, or one or two pupils. If you are working with the whole class or a group, it is unlikely that you will be able to take notes at the same time. You may be able to note down observations after the lesson but these are likely to be of the most general kind: what was talked about; who seemed to have a lot to say; any particularly salient feature, such as a dispute that broke out. If you wish to look at talk in any more detail you will need to observe on the spot as a (relative) non-participant—to observe while someone else is teaching, or to observe a small group working independently.

If you are chairing a meeting, or aiming to make major contributions to discussion, you will be in a similar position to a teacher taking a leading role in class discussion. It will be difficult to take systematic notes, but you could ask a colleague to help.

The examples of observation methods in this section are all designed for observers who are not (simultaneously) taking a leading part in discussion. I shall contrast field-notes, which allow you to record observations in a relatively open-ended way; and observation schedules, which usually record specified categories of behaviour.

Taking field-notes

An observer may use field-notes to record details of class or group interactions; or to focus on the behaviour of an individual speaker. Such notes may be your main source of information, or they may supplement other forms of recording. If you are taking notes on the spot, you will find that the talk flows very rapidly. This is likely to be the case particularly in informal talk, such as talk between pupils in a group. More formal talk is often easier to observe on the spot. In whole-class discussion led by a teacher, or in formal meetings, usually only one person talks at a time, and participants may wait to talk until nominated by the teacher or chair. The teacher or chair may rephrase or summarize what other speakers have said. The slightly more ordered nature of such talk gives an observer more breathing space to take notes.

It is usual to date notes and to provide brief contextual information. The format adopted is highly variable—depending on particular research interests and personal preferences. Figure 1 shows extracts from field-notes made by Janet Maybin while watching an assembly in a middle school. Janet Maybin's observations form part of a larger study of children's collaborative language practices in school (the study is discussed in article 8 in this volume). In this extract, she was interested in identifying the values laid down in school assemblies. She wanted to see whether, and how, these might resurface later in children's talk in other contexts.

As Janet Maybin was not taking an active part in the assembly, she could jot down observations and brief comments at the time. She also tape-recorded the assembly for later analysis (she occasionally jots down counter numbers in her field-notes). After school, she wrote up her field-notes, separating observations (what actually happened) from a commentary (her questions, reflections, interpretations, ideas for things to follow up later).

Separating 'observation' from 'commentary' is useful in that it encourages the observer to think carefully about what they have observed, and to try out different interpretations. Bear in mind, however, that no observation is entirely free from interpretation: what you focus on and how you describe events will already depend on an implicit interpretive framework.

Figure 2 provides an example of detailed field-notes made at a school governors' meeting. The notes were made by Rosemary Deem as part of a research project on school governing bodies, carried out with two other researchers, Sue Hemmings and Kevin Brehony. As well as observing governors' meetings, the researchers issued questionnaires to a sample of governors and interviewed some chairs of governing bodies and head teachers. Observations of meetings provided information on

Tape Counter	Notes	Comments / questions
134	3 children take it in turn to read out poems about animals which they have written. Seated classes quiet and attentive.	I can't hear any of this – neither I suspect can most other children in the assembly. What is being communicated here?
	1 child asks teachers to come and sit on two rows of chairs placed diagonally at the front. Teachers go up to the chairs, acting as if reluctant (sounds of 'Oh no').	I immediately realise teachers are being asked to pretend to be pupils, and the child will be their teacher. Air of puzzled anticipation among seated children. Maybe they aren't familiar with this kind of 'role-reversal' sketch?
142	Teachers mess about, pretending to punch each other, pull hair, tip chair etc. Child 'teacher' stands in front looking embarrassed. Seated children laugh and make occasional comments.	Seated children don't seem at ease with this situation and don't quite know how to react. Who exactly is in authority, now? Teachers' acting out of pupil unruliness is exaggerated – to make it unreal?
	The child at the front is pretending to try and restore order to his 'class'.	The child 'teacher' in acting out his role is managing to remain respectful to his teacher 'pupils', so he's really acting two roles simultaneously (pupil and teacher)?
	The seated children watching now start to freely imitate the antics of the teachers at the front, and several scuffles break out as the noise level rises.	It's difficult for the watching children to cope with these two conflicting systems – teacher = fonts of authority v. teachers = naughty pupils. They seem very confused.
	Mr. Brown quickly steps out of the role of naughty pupil, and gives the watching children a threatening look as he says 'sh'.	Watching children seem almost relieved that traditional power relations are restored. They settle down very quickly.

Figure 1 Field-notes of an assembly.

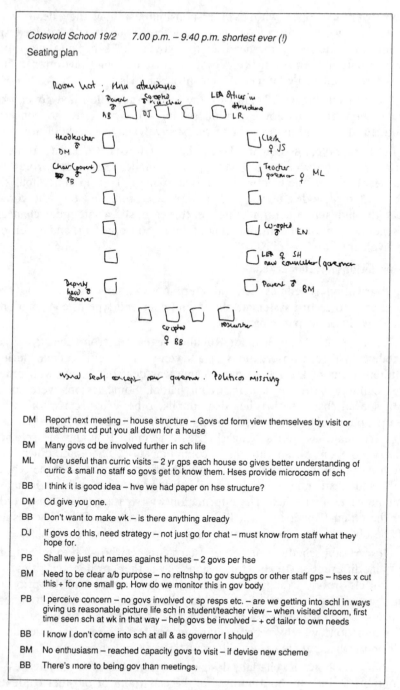

DM   Report next meeting – house structure – Govs cd form view themselves by visit or attachment cd put you all down for a house

BM   Many govs cd be involved further in sch life

ML   More useful than curric visits – 2 yr gps each house so gives better understanding of curric & small no staff so govs get to know them. Hses provide microcosm of sch

BB   I think it is good idea – hve we had paper on hse structure?

DM   Cd give you one.

BB   Don't want to make wk – is there anything already

DJ   If govs do this, need strategy – not just go for chat – must know from staff what they hope for.

PB   Shall we just put names against houses – 2 govs per hse

BM   Need to be clear a/b purpose – no reltnshp to gov subgps or other staff gps – hses x cut this + for one small gp. How do we monitor this in gov body

PB   I perceive concern – no govs involved or sp resps etc. – are we getting into schl in ways giving us reasonable picture life sch in student/teacher view – when visited clroom, first time seen sch at wk in that way – help govs be involved – + cd tailor to own needs

BB   I know I don't come into sch at all & as governor I should

BM   No enthusiasm – reached capacity govs to visit – if devise new scheme

BB   There's more to being gov than meetings.

Figure 2 Field-notes from a governors' meeting.

how governors coped with their responsibilities (how they dealt with issues that were referred to them; whether issues were resolved in meetings or referred to the head, or to a governors' sub-group, etc.); on power relations in meetings (e.g., who contributed and how often); and on the roles taken by lay people and professionals.

The notes in Figure 2 begin with the head's suggestion that governors attach themselves to houses within school. This gives rise to concern about the level and nature of governors' involvement in school life.

In these notes, Rosemary Deem has tried to note down, as near verbatim as possible, the points people made. She also wrote up recollections after the meeting in a research diary. To help in her analysis she created an index of issues that were discussed, and that she could track through subsequent meetings. In this case, she would index changes in school structure (the introduction of a new house system) and governor involvement in school life.

Using an observation schedule

Observation schedules help structure observations of talk, and are often used to record systematically the number and type of contributions made by different participants.

For instance, Beate Schmidt Rohlfing, a teacher from Leeds, used a schedule to record observations of a seven-year-old girl, Asima, during different parts of the school day. Asima was deaf but, along with other deaf children, attended a mainstream school. Some lessons were spent in a special 'base' with other deaf pupils, others in a classroom with hearing pupils. The school had a bilingual policy—deaf pupils used British Sign Language as well as English. Beate Schmidt-Rohlfing focused her observations on overall patterns of communication. She noted down how often Asima initiated communication with others (members of the school staff and deaf and hearing peers) and how often others initiated communication with her. The information was written up as a case study for the Open University pack P535 *Talk and Learning 5–16*. The results of the observation were presented as a chart, reproduced as Figure 3.

Observation schedules are often used by those who wish to investigate talk in different contexts—for instance, whether certain activities, or certain classroom arrangements, encourage a more even distribution of talk, or different types of talk. They have also been used by those concerned about inequality in meetings, classroom talk or other forms of interaction: whether certain participants, or groups of participants, talk more than others or use different types of talk from others.

Figure 4 shows a schedule designed to detect gender imbalances in group discussion. It could be used in the classroom or in other contexts.

Several published schedules are now available that focus on gender

	'A' to deaf peers	deaf peers to 'A'	'A' to hearing peers	hearing peers to 'A'	'A' to deaf Instructor	deaf Instructor to 'A'	'A' to support staff	Support staff to 'A'	'A' to class teacher	class teacher to 'A'
1. session base 9 – 9.40	26	24			17	12				
2. session classroom 9.40 – 10.30	14	15	3	6			18	21	0	1
playground	8	5	4	3						
3. session base 10.50 – 11.55	21	23					16	22		
lunch 12.00 – 12.20	12	12	4	6						
4. session classroom 1.05 – 2.25	25	26	4	7			23	15	2	2
playground	5	7	2	5						
5. session base 2.45 – 3.15	9	8			10	10				

Figure 3 Chart showing whom a child communicated with (The Open University, 1991: A101).

imbalances—see for instance *Genderwatch After the Education Reform Act* (Myers, 1992).

I have found it difficult to use published schedules such as the NATE 'matrix'—the categories of talk identified do not usually correspond to my own interests, or may not be relevant to the types of talk I wish to observe and you may have similar problems. It is possible to adapt published schedules, or to devise a schedule focusing on the aspect(s) of talk in which you are interested. Whether you use a published schedule or devise your own you should *pilot* this first to check that it is manageable and that it provides the information you need.

There are certain advantages and disadvantages attached to the use of open-ended observation using field-notes and more structured observation using schedules. Because these apply also to talk recorded by other means I shall mention them separately at the end of the article.

'On the spot' observations, whether using field-notes or some form of schedule, can provide useful evidence about the quality of an interaction and about broad patterns in the distribution of talk between participants. They are relatively simple to set up, and do not require any technical equipment. On the other hand, they provide only limited amounts of data and, other than the notes themselves, there is no permanent record of the talk. Observations cannot be checked and categories, once allocated, cannot be changed.

Group member (identified by sex)	Initiates talk	Interrupts	Helps another to speak	Supports another's point	Offers opposing view	Adds to what has been said	Challenges	Breaks off	TOTALS
M^1									
W^1									
M^2									
M^3									
W^2									
W^3									
M^4									
Man TOTALS									
Woman TOTALS									

M = Man W = Woman

Figure 4 A matrix to monitor group interaction
(NATE Language and Gender Committee, 1989: 25; matrix devised by Pat Barrett).

Nor can 'on the spot' observations allow you to analyse talk in any detail. To do this you need first to make an audio or video recording.

Making Audio and Video Recordings

Audio- and video-recordings allow you to make a permanent record of spoken language. They provide excellent evidence for discussion with colleagues or pupils. Videos are particularly useful for those with an interest in non-verbal behaviour; they're also useful for showing how certain activities are carried out, or certain equipment used.

Audio- and video-recordings have advantages over 'on the spot' observations: they can be played and replayed, so that observations are likely to be more reliable than those made at the time. You can go back and check any point you're not sure of, and you can ask others to check or comment on your observations. Because you have time to think about and check observations, you can look at people's talk or other aspects of behaviour in considerable detail. You can also transcribe talk for close analysis.

Set against these advantages is the fact that making recordings often requires special arrangements such as collecting, setting up and checking equipment. Audio-recording in a classroom isn't a problem in this respect if cassette recorders are already routinely used. Otherwise, the arrangements take extra time and may not easily fit in with normal teaching. A further point to consider is that, while you can make detailed analyses of people's talk or other behaviour, playing and replaying recordings takes a lot of time. For researchers working individually on small-scale projects, audio- and video-recordings are best suited to collecting limited amounts of data (for instance, one or two meetings, or one or two group activities in the classroom). They are also most suited to recording small groups (rather than, say, whole-class discussion).

Audio-recordings

If you're thinking of using audio-recordings, there are several practical points to bear in mind.

- An audio-cassette recorder can be intrusive—though this is less likely to be the case in classrooms where pupils are used to being recorded, or recording themselves. Intrusiveness is more of a problem if cassette recorders are used in contexts where talk isn't normally recorded, and where there isn't the opportunity for recording to become routine (e.g. staff or other meetings).
- Intrusiveness can be lessened by keeping the technology simple and unobtrusive, for example by using a small, battery-operated cassette recorder with a built-in microphone. This also avoids the danger of trailing wires, and the problem of finding appropriate sockets.
- It is also better to use a fairly simple cassette recorder if pupils are recording themselves. In this case, go for a machine with a small number of controls, and check that young pupils can operate the buttons easily.
- There is a trade-off between lack of intrusiveness/ease of use and quality of recording: more sophisticated machines, used with separate microphones, will produce a better quality recording. This is a consideration if you intend to use the recordings with others, for example in an INSET session.
- A single cassette recorder is not suitable for recording whole-class discussion, unless you focus on the teacher's talk. The recorder will pick up loud voices, or voices that are near to it, and probably lose the rest behind background noise (scraping chairs and so on). Even when recording a small group, background noise is a problem. It is worth checking this by piloting your recording arrangements: speakers may need to be located in a quieter area outside the classroom.
- With audio-recordings you lose important non-verbal and contextual information. Unless you are familiar with the speakers you may also find it difficult to distinguish between different voices. Wherever

possible, supplement audio-recordings with field-notes or a diary providing contextual information.

Video-recordings

As with audio-recordings, there are several points to bear in mind when planning to use a video camera:

- Video cameras are more intrusive than audio-cassette recorders. In contexts such as classrooms, intrusiveness can be lessened by leaving the recorder around for a while (switched off!).

- A video camera is highly selective—it cannot pick up everything that is going on in a large room such as a classroom. If you move it around the classroom you will get an impression of what is going on, but will not pick up much data you can actually use for analysis. A video camera may be used to focus on the teacher's behaviour. When used to record pupils, it is best to select a small group, carrying out an activity in which they don't need to move around too much.

- As with audio-recordings, it is best to have the group in a quiet area where their work won't be disrupted by onlookers.

- The recording will be more useable if you check that the camera has all that you want in view and then leave it running. If you move the camera around you may lose important information, and you may introduce bias (by focusing selectively on certain pupils or actions).

- Video cameras with built-in microphones don't always produce good sound recordings. You will need to check this. A common problem is that you may need to locate a camera a long way from the group you are observing both to obtain a suitable angle of view, and to keep the apparatus unobtrusive. If it is important that you hear precisely what each person says, you may need to make a separate audio-recording or use an external microphone plugged into the video camera.

After you have made recordings, it is useful to make a separate note of the date, time and context of each sequence, and then summarize the content. When you come to analyse your recording, you can adopt an open-ended 'field-notes' approach, playing the recording through several times and noting points relevant to the questions you wish to investigate. In this case, use the cassette player counter to make an index of your tape and help you locate extracts again. Alternatively (or in addition) you can use a structured 'observation schedule' approach, focusing on the number and types of contribution made by different participants. Because you can replay the recording it should be easier to distinguish different categories of talk.

Transcribing From Audio and Video-recordings

Transcripts provide a permanent and readily-accessible record of spoken language and they can allow you to look at this in considerable detail. They may be used to examine quantitative or qualitative aspects of talk, or a mixture of the two. A disadvantage (perhaps the main disadvantage) is that transcription is very time-consuming. Edwards & Westgate (1987) suggest that every hour's recording may require 15 hours for transcription. I find that I can make a rough transcript more quickly than this, but a detailed transcript may take far longer, particularly if a lot of nonverbal or contextual information is included. However transcripts may be used selectively, and alongside other methods. Julie Fisher, in article 10 in this volume, transcribed only the first 10 minutes of each of her video-recordings. In a study I carried out with David Graddol (reported in article 9) we made a rough transcript of two video recordings that allowed us to identify general patterns in the data, followed by much more detailed transcripts of relevant extracts.

Like other forms of recording talk, a transcript provides a partial record: it cannot faithfully reproduce every aspect of talk. Transcribers will tend to pay attention to different aspects depending upon their interests, which means that a transcript is already an interpretation of the event it seeks to record. Elinor Ochs, in a now classic account of 'Transcription as theory', suggests that 'transcription is a selective process reflecting theoretical goals and definitions' (1979: 44). This point is illustrated by the sample layouts and transcription conventions discussed below.

Transcription conventions

Many published transcripts use conventions of written language, such as punctuation, in representing speech. But because written down speech is not the same as writing it can be quite hard to punctuate.

If you do wish to punctuate a transcript bear in mind that in so doing you are giving the speech a particular interpretation. Compare the following two methods of punctuating a teacher's question(s):

> Now, think very carefully. What would happen if we cut one of those hollow balls in half? What would we find inside?

> Now, think very carefully what would happen if we cut one of those hollow balls in half. What would we find inside?

Use of punctuation represents a trade off between legibility and accessibility of the transcript and what might be a premature and impressionistic analysis of the data. It is probably best to use as little conventional punctuation as possible. Several sets of transcription conventions are available to indicate features of spoken language. Some of these are highly detailed, allowing transcribers to record intakes of breath, increased volume, stress, syllable lengthening etc. (see, for instance, Sacks, Schegloff & Jefferson, 1974; Ochs, 1979). Such conventions are designed to produce accurate transcriptions, but there is a danger that they will lend a misleading sense of scientific objectivity to the exercise. Rather than being 'objectively identified' such features of language are likely to correspond to the transcriber's initial interpretations of their data.

Bearing in mind this caveat, Figure 5 illustrates a simple set of conventions for transcribing spoken language.

Further conventions may be added if need be. Alternatively, as in Figure 5, you can leave a wide margin to comment on features such as loudness, whispering, or other noises that add to the meaning of the talk (as with other aspects of transcription these will necessarily be selective).

	Transcript		Comment
1	**Lucy**:	This girl always wins anyway	
2		she's (brilliant) at losing money	
3		[laugh] [general laughter]	
4	**Kathryn**:	<u>I know</u>	quietly
5	**Lucy**:	Same as me I hate taking money	dice thrown
6		out of my bank account (.)	
7	**Kate**:	Yeah seven again <u>one two three</u>	several voices
8		<u>four five six seven</u>	join in counting
9		(2 secs)	
10	**Lucy**:	You and one opponent each	
11		throw a dice high roller gets	
12		50,000 from opponent ( ) I'm	
13		not choosing Kate ⌠ she's good	
	Kate:	⌡ Just throw	

Key

<u>I know</u>	underlining indicates any feature you wish to comment on
(.)	brief pause
(2 secs)	timed pause—2 seconds
(brilliant)	transcription uncertain: a guess
( )	unclear speech—something you can't transcribe
⌠ She's good ⌡ Just throw	overlapping speech
[laugh]	transcription of a sound etc. that forms part of the utterance

Figure 5 Extract from a transcript of teenagers' talk while playing a board game, illustrating some transcription conventions.

Figure 5 uses conventional spellings but note that 'yeah' rather than 'yes' is used to indicate a feature of Kate's pronunciation (line 7). Again, this is an attempt at accuracy (Kate did say 'yeah', not 'yes') but there is a tendency in such cases to home in certain readily identifiable features: *yeah*, *'cos*, *wanna*, *gonna*, *laughin'*, *innit*, rather than to transcribe all pronunciation accurately (e.g. to attempt a complete phonetic transcription). There is a particular danger here if transcribers resort to what are effectively comic strip conventions to represent certain types of speaker (pupils? working class speakers?) but not others.

Laying out a transcript

The most commonly used layout, which I shall call a 'standard' layout, is set out rather like a dialogue in a play, with speaking turns following one another in sequence. This is the layout adopted in Figure 5, and in several articles in this volume. One of the better known alternatives to this layout is a 'column' layout, in which each speaker is allocated a separate column for their speaking turns.

Figures 6 and 7 illustrate respectively 'standard' and 'column' layouts applied to the same extract of talk. This extract comes from a longer transcript of a video-recording showing two pairs of children talking while building cranes from different construction materials. The recording comes from the Cumbria Oracy Project *Talking Sense* pack (Cumbria Oracy Project, 1988). My interest in this data was in the way the children negotiated a working relationship—and particularly with James' attempts to dominate the interaction and Ruth's attempts at resistance.

	Transcript		**Comment**
1	**Ruth**:	Now what do we need	
2	**James**:	Bring it over here then I can	
3		reach	
4	**Ruth**:	All right (.) bring it over here (.)	
5		how many of them do we need	
6	**James**:	Er (.) How big do we want it (.)	
7		about that high	Seems to be a question
8	**Ruth**:	I think a bit bigger	
9	**James**:	OK	
10	**Ruth**:	Only if you want it (.) whoops	
11	**James**:	Ruth get two er	Command or talking to himself?

Figure 6 Transcript of two infant children talking while constructing a lego crane: standard layout.

Ruth	James	Comment
1 Now what do we		
2 need		
3	Bring it over here	
4	then I can reach	
5 All right (.)		
6 Bring it over here		
7 (.)		
8 How many of them		
9 do we need		
10	Er (.) how big do	
11	we want it (.)	
12	About that high	Seems to be a question
13 I think a bit bigger		
14	OK	
15 Only if you want it		
16 (.)		
17 Whoops		
18	Ruth get two er	Command or talking to himself?

Figure 7 Transcript of two children talking while constructing a lego crane: column layout.

The way transcripts are set out seems to highlight certain features of talk. For instance:

- The standard layout suggests a connected sequence, in which one turn follows on from the preceding one. But conversation doesn't always work this way. Is James' first turn 'Bring it over here then I can reach' (Figure 6, lines 3, 4) a response to Ruth's 'Now what do we need' (lines 1, 2)? There are several instances in the complete dialogue when the children's speaking turns do not seem to follow one from another. This is suggested more readily by the column transcription than by the standard one.
- Column transcripts allow you to track one speaker's contributions: you can look at the number and types of contribution made by a speaker, or track the topics they focus on—or whatever else is of interest.
- In a column transcript, it's important to bear in mind which column you allocate to which speaker. Because of factors such as the left-right orientation in European scripts, and associated conventions of page layout, we may give priority to information located on the left hand side. (Ochs, 1979, points out that, in column transcripts of

adult-child talk, the adult is nearly always allocated the left hand column, suggesting they are the initiator in the conversation.)

Other aspects of layout are important. In Figure 7 I have separated out what I think are distinct utterances within the same child's speech. So, Ruth's 'How many of them do we need' (lines 8, 9) counts as a separate utterance, rather than the final part of a longer utterance. This seemed to me more accurately to reflect the children's speech: consecutive utterances in the same child's speech were often separated by a pause during which some activity took place and they seemed to be distinct.

This raises the issue of what one counts as separate speaking turns. I would be inclined to count 'All right', 'Bring it over here' and 'How many of them do we need' as separate turns, but conventions vary. Some accounts would probably classify these utterances as a single turn.

Accounts of turn-taking have often assumed that one person talks at a time (e.g. Sacks, Schegloff & Jefferson, 1974) but such a model does not stand the test of informal group talk where there is lots of overlapping talk and where speakers frequently complete one another's turns (for an interesting account of turn-taking in meetings see Edelsky, 1981; see also Jennifer Coates' transcription and analysis of collaborative talk among women friends in this volume, article 11).

The method one chooses to display speaking turns is particularly important if you intend to use these as units of analysis—i.e. as the basis for identifying certain types or categories of talk.

The layout you choose for a transcript will depend on what you're transcribing and why. Here I've tried to show how different layouts highlight certain aspects of talk and play down others. You will need to try out, and probably adapt, layouts till you find one that suits your purposes—bearing in mind, as ever, that such decisions are already leading you towards a particular interpretation of your data.

Including nonverbal and contextual information

Transcriptions tend to highlight verbal information but nonverbal signs, such as gesture and eye gaze, also convey important information. Figure 8 shows part of the interaction transcribed in Figures 6 and 7 above. In this case I have allocated each speaker a column for nonverbal acts that I thought were important—and that might count as nonverbal 'turns' alongside verbal turns.

When working on the video it seemed to me that the children's moves while constructing the crane were not simply part of the context for the talk but an integral part of the interaction. James' attempts at dominance and Ruth's resistance seemed to operate verbally and nonverbally—e.g. James began the activity and set a pattern that Ruth initially mirrored

Dialogue Ruth and James		Action R	J
		Watching J.	Holding base + 1 lego piece.
Ruth:	Now what do we need		
			Attaches piece to base.
James:	Bring it over here then I can reach	Turns to box, picks up piece.	Turns to box, holds out hand.
Ruth:	All right(.)		Takes piece from R.
Ruth:	Bring it over here (.)	Points to floor near her.	Attaches piece to base to start crane.
			Pushes crane to R.
		Takes crane. Other hand in box.	Puts hand in box.
		Watches J., one hand on box and one on floor.	Takes crane. Attaches another piece.
Ruth:	How many of them do we need	Feels in box for more pieces.	
		Hand on crane, turns towards her.	One hand on crane, the other in box.
		Attaches piece at opposite end to J's.	Adds another piece.

Figure 8 Transcript of two infant children talking while constructing a lego crane, including nonverbal information.

on 'her' side of the crane; Ruth's insistence that the Lego base be placed where she could reach it was accomplished verbally ('Bring it over here') and nonverbally (by simultaneously pointing at the floor).

It's possible to use a column transcript for children's speech, as well as columns for actions, but when I tried this for Ruth and James the transcript became too complicated to read so I had to fall back on a standard layout for speech.

Even if you don't want to record actions as the equivalent of verbal turns, you can still record nonverbal information in a separate 'comment' column. Figure 5 does this to some extent. You can also use a 'comment' column to provide an explicit interpretation of the talk—I went some way towards this in Figures 6 and 7. If you want to include different types of information, such as nonverbal information and comment/ interpretation, it's best to allocate separate columns for these.

Analyses Involving Transcripts

You can adopt the same general principles in analysing transcripts as 'in analysing talk recorded in other formats. Articles 9 and 10 in this volume show how transcripts may be drawn on to provide quantitative analyses of small group talk, in which speaking turns are counted, or categorised and counted. In this case it's possible to make a more detailed analysis than when counting and coding on the spot or directly from audio or video recordings; the analysis can also be mulled over at length and discussed with others.

Transcripts can also help you look more closely at qualitative aspects of talk—and it's perhaps in this respect that teachers, and many researchers, have found them particularly useful. Qualitative information can be used to supplement or help explain other types of analysis: an analysis of pupils' contributions to group talk could be accompanied by a transcript illustrating certain characteristics of talk (Article 9 provides an illustration of this).

More open-ended exploration of extracts of talk can provide information on the formal properties of talk, or on the functions it fulfills: for instance, how relationships are established and maintained or how pupils achieve an understanding of particular concepts. There are examples of such analyses of transcripts in this volume (see, for instance, articles 8, 10 and 11).

Close scrutiny of class or group talk is time consuming and may be extremely frustrating. John Richmond describes his experiences as a member of a Talk Workshop Group at Vauxhall Manor School, a girls' comprehensive in south London:

> There are times when you stare at the video, or at transcripts, or at writing, and ask yourself, 'Well, is there anything here at all?' and for a while you lose your nerve. Or there are periods of impatience for answers, when there may be no answers. (Richmond, 1984: 60–1)

On the other hand, working with recordings and transcripts can provide unexpected insights into pupils' understanding. Richmond describes a detailed examination, running over several weeks, of a group discussion in a third year chemistry lesson. The discussion concerned an experiment illustrating endothermic and exothermic reactions (in which heat is, respectively, taken in and given out).

> After repeated playing of the tape, reading aloud and discussion of the transcript, we realised that at the two significant moments of the experiment the children were aware that the reaction could be described as both endothermic and exothermic, depending on how you looked at it. The chemistry teacher confirmed the validity of

the children's understanding, and admitted that on both occasions when he had intervened in the group to push them towards the answers he wanted he had been unaware of the complexity of what they were trying to say. The realization that the pupils were using talk to struggle with an abstract reality more subtle than the teacher at the time was even aware of was a piece of knowledge with impetus in it. It rebounded directly into the chemistry teacher's assumptions and practice, and, by analogy, into the classrooms of all of us. (Richmond, 1984: 59)

Such close examination and discussion of recordings and transcripts has been termed 'insightful observation'. It became particularly well-known in the work of Barnes, Britton & Rosen (1969). While it has been found very revealing, it isn't without its critics. Michael Stubbs (1984) comments on the work of Douglas Barnes:

There is no doubt that many teachers find Barnes' work very helpful: it has made them aware of all kinds of things they had never noticed before, and Barnes is a very sensitive observer. This is precisely one of the problems; there is no method or guiding principle for those of us who are not so sensitive or full of insight as Barnes. (Stubbs, 1984: 220)

You will need to weigh up the pros and cons of carrying out such open-ended explorations of talk. You may find these particularly productive if worked through, or at least discussed, with colleagues or pupils.

Quantitative and Qualitative Approaches

At the beginning of this article I set up a broad distinction between quantitative and qualitative approaches to research, while pointing out that the distinction between the two sometimes blurred. I shall summarise here how these approaches may be drawn on in the observation and analysis of spoken language, and also some advantages and disadvantages attached to their use.

A quantitative approach allows you to represent your data in terms of numbers. You can make a numerical comparison between talk produced by different people or during different events: article 9 in this volume shows that during two interactions boys took more speaking turns than girls, but there was also variability between boys and between girls; article 10 shows variability between the amount spoken by girls and boys in different contexts.

When representing data that has been analysed using quantitative methods it is usual to display this in a table (as in articles 9 and 10).

Alternative forms of representation such as histograms or bar charts may be used to point up comparisons between people or events.

Data may be analysed using prespecified categories of talk: the observation schedule in Figure 4 requires the observer to allocate talk to such categories at the point of observation.

Alternatively, categories may emerge from close scrutiny of data. In article 9 David Graddol and I discuss how we categorised different ways in which pupils began a speaking exchange with the teacher. These categories emerged from playing, and replaying, a video-recording of the interaction. Such categories are not 'naturally' present in the data, but will depend upon your own research interests.

Article 9 identifies discrete categories: ways of beginning an exchange fall either into one category or another. However, categories need not be discrete: you may devise a set that allows you to allocate the same stretch of talk to more than one category.

Representing talk in terms of numbers has the disadvantage that it is necessarily a reductive exercise: talk is reduced to a set of categories; it is abstracted from its original context; it is unambiguously pigeon-holed, masking the rather fluid, uncertain and negotiated meanings that are evident when talk is examined in context.

Talk may be recorded and analysed in a more open-ended way. Researchers adopting a qualitative 'field-notes' approach to recording can note down and explore any interesting aspects of their data. What count as interesting aspects will depend upon the questions the researcher is concerned to investigate, but sometimes points emerge that are quite unexpected.

Aspects of the data may only begin to make sense when mulled over and compared with other information, or perhaps discussed with speakers. Sometimes interpretations may change, or you may want to allow for a number of different interpretations.

When presenting and discussing data that has been recorded and analysed using a qualitative approach, researchers frequently quote selectively from field-notes or transcripts to support points they wish to make. Transcripts may be supported by a detailed commentary, as in article 8.

Such ways of analysing and presenting data allow the researcher to preserve important contextual information that affects the meanings of utterances, and also to preserve the ambiguity and fluidity of these meanings. The approach is selective in that two researchers may (legitimately) notice different things about a stretch of talk or provide different interpretations of utterances. There is also a danger of unintended bias, in that researchers may notice features of talk that support a point they wish to make and ignore counter-evidence.

I mentioned that the qualitative/quantitative distinction is not always clear-cut in practice, and that researchers may choose to draw on a range of approaches. In article 10, Julie Fisher provides a quantitative analysis of speaking turns, finding considerable variability across contexts. She seeks to explain this by adopting a more open-ended, qualitative approach to her data. It is often useful to draw on a combination of methods— these may complement one another and provide a more complete picture of spoken language.

References

Barnes, D., Britton, J. and Rosen, H. (1969) *Language, the Learner and the School*. Harmondsworth: Penguin.

Cameron, D., Fraser, E., Harvey, P., Rampton, M.B.H. and Richardson, K. (1992) *Researching Language: Issues of Power and Method*. London: Routledge.

Coolican, H. (1990) *Research Methods and Statistics in Psychology*. London: Hodder and Stoughton.

Cumbria Oracy Project (1988) *Talking Sense: Oracy Group Work in Primary Classrooms*. Carlisle: Cumbria County Council.

Edelsky, C. (1981) Who's got the floor? *Language in Society* 10, 383–421.

Edwards, A.D. and Westgate, D.P.G. (1987) *Investigating Classroom Talk*. London: Falmer Press.

Hitchcock, G. and Hughes, D. (1989) *Research and the Teacher: A Qualitative Introduction to School-based Research*. London: Routledge.

Labov, W. (1970) The study of language in its social context. In W. Labov (1972) *Sociolinguistic Patterns*. Oxford: Basil Blackwell.

Myers, L. (1992) *Genderwatch After the Education Reform Act*. Cambridge: Cambridge University Press.

National Association for the Teaching of English (NATE) Language and Gender Committee (1988) *Gender Issues in English Coursework*. Sheffield: NATE.

Ochs, E. (1979) Transcription as theory. In E. Ochs and B.B. Schieffelin (eds) *Developmental Pragmatics*. London: Academic Press.

Open University (1991) *P535: Talk and Learning 5–16: An Inservice Pack on Oracy for Teachers*. Milton Keynes: The Open University.

Richmond, J. (1984) Setting up for learning in a cold climate. In M. Meek and J. Miller (eds) *Changing English: Essays for Harold Rosen*. London: Heinemann Educational Books.

Sacks, H., Schegloff, E. and Jefferson, G. (1974) A simplest systematics for the organization of turn-taking for conversation. *Language* 50(4), 696–735.

Stubbs, M. (1984) Applied discourse and educational linguistics. In P. Trudgill (ed) *Applied Sociolinguistics*. London: Academic Press.

Walker, R. (1989) *Doing Research: A Handbook for Teachers*. London: Routledge.

4 Negotiation as a Criterial Factor in Learning to Read in a Second Language

EVE GREGORY

Introduction

Research studies have concentrated largely upon the difficulties young minority group children are likely to encounter upon beginning reading in school rather than analysing why some might succeed. According to the field of inquiry, children new to the mainstream language and culture have been viewed as linguistically, socially or culturally 'disadvantaged' in facing classroom demands. The theme of cultural conflict and its reflection in different uses of language by teachers and pupils in the classroom has received detailed investigation from both linguists and social anthropologists. Their ethnographic and longitudinal research has produced evidence to illustrate the problems young minority children might meet through different expectations of how and when to speak with the teacher (Phillips, 1972; Michaels, 1986) as well as understanding what might be involved in reading in school (Schieffelin & Cochran-Smith, 1984; Anderson & Stokes, 1984). These studies centre on negative rather than positive classroom interactions; on the general experience of different minority groups rather than the specific experience of individual minority group children.

Other studies have focused more directly on particular cultural practices and how their mastery might benefit children in school. One specific cultural practice picked out as vital to early school literacy is that of story-reading. Studies on young monolingual children have shown a significant correlation between familiarity with written stories from home and reading progress in school (Scollon & Scollon, 1981; Wells, 1985). These studies see familiarity with a cultural practice primarily in terms of gaining access to patterns of narrative which will be reinforced in school 'literacy events', thus enabling a child quickly to become initiated into the 'membership' of the group of school readers. Detailed evidence

49

has been provided on how some young monolingual children learn this cultural practice both at home (Dombey, 1983) and in the nursery school (Cochran-Smith, 1984). It shows us clearly how children develop particular cognitive and linguistic strategies as part of the interactional process between care-giver and young child during shared story-readings. These children are then able to apply familiar patterns of language and learning from home to reading in school.

In her study 'What no bed-time story means . . .' (1982), Brice-Heath investigates what lacking this particular cultural practice with its accompanying cognitive and linguistic advantages might mean for minority children upon school entry. She maintains that these children will need to learn to employ an 'analytic field-independent cognitive style' which is vital for successful school learning. In other words, they will need to develop different habits of learning to gain early reading success in school. Brice-Heath itemises ways in which one group of minority children will have to learn to extend its labelling habits to other domains, learn distinctions in discourse strategies and structures and become active information-givers within a participant frame of reference to books. Thus, they need somehow to gain access to what the mainstream children have already learned through story-readings. In this paper, I shall investigate how one non-mainstream bilingual child begins to tackle early school literacy and the ways in which negotiation between teacher and child helps facilitate his task.

Defining 'Negotiation'

In everyday usage, we often understand 'negotiation' as signifying conflict and assertion. For example, we refer to business or financial deals being 'negotiated' by parties with different interests. However, this is only one sense of the term. In this paper, I shall call upon three definitions (Concise Oxford Dictionary, Fowler & Fowler, 1968) and use 'negotiation' to mean the following:

(i) *Negotiation is to confer, consult together, take advice or to discuss in order to reach agreement.* This interpretation of negotiation is central to theories of language and child development which view learning as a collaborative process within a social framework. Thus, human cognitive understanding arises from an 'intersubjectivity' (Newson & Newson, 1975), a process of negotiation between two or more human beings. This negotiation begins in early infancy with visual 'turn-taking' and develops through communicative gestures and dialogue. Of key importance is the role of the adult in these collaborative activities. A 'loan of consciousness' (Bruner, 1986) is given whereby the infant becomes familiar with the role of a skilled communicator, participating in forms of communication even before s/he is able to understand the full content of what is being communicated. Adults, therefore, 'scaffold' a child's language development by pitching their talk at a level the young child can understand (Ninio & Bruner, 1978) and making 'rich interpretations' of the child's talk, enabling the young learner to master meanings in new contexts (Brown, 1977).

Conversation has been seen as a particularly important site for this to take place. A young child is able to negotiate meanings through 'conversational acts' (Dore, 1979) where adults model conventional interpretations of intentions. Young children learning a second language may gain similar benefits but conversation (and, therefore, negotiation of meaning) is said to be more limited as less information will be shared by adult and child (Hatch *et al.*, 1979). Such a negotiation of meaning is, therefore, less intensive than between care-giver and young child. The scope of these studies in any case does not include the negotiation of the meaning of print in school.

The nature and potential of the scaffolding process within a formal instructional setting has been documented by Wood, Bruner & Ross (1976). Young children between three and five were given the task of building a pyramid of blocks with controlled and systematic tutoring. It was found that successful 'scaffolding' by the teacher was typified by the following features:
(a) a reduction in the degree of freedom; i.e. reducing the size of the task for the child and 'filling in' the rest;
(b) keeping the child 'in the field' and motivated;
(c) marking critical or relevant features;
(d) 'modelling' an idealised version of the task.
Here we see a conscious use of negotiation on the part of the teacher where the 'scaffolding' provided enables the child to reach a considerably higher level of cognitive development than that which can be attained in isolation.

This difference in the level of social and cognitive attainments between the child working alone or together with the guidance of an adult or more capable peers has been coined 'the zone of proximal development' or ZPD (Vygotsky, 1978). Key conditions for this process are joint activity by both where the partners have differential responsibility and expertise (Cole, 1985). The child is never forced beyond its capacity.

Negotiation in this definition is, therefore, synonymous with 'collaboration'. It is an important feature of the negotiation taking place between the teacher and child in this paper.
(ii) *Negotiation is to compromise or meet half way.* Linguists show

how adults often incorporate the meanings and utterances of a young child into the conversation taking place even if it involves changing what they originally set out to say (Wells, 1987). This often happens during discussions on shared stories in the home but is far less likely during school reading lessons (Heap, 1985). The child and teacher in this paper, therefore, counter expectations from previous studies.

(iii) *Negotiation is to overcome a difficulty.* This is a figurative use of the term, i.e. to negotiate a difficulty. In this paper, I shall illustrate how Tajul negotiates his difficulty with getting to know the English language and culture by deliberately trying out the limits of what is acceptable within them. He exaggerates his lack of familiarity of English customs which results in considerable help and direct answers from his teacher.

Both cultural studies and those on child and language development take us some way in understanding our young bilingual child's task. We read that Tajul will need to develop new habits of learning successfully to participate in British schooled literacy events but we know that he has already successfully negotiated meaning through the aid of adult scaffolding in his early cognitive and linguistic development. However, what studies do not show us is how he might use such negotiating skills to begin a different kind of learning in school. The purpose of this paper is to begin an investigation of this.

In the following sections, I shall pick out features of this negotiation in discourse. We must not forget, too, that both teacher and child play out their roles within the setting which has been staged—in this case, it is the stories and the text. This will place an important framework around their negotiations.

Methodology and Data Collection

My data comes from dialogues between the teacher and child as they 'share reading' together during his first eighteen months in school. 'Shared reading' is now a commonly adopted approach to teaching reading in British Infant schools and such reading 'lessons' facilitate data collection of interactions between teacher and individual child.

But what is 'shared reading' exactly? The approach is the practical result of research showing the importance of 'sharing' a story with a caring adult (Cochran-Smith, 1984; Wells, 1985). Teachers are aware of studies showing the value of choosing 'real' books where the story is exciting and the text and illustrations polysemic (Meek, 1988). Adopting a similar role to that of caretaker with young child, teachers at first read stories then gradually encourage children to take over the reading themselves. Practitioners have shown how such an 'apprenticeship' approach can take place in the classroom (Holdaway, 1979; Waterland, 1985) and publishers have responded by producing both scheme and well-loved stories as 'Big Books' for whole class 'sharing'.

British Infant schools are usually organised around an integrated day which allows the teacher to share books with individuals or small groups whenever time allows. The teacher in this class encourages children to bring a book to share with her at any time. Working as a colleague from the local College of Education with students training in the school, I taped and observed her 'book-sharings' with individuals and groups during the children's first two years in school. This information together with interviews with the teacher and the children's families contribute to a corpus of data showing children from different backgrounds beginning reading in school. Significant differences between children's 'sharings' of reading with the teacher are being noted for closer analysis.

The excerpts of dialogue presented here span Tajul's first eighteen months in school and they are typical of the teacher's interactions with this child. Tajul is a five year old Bengali speaking child who entered school a few weeks ago speaking and apparently understanding very little English. He is doing exceptionally well 'against all the odds'. By relying here on classroom discourse for my data, I am focusing on only one part of the 'literacy event' thereby basing my argument upon the productionist position of knowledge, where meaning is viewed as being made collaboratively through the exchanges between teacher and child in the lesson (Heap, 1985). I shall, however, use the term 'reading event' as I bring some details of the context as evidence.

The ethnographic approach used means that analyses are subjective in the sense that I am giving my own interpretations of classroom dialogues. As I cannot know the motives or intentions of the participants, I am presuming that they share my own frame of reference; that what makes sense for me will have a similar meaning for them. This is particularly pertinent when I interpret the intention behind the words of a child just beginning to learn English, whose life-space is very different from my own. As far as possible, I attempt to overcome this limitation by (i) grounding conclusions in the consequences or functions of the child's words, i.e. how the teacher verbally interprets or responds to them; (ii) using the teacher and my own role as participant-observer as 'typical actors' in the 'typical situation' of the classroom (Schutz, 1964). But what does negotiation in school discourse look like? In the following exchanges, I shall show some of the features of negotiation as defined above and go on to discuss how we might generalise Tajul's experience.

Negotiating the Formulae of 'Shared Reading'

Teacher: Which one shall we look at first? That one?
Tajul: That's very good.
Teacher: Is it?
Tajul: Yes.
Teacher: Do you know that story?
Tajul: No.

Tajul started school six weeks before this exchange took place. How does negotiation take place here? I propose that Tajul has learned the formula for 'getting the teacher to share reading with you' and is using it but at the same time, he steps outside the formula to make his own position clear. The formula is 'liking the story' which will ensure a reading. At the same time, he maintains in no uncertain terms that the story is new to him. To any teacher of a child just coming to English this is a clear indication of how much help she needs to give. By offering the comment 'That's very good', Tajul is opening the discussion. His later 'No' negotiates the level and kind of feedback he requires. The apparent contradiction in his words makes complete sense within the context of the task in hand.

Negotiating the Role of Prediction in Reading

Two months later, the following exchange takes place:

Tajul: What's that? (pointing to half-hidden figure in picture)
Teacher: I don't know. Turn over the page and we'll find out. (Reads) '. . . and it flopped and wriggled and jiggled.' It looked terrible!
Tajul: Yes.
Teacher: (whispers) What do you think it could be?
Tajul: Terrible.
Teacher: A terrible monster, I think, don't you?
Tajul: Yes.

Again, Tajul initiates the exchange. There is, indeed, a collaboration whereby, like the care-giver with a young child, the teacher is able to provide a firm scaffold around his few words. However, such scaffolding transcends the strict limitations of the actual shared information we have been told typifies teacher/second language learner interactions (Hatch, 1979). If Tajul had simply pointed at any object in the picture and asked 'What's that?' he could well have just received the answer 'It's a —'. I suggest that negotiation hinges on asking a question which is a real and urgent request for information and leads to a discussion 'What can it be?' At no point does the teacher see this as a 'labelling' question, for they are both within the context of 'story-reading'. She leads Tajul to try to guess, hypothesise and predict, importantly showing him what reading involves. At the same time, she provides him with a wealth of English, hardly comparable with the 'label' he might possibly have received if the question had been a labelling one—or the context different. For it is the story which at the same time widens the possible feedback '. . . and it wriggled' etc., and yet gives the discussion a very definite frame '. . . We'll find the information from the book soon' which conversation cannot share.

After six months in school, Tajul is more skilled in negotiating this language of hypothesis with his teacher and is beginning to use it himself:

Tajul: Look! They're gonna find gold! (pointing to a picture of a fireman entering a burning house).
Teacher: (laughs) Do you think so?
Tajul: Yes.
Teacher: (laughs) I don't know. They might be.
Tajul: And there might be fish and water.
Teacher: Do you think so? Might be.
Tajul: In there, there's water (points to bubbles under fire-hose)
Teacher: Underneath, you mean? Under the bubbles?
Tajul: Yes.
Teacher: Could be.

With his words 'They're gonna find gold', Tajul is playing the game of 'make believe', creating the meaning of the text for himself and, importantly, negotiating what reading entails. The teacher believes that an important part of learning to read lies in taking the text into life, so she negotiates with him what might happen. In this way, she confirms to him that this is how to go about story-reading. At the same time, she responds playfully, supporting his early attempts at the language of hypothesis.

Negotiating How Reading Must Make Sense

Perhaps encouraged by such firm support, Tajul is assertive, daring to experiment and take risks. After seven months in school, he initiates this exchange:

Tajul: You know, lions . . . (on sharing 'The Tiger who came to Tea')
Teacher: They're like tigers, aren't they?
Tajul: Yes.
Teacher: But tigers have got stripes.
Tajul: And tigers . . . and lion is tiger's friend.
Teacher: Yes. That's right.

Who knows what Tajul originally wanted to say about lions? Earlier, he had simply mistaken the English word 'tiger' for 'lion':

Tajul: That lion.
Teacher: Tiger.
Tajul: Yes.

and it is quite possible that he is doing so again. However, the teacher attempts to read his intention within the context of the story and express what she thinks he cannot yet say; 'They're like tigers, aren't they?' Tajul's response, 'And tigers . . . and lion is tiger's friend' shows he is probably misinterpreting the word 'like'. However, in negotiating the double meaning of this word, he seems to be working hard to make the story 'make sense'. One interpretation is that Tajul realises that 'lion' and 'tiger' must have some coherence within 'reading a story' and that he is linking them as best he can. He is, indeed, narrating at a simple level. At the same time, he appears to be aiming to share the teacher's intention and keep the 'shared reading' going. This demands a considerable 'decentring' in Donaldson's (1978) terms.

These strategies of predicting, sense-making and stepping into the world of 'Let's pretend' correspond to his teacher's interpretation of 'reading' and she reacts by giving considerable feedback. Notice how his lack of English is certainly no detriment and may even push him into both using metaphor and entering the playful world of make-believe in a way which would be less acceptable for a monolingual child of this age in school. Here, Tajul has been in school for four months:

Teacher: (reads from 'Meg at Sea') That's the magnifying glass . . . There's the fire. Can you see?
Tajul: Yes. There?
Teacher: Yes.
Tajul: There's the window. (points to the magnifying glass).
Teacher: That's the magnifying glass. It's nearly the same as a window, isn't it?

Negotiating the Boundaries of 'Reading a Story'

We have already seen how it can be valuable to use certain formulae to partner your teacher in 'shared reading'. But there are certain rules, too; boundaries which delimit the event. During some stories, Tajul challenges his teacher to show him what may or may not be included within 'reading'. Tajul uses both playful and real questions to negotiate what is acceptable to the 'story reading' framework. Reading is thus one special type of play and, as such is 'rule-bound' (Vygotsky, 1978). But rules can be learned through negotiation too. The rules of 'shared reading' as it takes place in this classroom are few and simple. Sometimes, playfulness and wondering and the resulting language of hypothesis are fully acceptable within the teacher's interpretation of a text-to-life approach to reading (Tajul has been in school for six months):

Tajul: Is that a mummy? (pointing to a picture of a woman in Ladybird's 'The Fireman')
Teacher: (doesn't understand) Pardon?
Tajul: Is that a mummy?
Teacher: Might be.
Tajul: Yes. (definitely).
Teacher: Could be . . .
Tajul: And that's a mummy and that's daddy.
Teacher: Might be!
Tajul: It is!

There are many such examples. On other occasions, however, the teacher realises that discussion is going beyond the boundaries of the story and 'reading' as the task in hand. Then she is careful to 'pull' Tajul back to the task in hand which is the framework of the text and the story embedded in it.

Teacher: (reading from 'Meg at Sea') That's the fish.
Tajul: And that?
Teacher: That's the octopus. That's an octopus.
Tajul: (points) That's the fish.
Teacher: (reads) A present for you . . . (out of text) Yes, there's the fish. (reads again) Meg cooked the fish . . .
Tajul: And, do you like?
Teacher: Mmm. And they like to eat octopus, too, I think. Do you like octopus?
Tajul: (hesitantly) No. Do you?
Teacher: No. Some people do. (Reads) Meg and Mog had a rest.
Tajul: English do?
Teacher: Well, some English do. Not many . . . (reads) Chopper ahoy! They saw a helicopter . . .

Through both real and playful questions, Tajul negotiates where the boundaries of 'reading a story' lie. The basic rule which emerges from a number of teacher/child interactions is that the dialogue is purposeful. Neither teacher nor child must stray too far from the text.

Negotiating how Stories are Seated Within Culture

The above exchange shows Tajul beginning to sort out the boundaries of play and reality in life. To the teacher, getting meaning from print involves understanding the cultural framework in which the text is set. On occasions where Tajul is working out the host community's habits, she is prepared to stay away longer from the text. After a year in school, we see the limits of Tajul's knowledge of British habits and how he negotiates his difficulties through shared reading. The story is 'The Hungry Giant', a 'Big Book' which Tajul is very familiar with from whole class readings:

Teacher: (reads) And the giant got some bread.
Tajul: (points to bread) This not bread. These are finger.
Teacher: It's supposed to be bread, actually. Some bread looks like that. It's not supposed to be fingers, it's supposed to be bread.
Tajul: It's not bread.
Teacher: Well, if you go into Tesco's supermarket you can find some long thin bread like that. What does your bread look like? Does your bread look different from that?
Tajul: No. My bread is square.
Teacher: Oh, your bread is square, is it? Well, some bread is long and thin and some bread is square.

Tajul plays using metaphor, but this time the teacher prefers to give him a serious explanation of British cultural habits. Tajul's familiarity with the story means there can be little doubt that he realises this is not supposed to be a finger, whatever it may look like. We cannot be sure whether he is working out the limits of 'bread within a story', asking 'What does your bread look like that?' or simply playing 'Let's pretend' within the story. Whatever may be the case, he has successfully negotiated this particular difficulty and found out what British bread may look like, where it may be purchased and that it is not just 'storytime' bread. After a number of such exchanges, he will begin to realise that getting meaning from print involves understanding the culture in which it is set too.

The above exchanges, I argue, are radically different from those presented in studies on school reading lessons or early literacy events at home. Both of these assume a common literacy or cultural 'base', meaning that expectations are shared by participants; they thus provide a different starting-point from that of minority group children in 'shared reading' lessons. Reading comprehension lessons, dominated by the ERF formula, take as given the child's understanding of what is actually required in reading, are carefully controlled by the teacher and allow no space for negotiation. Young children in early literacy events with their care-giver are learning a whole cultural practice as part of the fabric of their 'home' cultural base. These exchanges differ, too, from the few examples we have of literacy events between minority group care-givers and young children which have been shown to be dominated by 'labelling' questions (Brice-Heath & Branscombe, 1986).

I suggest that the 'shared reading' event may be a means of entry for minority group children into a cultural practice and the uses of language relevant to it as they are performed in school. Tajul shows us that becoming familiar with a cultural practice means more than mastering language forms. Particularly, we see how he and his teacher negotiate opinion on the story, the role of prediction, moving from text to life and the place of local cultural habits in understanding what is going on. The relevant language is, indeed, one essential part and to some extent can act as a 'code' for mastering the practice itself. Notice how there is no contradiction for Tajul or the teacher when Tajul announces liking a story he is totally unfamiliar with.

Embedded within the wider frame of 'shared reading' are the stories. An understanding of how these work as well as realising their importance in school are likely to be key factors in deciding a child's future reading performance. The stories themselves act as scaffolds; they provide security through being 'encapsulated' in the book; they allow experiment through being playful. The stories are so framed to allow teacher and child to suspend reality. Through play and the use of metaphor, a different kind of language evolves from that of conversation. Tajul would have floundered helplessly if participating in the 'sharing time' Michaels (1986) has described, yet here the story provides both the backcloth and support to the necessary structures of language and culture as well as being a forum for negotiation to take place.

But how can we generalise Tajul's experience and what implications might the above examples have for teaching strategies with young minority group children? In the above discourse, Tajul has generated a number of hypotheses about the written word. He has done this through questioning and challenging the teacher as she 'shares' the text with him. Through play, he is searching out the boundaries of 'what counts as reading in school'. His teacher, in return, picks upon and negotiates exactly those features which she sees to be vital to beginning to get meaning from text. The exchanges show a synchrony of movement from text to fantasy to real life and back to text again which both initiate.

The teacher's role, however, is to orchestrate the boundaries of reading, to ensure the final return to text and we see her doing this throughout the reading event. Analysis of exchanges with a child 'doing exceptionally well' show her using distinct strategies which translate into practice her own ideas on what becoming a reader involves. Specifically, these mean enjoyment, trying to predict, making sense of the text and the story through drawing on experiences from life and playing 'What if?' when these are lacking. Between this child and the teacher such strategies seem to come 'naturally' and become obvious only upon closer scrutiny. With other minority group children who are not so quickly successful exchanges are not taking this pattern.

When young children step quickly and easily into reading in school, it is tempting for us to take it for granted that they have already 'absorbed' ways of seeing meaning in print through familiarity with the cultural practice of story-reading at home. Studies on narrative genre show us clearly that the systematic structures and linguistic habits we use for narratising experiences are not 'absorbed' but quite definitely learned and are culturally specific (Rosen, 1982). When young minority group children, for whom this practice is new, take on reading just as quickly we tend to regard them as 'exceptions' learning through a process rather like 'osmosis' in their contact with the teacher and 'schooled' children. This is not surprising for studies on early linguistic and cultural competence naturally focus more on 'learning' rather than the teaching which is taking place. For minority group children in school, however, this may mean alighting more by luck upon what they are supposed to do.

In this paper, I claim that Tajul is being given a number of quite specific reading 'lessons' which I have outlined above. The teacher is teaching Tajul to read by discussing with him exactly what is required of him as a reader in school. It sometimes appears that he is teaching himself and to a certain extent this is true: but she is quite carefully drawing up the boundaries of 'reading' and making sure he stays within them. Tajul and his teacher show us the importance of making precise and clear to minority group children exactly what we in school understand by 'seeing meaning in print' together with the steps needed to get there. This will mean taking stock of our own ideas of what 'makes' a reader before devising and practising distinct strategies in our teaching. Only in this way, I believe, can we ensure that all minority group children get an equal 'share' in our reading lessons.

References

Anderson, A.B. and Stokes, S.J. (1984) Social and institutional influences on the development and practice of literacy. In H. Goelman, A. Oberg and F. Smith (eds) *Awakening to Literacy*. London: Heinemann Educational.

Brice-Heath, S. (1982) What no bed-time story means. *Language in Society* 2(1), 49–74.

Brice-Heath, S. and Branscombe, A. (1986) The book as narrative prop in language acquisition. In B. Schieffelin and P. Gilmore (eds) *The Acquisition of Literacy: Ethnographic Perspectives*. Norwood, NJ: Ablex.

Brown, R. (1977) Introduction. In E.E. Snow and C.A. Ferguson (eds) *Talking to Children: Language Input and Acquisition*. Cambridge: Cambridge University Press.

Bruner, J. (1986) *Actual Minds, Possible Worlds*. Cambridge, Mass.: Harvard University Press.

Cochran-Smith, M. (1984) *The Making of a Reader*. Norwood, NJ: Ablex.

Cole, M. (1985) The concept of internalisation: Vygotsky's account of the genesis of higher mental functions. In J. Wertsch (ed.) *Culture, Communication and Cognition. Vygotskian Perspectives*. Cambridge: Cambridge University Press.

Dombey, H. (1983) Learning the language of books. In M. Meek (ed.) *Opening Moves*. London: Institute of Education Press. (Bedford Way Papers 17).

Donaldson, M. (1978) *Children's Minds*. Glasgow: Fontana.

Dore, J. (1979) Conversational acts and the acquisition of language. In E. Ochs and B. Schieffelin (eds) *Developmental Pragmatics*. Norwood, NJ: Ablex.

Hatch, E., Peck, S. and Wagner-Gough, J. (1979) A look at process in child second language acquisition. In E. Ochs and B. Schieffelin, *Developmental Pragmatics*. New York: Academic Press.

Heap, J. (1985) Discourse and the production of classroom knowledge. *Curriculum Inquiry* 16(1), 73–86.

Holdaway, D. (1979) *The Foundations of Literacy*. Sydney: Ashton-Scholastic.

Meek, M. (1988) *How Texts Teach What Readers Learn*. Bath: Thimble Press.

Michaels, S. (1986) Narrative presentations: An oral preparation for literacy with 1st graders. In J. Cook-Gumperz (ed.) *The Social Construction of Literacy*. Cambridge: Cambridge University Press.

Newson, E. and J. (1975) Intersubjectivity and the transmission of culture. *Bulletin of the British Psychological Society* 28, 437–46.

Ninio, A. and Bruner, J. (1978) The achievements and antecedents of labelling. *Journal of Child Language* 5, 5–15.

Fowler, H.W. and F.G. (1968) *The Concise Oxford Dictionary of Current English*. Oxford: Clarendon Press.

Phillips, S.U. (1972) Participant structures and communicative competence: Warm Springs children in community and classroom. In C.B. Cazden, V.P. John and D. Hymes (eds) *Functions of Language in the Classroom*. New York: Teachers College Press.

Rosen, H. (1982) *The Nurture of Narrative*. Paper to Annual Meeting of IRA, Chicago.

Schieffelin, B.B. and Cochran-Smith, M. (1984) Learning to read culturally: Literacy before schooling. In H. Goelman, A. Oberg and F. Smith (eds) *Awakening to Literacy*. London: Heinemann.

Scollon, R. and B.K. (1981) *Narrative, Literacy and Face in Interethnic Communication*. Norwood, NJ: Ablex.

Schutz, A. (1964) *Collected Papers, II: Studies in Social Theory*. The Hague: Martinus Nijhoff.

Vygotsky, L. (1978) *Mind in Society: The Development of Higher Psychological Processes*. Cambridge, Mass.: Harvard University Press.

Waterland, L. (1985) *Read with Me*. Bath: Thimble Press.

Wells, G. (1985) Pre-school related literacy activities. In D.R. Olson, N. Torrance and A. Hildyard (eds) *Literacy, Language and Learning*. Cambridge: Cambridge University Press.

——(1987) *The Meaning Makers*. London: Hodder and Stoughton.

Wood, D., Bruner, J.S. and Ross, G. (1976) The role of tutoring in problem solving. *Journal of Child Psychology and Psychiatry* 17, 89–100.

5 Through Whose Eyes? Exploring Racism Through Literature with White Students

BEVERLEY NAIDOO

The Research Project

This article discusses a research project I conducted in 1988/89 which involved a year's course of literature for a class of Year 9 (13–14 year old) white secondary school students, through which issues of racism could be explored, with the selected books all being written from a perspective strongly indicting racism. I was not the teacher but a participant observer, my presence being explained to the class in terms of my interest in their responses to the literature. The students' attention was drawn to the reader-response work in which they would be engaging, but not to my particular interest in their responses to issues of inequality and racism.

I began with five main objectives. The first was to establish initially what were the significant frames of reference amongst the students in relation to 'race'. A survey I devised was administered (not by myself) to the whole year group (177 students) a couple of months before the course began and again four months after the course ended. Part of the survey involved the students agreeing or disagreeing with a range of explicitly racist and non-racist statements. This provided me with a limited amount of quantitative information that might not otherwise have come to light and which proved useful in interpreting some of my qualitative findings (see Appendix).

Secondly, using selected works of literature, it was my intention to develop, in collaboration with the teacher, ways of exploring these texts which encouraged empathy with the perspective of characters who were victims of racism but who resisted it. The project methodology involved a strong emphasis on students responding directly to the texts, for example in reading journals and in small group discussions.

Thirdly, I intended to provide specific interventions, promoting perspectives that would challenge the students, through inviting a number of visitors to work with them—including an elderly Jewish couple, who had escaped from Vienna after the Nazi invasion, and various black artists.

My fourth objective was to document and monitor the processes at work, particularly those which indicated any change in perceptions, or obstacles to change. The major part of my data was qualitative. Apart from keeping my own diary of observations, I had access to all the students' reading journals in which they wrote responses to what they were experiencing. In addition they were asked to respond in a variety of ways to key points in the texts either in writing or in discussion. All the class and small group discussions were tape-recorded throughout the year and I tape-recorded a number of interviews with various people, including all the female students with the help of an assistant.

My final objective was to complement the above data with the students' evaluations of the year's course at the end and to investigate whether there was any notable change in their frames of reference relating to 'race'.

The form my research project took—with a particular focus on the responses of the students as readers—developed partly out of my own curiosity as a writer of children's fiction (Naidoo, 1985; 1989) attempting to uncover something of 'the reader as ideologist' (Hollindale, 1988). How do readers' frames of reference affect their reading and the ways in which they follow or diverge from the paths authors offer their 'implied readers' (Iser, 1978) within texts? I was furthermore attracted by the possibilities of reader-response study and an ethnographic approach, as characterised by Michael Benton (1988): reflexivity of the researcher who forms part of the phenomena as a 'participant' rather than an 'objective' observer; recognition of the context of reading; description leading to the theorising of the process of response; and flexibility of enquiry, given that one is not tied to testing out a preconceived theory.

In summary, my original aims were:

- to investigate the potential for certain works of literature, which contain strong indictments of racism from the writer's perspective, to extend white students' empathies;
- to challenge ethnocentric and racist assumptions and concepts;
- and to develop critical thinking about the nature of our society.

By using various reader-response strategies I hoped to uncover something of the reading transactions amongst a class of white teenage readers. Apart from the personal perceptual filters through which each student would view and respond to a text, could I detect the workings of a more common filter connected with 'race'? My concern was not only to uncover the students' frames of reference but to observe whether any apparent shifts occurred in these frames through their reading of the selected texts, through discussions, or through other specific interventions including drama and the work with visitors.

As an action-researcher I acknowledged a dual role. On the one hand, as activator and instigator of the project, I had devised a year's course of literature which I hoped would have the maximum chance of challenging racist frames of reference. On the other hand, as researcher, I was required to observe as accurately and fully as possible what seemed to be occurring. Both roles involved subjective judgement and the study was largely ethnographic in character. My intended primary focus was to have been on the interaction of students and texts. Recognising the close web of content and context, when devising my research, I had envisaged a collaborative learning framework within the class—one in which the students would not feel 'over-weighted' by the teacher's authority (Hall, 1981). In the event, although the reader-response methodology ensured a certain amount of space for students to express themselves without being directly led by the teacher, the classroom I found myself observing was far more traditionally teacher-centred than I had anticipated. I thus rapidly found my intended primary focus widening from that of students and texts to one encompassing the context of the traditional classroom in which the texts were being presented and 'constructed' by the teacher. The classroom in turn could not be extrapolated from the school, nor the school from the society.

A Framework for the Research

Literature and the reading process

My decision to devise a project with literature at its core, for a school in a predominantly white area, was undertaken in full knowledge of the limitations of addressing racism in isolation, compared with change through the whole of a school's formal and informal curriculum. Apart from practical considerations, the rationale for using the framework of an English course was that literature and drama provide a 'legitimate' arena for students to enter at least imaginatively into someone else's reality.

As I see it, literature's prime quality is the ability to carry human voices across time, place, experience, society, culture—albeit through an author's rendering of those voices. Having been brought up as a white, middle-class South African child—with all that entailed in terms of the construction of blinkered, racist childhood perceptions—I have personally found books written by writers from very different backgrounds a major resource in enabling me to listen to other voices. Significant literature, to me, is that in which the lives of characters are represented in relation to deep currents in their society. Characters are contextualised, so that in so far as one observes them or empathises with them, one can learn something of what it is to be human in that time, that place, those circumstances. In questioning what it is in a text that invites or inhibits a reader, Margaret Meek writes that 'it is not necessary for him (sic) to recognise his social milieu in the setting, but to find his interior fiction as part of a writer's intention' (Meek, 1980: 36). One of my criteria for selecting key texts for the research project was that although some of the settings might be alien to the readers, the texts should contain enough points of connection for the readers to enable an imaginative leap and reveal a certain universality of 'interior fiction'.

But readers do not approach texts as culturally neutral. Reading is a transaction, as Louise Rosenblatt (1938) has been asserting for over fifty years against those critics ('the formalists') who would prioritise the text (Rosenblatt, 1938; 1985). The reader brings to the text 'a network of past experiences in literature and life' (Rosenblatt, 1985: 35), while the author has created the text out of her or his own such network. The text that is 'evoked during the transaction between reader and text' will therefore vary according to the reader, bearing in mind also that personal readings are framed within wider cultural contexts (Eagleton, 1985). Ideology, as Hollindale (1988) argues in relation to children's literature, is not something passively transferred from an author's text to young readers as empty receptacles. Young people already possess ideology, 'having drawn it from a mass of experiences far more powerful than literature' (Hollindale, 1988: 17). Given the diversity of readers, the text will not necessarily be read in the manner implicitly constructed by the author for his or her 'implied reader' (Iser, 1978).

In her important study covering a wide range of research into the relationship between reading and prejudice, Sara Goodman Zimet comments:

> that while our attitudes, values and behaviours may be influenced by what we read, when left to our own initiative we read what we are. In other words, we select our reading to support our predispositions rather than in order to change them. (Zimet, 1976: 17)

The critical qualification here is, however, 'when left to our own devices' and Zimet offers evidence of studies suggesting that it is possible to modify attitudes and behaviour so that 'we are what we read'. It is the circumstances **under which the reading** is done (including, for example, related teaching) which she claims 'will determine which will have the greatest impact, the reader or the printed message.'

'Those kinde of people': Defining racism

In considering the framework of the research, it is also necessary to spell out the conception of racism with which I was working. While racism is evident in many societies and not unique to Britain, the roots of racism and its attendant discourse lie deep within British history. Echoes of the concepts, language and agenda of Elizabeth I's Privy Council reverberate nearly 400 years later in pronouncements of politicians of the last two decades:

> there are of late divers blackamoors brought into this realme, of which kinde of people there are already here to manie. . . her Majesty's pleasure therefore ys that those kinde of people should be sent forth of the lande. . . (Acts of the Privy Council, XXVI, 1596–7, cited in Greater London Council, 1986)

> The nation has been and is still being, eroded and hollowed out from within by implantation of unassimilated and unassimilable populations. . . alien wedges in the heartland of the state. (Enoch Powell, 9.4.76, cited in Gilroy, 1987)

> People are really rather afraid that this country might be rather swamped by people with a different culture and you know the British character has done so much for democracy, for law, and done so much throughout the world, that if there is any fear that it might be swamped, people are going to react and be rather hostile to those coming in. (Margaret Thatcher, ITV World in Action 30.1.78)

Enslaved, and desired only for their labour, 'blackamoors' were clearly presented to the native Elizabethan English as different in 'kinde' and quite distinguishable from 'people of our owne nation'. While there has been a subtle shift from the colonial language of overt racial superiority to that of cultural difference, there still remains a widely-held 'commonsense' notion that people have biologically distinguishing features which separate one 'race' from another. This idea persists despite the evidence that 'race' itself has no objective biological validity, with greater biological variation existing within any designated racial group than between any two such groups (Hiernaux et al., 1965; Rose et al., 1978; Lewontin, 1987). 'Race' is in fact a product of the human mind and behaviour—in other words, a social construction (Figueroa, 1984; 1991). Stuart Hall (1978) has given us a useful analogy in likening it to a lens through which people view and experience reality.

While racism maintains common elements—or an 'echo'—over time, it is also historically specific to each period (Hall, 1978), its 'shape' adapting to new conditions. Deeply structured into our economic, political and social life, racism is also deeply embedded ideologically within popular culture (Mullard, 1980) and within the society's frames of reference (Figueroa, 1984). Shared by the majority of Britons and closely associated with British identity, these frames of reference are the 'largely unacknowledged and unverbalised substratum of beliefs, assumptions, feelings, quasi-memories, etc. which underlie, sustain and inform perception, thought and action' (Figueroa & Swart, 1986).

My understanding of racism is that it is more complex than is suggested by the 'racism = power + prejudice' formula. Power clearly also functions in terms of features such as class, gender, sexuality and able-bodiedness, as well as 'race', and the operation of power in black/white interactions may be both complicated and dynamically shifting when these come into play. Furthermore there is no room within the simplified 'power + prejudice' formula for Gramsci's concept of hegemony and the way power is maintained partially through the compliance of the oppressed (Gramsci, 1971), nor for the way in which language shared by oppressor and oppressed functions in this process.

My own working definition of racism is a broad one. It was sufficient for the purpose of my study to conceive of racism as a highly complex phenomenon of discrimination and oppression, which is historically specific in both its structural and ideological forms in each society, and which is based on, as well as sustained by, a socially-constructed belief in the existence of inherently different 'races'. Language not only plays a key role in reflecting racism within the society but in transmitting and constructing the racist frames of reference which help perpetuate it.

Racism, schooling and the space for change

In Britain conceptions of 'race' are currently shaped within the duality of a highly efficient framework of nationality and immigration legislation—promoting 'British' equals 'white'—and constrained Race Relations legislation, attempting to counter some of the racist effects of the former. The same duality can be seen within education. The 1988 Education Reform Act furthers divisions between schools, particularly between those that 'have' and those that 'have not', thus reinforcing black disadvantage, inequality and injustice (Verma, 1990; Richardson, 1988, 1989; Hatcher, 1989; Ball & Troyna, 1989). Whatever useful statements we may find within some documents of the National Curriculum reflecting Britain as a diverse society—and which contrast strongly with its fundamental nationalism elsewhere—it would be naive to disregard the over-arching discriminatory effects of the Education Reform Act. However, it is precisely because there are contradictions that there is room for manoeuvre. Given the role of schools in the business of cultural transmission (Lawton, 1973; Bowles, 1976; Bourdieu, 1976), it is quite unrealistic to conceive of schools having the power of directly changing structures in society. Nevertheless the curriculum is not monolithic and space still remains for teachers and students to question and challenge contradictions. Developing a school culture in which racist frames of reference are questioned is an important contribution to the roles students will be capable of taking on beyond the school gates, both in the present and the future.

The Context

Why focus on a predominantly white area?

It can be argued that the most difficult areas in which to combat racism are those where it is least obtrusive, namely those places where few black people live. Although actual instances of overt racist abuse are thereby reduced—partly accounting for the ubiquitous 'no problem here' response from many teachers in such places (Gaine, 1987)—there is consistent evidence of the persisitence of wide-spread racist attitudes amongst young white people (British Social Attitudes 1984; Swann Committee, 1985; Williams, 1986; Tomlinson, 1990). Furthermore, as Stuart Hall points out, racism is as much 'a structured absence—a not-speaking about things—as it is a positive setting up of attitudes to 'race'.' (Hall, 1985). This is what makes challenging racism so difficult in a predominantly white area. Raising the issue is immediately outside the norm—and looking too deeply into racism and its origins in the colonial past creates a profound uneasiness amongst the ethnic majority.

It was, however, in the context of a county of wide-spread 'not-speaking' that I decided to set up my research project. With no significant black community to pressure for change, how does one begin to challenge Eurocentric, racist complacency in the education system?

The school, teacher, class

The school in which I conducted the project was a Church Comprehensive school in the south of England. It had no multicultural/anti-racist policy but senior management was in the process of reviewing the school's philosophy. Draft papers included references to racism being unacceptable and to the importance of developing in pupils a sense of justice. In the school body of over 1000 students, about half a dozen were black. The Head of English, who was openly committed to challenging racism, was keen to be the project teacher and almost certainly would have been, had he not moved to another school. Had he remained—as an insider catalyst—the outcomes both within the class and the wider school would very likely have been different. I had however started from the position that I would work with whomever was prepared to work with me, knowing my agenda. Fortunately another English teacher volunteered to take on the project, offering two 40 minute lessons and a drama session each week.

The selected class formed part of the school's third year 'middle band' and consisted of thirty 13/14 year olds—eighteen boys and twelve girls.

The course

The sequence in which the literature was introduced was important. We started with *Buddy* by Nigel Hinton, where the context was a familiar British one and where racism remains only a side issue but links are suggested between different oppressions. Buddy, a white working class lad whose mother has left home, is befriended by black twins—also outsiders in an otherwise snobbish class where racist jokes are openly condoned by the teacher. Hans Peter Richter's *Friedrich* focuses on racism in a European context. Written almost like a diary, a non-Jewish boy charts the increasing compromises in his friendship with a Jewish boy in Germany between 1925 and 1942. From Europe we moved to the American south in the 1930s with Mildred Taylor's *Roll of Thunder, Hear My Cry* where events are seen through the perceptive, indignant and resistant eyes of nine year old Cassie Logan. This was the first class novel the students had read by a black author. It was followed by *Waiting for the Rain* by Sheila Gordon. Set in South Africa, it maps the course of a relationship between Frikkie (nephew of a white farmer) and Tengo (son of the farm's foreman). The reader is repeatedly shifted from one character's consciousness to the other. Tengo's growth in awareness of himself and his position leads to a final confrontation between the two as young men. The book's strength is that racism is located in the structure of social relationships, revealing that it is more than personal prejudice. This is also the case in *Friedrich* and *Roll of Thunder, Hear My Cry* and I was curious to know whether students would perceive this.

To help develop an understanding of unfamiliar contexts, students were provided with a range of background resources including videos, author interviews and related activities. Poetry and drama sessions were linked to issues arising in the literature, mostly indirectly. Students were frequently asked to make individual responses either in their journals or on specially devised sheets. Sometimes they would be asked to jot their thoughts freely around a section of photocopied text, while on other occasions their responses were more structured, for example, advising a character, making a prediction or directly commenting on a particular action or attitude. Students also regularly discussed their responses with each other in small groups and were encouraged to use their journals to record the development of their responses and thoughts. The drama technique of 'hotseating' was used at times in relation to the texts, with people taking on the roles of characters and answering questions in role.

While literature remained at the core of the course, towards the end of the year, circumstances led to a new direction and issues of racism were addressed directly with the students without the intervening medium of fiction. The students viewed the BBC series *Getting to Grips with Racism* during Religious Education, with discussions of racism brought very directly into the arena of considering themselves and their society. This move from fiction to 'real life' provided a new and contrasting dimension in which to study responses.

Visitors were a significant element throughout the course. The culmination was a final 'Media Week' when drama director/writer Olusola Oyeleye led five afternoon workshops in which students met a variety of people concerned with racism in their working lives including the producer of the BBC series *Getting to Grips with Racism*.

Interpreting the Students' Responses

Given the wealth of data, I shall not attempt in this paper to summarise them or the extent to which the original aims of the project were met. Readers may refer to my narrative reflection of that year in the classroom in *Through Whose Eyes? Exploring Racism: Reader, Text and Context* (Naidoo, 1992) or to the original research thesis (Naidoo, 1991). Instead I shall focus briefly on a few of the critical issues which arose in interpreting the data: concerning gender, 'contradictory consciousness', acknowledgement of white identity and the challenge of a black perspective, and conceptions of racism beyond notions of personal hostility.

Gender

Many of the project findings had gender implications. A greater tendency amongst the girls towards openness in their responses and towards use of a non-racist discourse was borne out by a marked gender difference in average scores across the whole year group on the Racist Perceptions Survey on both occasions it was administered. This finding, which concurs with that of others (Gaine, 1987, Cohen, 1987), suggests that we need to know more about how different socialisation processes, as well as the experience of sexism, may affect the openness of students to addressing issues of racism.

This gender difference does not mean that girls in the project class never engaged in racist discourse. However, at a number of key points in the novels significantly more girls than boys revealed not only sympathy with the perspective of characters who had been victimised by racism, but identified with a spirit of resistance. For instance at the end of *Waiting for the Rain*, almost all the girls—despite some feelings of sympathy for the young white man Frikkie—supported the final oppositional stance taken by Tengo, the young black man. This contrasted with less than a third of the boys supporting Tengo.

At the end of *Friedrich*, the majority of girls felt the narrator's family had not done enough to save Friedrich's family from persecution, whereas almost all the boys exonerated the non-Jewish family on the pragmatic grounds that they would have endangered themselves by doing anything else. While the boys had shown empathy in their responses to the Jewish family, the vast majority seemed to give such empathetic feelings less weight when making their final judgements. (Indeed the only two boys who felt the narrator's family should have done more to save Friedrich despite the risks, turned out themselves to have Jewish relatives.)

Another gender difference, well noted by other researchers (Stanworth, 1981; Spender, 1982), was a sharp contrast in the degree of female participation in small group discussions compared with whole class discussions. In the latter, conducted in teacher-centred question-and-answer style, only a minority of girls ever volunteered an answer or an opinion. This contrasted with their use of the reading journals, in which they generally wrote more prolifically and more reflectively than most of the boys. Interviews with the girls suggested they were generally far more conscious of being 'shown up' in public than many of the boys and were thus less willing to enter into adversarial style debate, even when they knew there was not necessarily a right or wrong answer. Given the greater tendency of the girls towards articulating non-racist perceptions, it is of prime importance to ensure that their voices are heard in the wider classroom. Clearly it is impossible to tackle racism effectively in isolation. Put bluntly, if a predominantly white classroom and school give priority to white male voices and experience, what is the likelihood that racism can be properly addressed?

Contradictory consciousness

It is important not to be simplistic nor suggest an overall uniformity in male or female responses. The contradictory discourses which exist within the society regarding 'race' were frequently evident within both male and female students, reflecting Gramsci's (1971) notion of 'contradictory consciousness'. A particularly striking example of this was provided by Angela, the most outspoken and self-confident girl in the class, who openly articulated strong views on equality. The latter were reflected in her low scores both times on the Racist Perceptions Survey. Despite her Southern British English accent, she was Irish-born, declaring boldly in the first survey: 'I think about how lucky I am to be Irish and I am never ashamed.' Nevertheless, when 'hotseated' as the black twin Charmian from *Buddy*—answering questions in role—she did not transfer this same sense of pride, but acknowledged feeling 'ashamed of my colour'. On another occasion, she allowed herself to be drawn into a racist joking session, unwittingly recorded by a group of students who had forgotten the presence of a tape recorder in the drama studio. Angela's contribution was a 'backwards Irish' joke.

Peer pressure is an important factor. Angela revealed an awareness of her own susceptibility to participating in the dominant discourse, even when it ran counter to her beliefs, during a drama role-play which focused on the bullying of a minority religious sect in school. She had been assigned a neutral role in the drama but had gradually shifted to joining in the verbal taunting. Questioned in the subsequent hotseating of the participants as to why she had joined in the abuse, she pleaded self-protection. If she had not, the bullies would have picked on her.

The duality expressed by Angela is a reflection of the contradictory discourses in the society. In Troyna & Hatcher's view:

> Society makes available to children a powerfully charged vocabulary of racist terms, but their use. . . does not necessarily imply a commitment to the racist ideologies from which they derive. (Troyna & Hatcher 1992: 76)

Whether or not engaging in racist discourse reflects actual beliefs, nevertheless, it still has the function of reinforcing racist 'common knowledge' and racist frames of reference within young people's culture. One of the implications for education is the need to create spaces in which students can give expression to ideas about equality, and where they can reflect on—and discuss in a supportive atmosphere—their own possible contradictions.

Acknowledgement of white identity and a black perspective

A feature of certain students' responses was their acknowledging a shared white identity with characters from the texts, mostly in the privacy of their reading journals. This is an important area to explore, requiring considerable sensitivity, in order to guide the students away from the realm of guilt towards an understanding of the construction of attitudes and identities. One student, Louise, was clearly making significant steps in that direction when she wrote:

> It made me feel angry and embaressed to admit to myself that my South African cousins are like that. . . It's disgusting the way black people are treated, after all, it is their country and white people took over the country and we treated them as heroes, as great explorers, when really they were invaders.

Louise's use of 'we' is significant. Reading *Waiting for the Rain* appeared to have engaged her in a dialogue with herself, surely an integral part of personal change.

There were a number of examples of journal writing which suggested personal disturbance and a movement beyond empathy into reperception. For instance Paul, for whom *Roll of Thunder, Hear My Cry* was 'powerful and sad, quite clearly one of the most brilliant books I've ever read', wrote that it had given him 'a new perspective' on the treatment of black people. There are obviously questions concerning the extent and effect of such experiences of reperception. To what extent, for example, do individual instances of reperception begin to 'add up'? Furthermore, when they do begin to connect—as seems to be the case with Paul's sense of 'a new perspective'—will this actually inform any aspects of every day life for him? Or is he just becoming a product of Eagleton's 'moral technology of Literature', namely 'an historically peculiar form of human subject who is sensitive, receptive, imaginative and so on. . . *about nothing in particular*' (Eagleton, 1985: 5). I should like to argue that the responses of Louise and Paul are 'particular' and at least provide a basis for further action. Reading *Waiting for the Rain* certainly caused Louise to reflect on her own South African cousins, their attitudes and behaviour in a meaningful way. Indeed the very act of attempting to make explicit such responses and perceived changes in themselves was, I believe, a step forward for these students. Admittedly we only have, as it were, their 'internal evidence' of change, but without external evidence to the contrary, it still deserves credit.

Conceptions of racism beyond personal hostility

While many of the students tended to see racism simply in terms of attitudes on a personal level and not in terms of structural dimensions related to power, I felt a number of students had the potential to break out from a conception of racism restricted to one of personal hostility. Given the right pointers and space to explore issues, there were students who were ready to see beyond the individuals to the racist structures in which those individuals were embedded. Indeed the tragedy for individuals in each of the Richter, Taylor and Gordon novels is how the fundamental inequality and oppression inescapably affect the quality of relationships possible between members of unequal groups.

It was perhaps the inability to understand fully the fundamental imbalance in the power relations between white and black characters in some of the novels that led some students, and indeed the project teacher, to be critical of black characters who were wary of the motives of white liberals. For instance, there was a strong perception that Cassie Logan's family in *Roll of Thunder, Hear My Cry* was unfair to the white child Jeremy by not reciprocating his efforts at friendship. Given the chasmic divide between white and black in 1930s Mississippi, the perception that Papa Logan was being too harsh suggests inappropriate expectations of 'balance'.

Questions of Pedagogy, the Role of the Teacher and the Wider School Context

While the project methodology ensured a certain amount of space both for student autonomy and collaborative learning, the personal style of the teacher who undertook the project turned out to be predominantly didactic and traditionally formal. Space precludes my elaborating the consequences of this, except to say that my observations strongly reinforce the findings of others (Lynch, 1987; Richardson, undated) about the importance of establishing an appropriate classroom context for raising issues of inequality. In addressing racism with white students, one is challenging them not only to extend their range of empathy but to question their frames of reference and thus elements of their own identities. This requires an ethos in which trust and respect form the basis for developing the self-esteem necessary to undertake such self-critical activity. In order to promote open-mindedness in students, it has also to be practised, and one therefore requires an ethos of tolerance. Finally, there is little point talking about equality and the inter-dependence of human beings if students are not encouraged to collaborate with each other. Clearly these features have implications not only for the ethos of the classroom but for the whole school.

In summary, it was possible to identify a number of features—or lessons to be learnt—relating to the course, pedagogy, teacher and school which could help to effect change. There is need for:

- a culturally diverse curriculum
- a combined focus on language and literature
- students to deconstruct their own 'knowledge'
- the integration of cognitive and affective learning
- learning to connect with the students' own experiences
- the creation of space for girls' voices
- development of a pedagogy which encourages self-esteem, open-mindedness and collaboration
- teachers to be both supportive and challenging
- teachers to develop their own awareness of racism
- the wider school context to reflect the collaborative, supportive but challenging context of the classroom.

Within the kind of pedagogical framework I am outlining as necessary for addressing racism, the role of the teacher is undoubtedly a difficult one. It is one both of support and challenge. Unless the teacher can create a trusting and supportive atmosphere, students will merely become defensive. And unless there is challenge, students will remain unchanged. Furthermore if the students are to come to understand that racism is not just a matter of negative and nasty attitudes and feelings, but that 'race' is a pervasive social lens which is constantly shaping their language and 'knowledge', then they need to see their teacher involved in the same process of questioning and self-scrutiny. The teacher has to enable what is often hidden and submerged, to come to the surface. The teacher expecting students to combine affective with cognitive knowledge, needs likewise to be prepared to offer heart as well as head.

Of the pedagogical skills outlined here most are not specific to anti-racist teaching but a reflection of a broadly liberal approach to education. However, there is also the central question of the teacher's own level of awareness about racism. A teacher who perceives racism only at the obvious personal or behaviourial level will not be able to take students very far. A teacher who has not begun to examine how living in a society culturally seeped in racism for centuries has infiltrated their own discourse and its substratum of beliefs, assumptions, perceptions and values, will not be in a position to help students engage in that difficult and often uncomfortable task. A teacher who has not begun to examine how racism is Hall's 'structured absence' (Hall, 1985), as well as how it is deeply embedded within the structures and institutions of our society, will not be in a position to help students uncover these realities.

But however desirable it is that teachers should have undergone their own process of awareness-raising in advance, it is unrealistic to think this represents the reality of teaching. One cannot assume that the majority of white English teachers reading *Roll of Thunder, Hear My Cry* with their students will necessarily have read much else by black writers themselves and thought in any depth about a black perspective or indeed about racism. Nevertheless, it is to be hoped that they will want to engage in the process of extending their own reading. Sharing the interest and stimulation of opening themselves out to new and challenging voices is probably the most valuable quality to be passed on to their students.

References

Ball, W. and Troyna, B. (1989) The Dawn of a New ERA? The Education Reform Act, 'Race' and LEAs. *Educational Management and Administration* 17, 23–31.

Benton, M., Teasey, J., Bell, R. and Hurst, K. (1988) *Young Readers Responding to Poems*. London: Routledge.

Bourdieu, P. (1976) The school as a conservative force: Scholastic and cultural inequalities. In R. Dale, G. Esland, and M. MacDonald (eds) *Schooling and Capitalism: A Sociological Reader*. Milton Keynes: Open University Press.

Bowles, S. (1976) Unequal education and the reproduction of the social division of labor. In R. Dale, G. Esland and M. MacDonald (eds) *Schooling and Capitalism: A Sociological Reader*. Milton Keynes: Open University Press.

British Broadcasting Corporation (BBC) (1988) *Getting to Grips with Racism*. London: BBC Television for Schools.

British Social Attitudes (1984). London: HMSO.

Cohen, P. (1987) *Reducing Prejudice in Classroom and Community*. PSEC/CME

Cultural Studies Project. London: University of London Institute of Education (mimeo).

Department of Education and Science (1985) *Education for All: The Report of the Committee of Inquiry into the Education of Children from Ethnic Minority Groups*. (The Swann Report). London: HMSO.

Eagleton, T. (1985) The subject of literature. *The English Magazine* 15, 4–7.

The English Centre (1984) *Roll of Thunder, Hear My Cry* (background book). London: ILEA English Centre.

Figueroa, P.M.E. (1984) Race relations and cultural differences: Some ideas on a racial frame of reference. In G.K. Verma and C. Bagley (eds) *Race Relations and Cultural Differences*. London: Croom Helm.

—— (1991) The *Social Construction of Race*. London: Routledge.

Figueroa, P.M.E. and Swart, L.T. (1986) Teachers' and pupils' racist and ethnicist frames of reference: A case study. *New Community* 13 (1), 40–51.

Gaine, C. (1987) *No Problem Here: A Practical Approach to Education and 'Race' in White Schools*. London: Hutchinson.

Gilroy, P. (1987) *There Ain't No Black in the Union Jack: The Cultural Politics of Race and Nation*. London: Hutchinson.

Gordon, S. (1987) *Waiting For The Rain*. London: Orchard Books.

Gramsci, A. (1971) *Selections from the Prison Notebooks*. Edited and translated by Q. Hoare and G. Nowell Smith. New York: International Publishers.

Greater London Council (1986) *A History of the Black Presence in London*. London: Greater London Council.

Hall, S. (1978) Racism and reaction. In *Five Views of Multiracial Britain*. London: Commission for Racial Equality.

Hall, S. (1981) Teaching race. In A. James and R. Jeffcoate (eds) *The School in the Multicultural Society*. London: Harper & Row/ Open University Press.

Hall, S. (1985) *Anti-racism in Practice: Stuart Hall Examines the Implications of Using ACER Materials* (video). Inner London Education Authority (ILEA): Afro-Caribbean Education Resource Centre (ACER).

Hatcher, R. (1989) Antiracist education after the act. *Multicultural Teaching* 7 (3), 24–7.

Hiernaux, J. *et al.* (1965) Biological aspects of race. *International Social Science Journal* XVII (1), 71–161.

Hinton, N. (1983) *Buddy*. London: Heinemann Educational.

Hollindale, P. (1988) *Ideology and the Children's Book*. Oxford: Westminster College/Thimble Press.

Iser, W. (1978) *The Act of Reading: A Theory of Aesthetic Response*. London: Routledge and Kegan Paul.

Lawton, D. (1973) *Social Change, Educational Theory and Curriculum Planning*. London: University of London Press.

Lewontin, R. (1987) Are the races different? In D. Gill and L. Levidow (eds) *Anti-Racist Science Teaching*. London: Free Association Books.

Lynch, J. (1987) *Prejudice Reduction and the Schools*. London: Cassell.

Meek, M. (1980) Prolegomena for a study of children's literature or Guess what's in my head. In *Approaches to Research in Children's Literature*. Southampton: University of Southampton, Department of Education (mimeo).

Mullard, C. (1980) *Racism in Society and Schools: History, Policy and Practice*. Occasional Paper No 1. London: University of London Institute of Education.

Naidoo, B. (1985) *Journey to Jo'burg: A South African Story*. Harlow: Longman.

—— (1989) *Chain of Fire*, London: Collins.

—— (1991) *Exploring Issues of Racism with White Students through a Literature-based Course*. PhD thesis, University of Southampton.

—— (1992) *Through Whose Eyes? Exploring Racism: Reader, Text and Context*. Stoke on Trent: Trentham Books.

Richardson, R. (undated) Justice and equality in the classroom: The design of lessons and courses. *World Studies Documentation Service* 7. York: World Studies Teacher Training Centre.

—— (1988) Opposition to reform and the need for transformation: Some polemical notes. *Multicultural Teaching* 6 (2), 4–8.

—— (1989) Manifesto for inequality: Some features of the new era. *Multicultural Teaching* 8 (1), 19–20.

Richter, H.P. (1978) *Friedrich*. London: Heinemann Educational.

Rose, S. *et al.* (1978) *Race, Education, Intelligence: A Teacher's Guide to the Facts and the Issues*. London: NUT.

Rosenblatt, L. M. (1938) *Literature as Exploration*. New York: Appleton-Century. (Revised edn, 1970, London: Heinemann.)

Rosenblatt, L. M. (1985) The transactional theory of the literary work: Implications for research. In C.R. Cooper (ed.) *Researching Response to Literature and the Teaching of Literature*. Norwood, NJ: Ablex.

Spender, D. (1982) *Invisible Women: The Schooling Scandal*. London: Writers and Readers Publishing Cooperative Society with Chameleon Editorial Group.

Stanworth, M. (1981) *Gender and Schooling: A Study of Sexual Divisions in the Classroom*. London: Women's Research and Resources Centre.

Taylor, M.D. (1987) *Roll of Thunder, Hear My Cry*. London: Heinemann Educational.

Tomlinson, S. (1990) *Multicultural Education in White Schools*. London: Batsford.

Verma, G.K. (1990) Identity, education and black learners: Are things improving?. *Multicultural Teaching* 8 (3), 18–19.

Williams, M. (1986) The Thatcher generation. *New Society* 75, 312–15.

Zimet, S.G. (1980) *Print and Prejudice*. Sevenoaks: Hodder and Stoughton/ United Kingdom Reading Association.

Appendix

The Racist Perceptions Survey below was devised to complement the mainly qualitative data from the project. It was not intended to be a sophisticated instrument for measuring attitudes, but proved useful in helping to paint a broad, descriptive picture of views held within the class and year group as a whole. Students wrote their names on separate forms with numbers linked to their survey papers and they were assured of anonymity. Only Section C was scored.

The survey was piloted with a comparable group of students in another school and several changes were made. There are a number of problems with attempting to tap into perceptions, feelings, values and beliefs through a formal questionnaire and those associated with my own survey are discussed in detail within my thesis (Naidoo, 1991). One fundamental problem, for instance, is how to develop a framework for eliciting racist perceptions without resorting to constructs which themselves derive from a racist frame of reference. The term 'Asian people' is a generalisation suggesting a common identity shared by people of many different and varied backgrounds. Likewise, there are problems with the term 'West Indians', but I decided to use it as I felt not all the students would have been familiar with the term 'Afro-Caribbeans'. To ask for a response to 'black British' following one to 'Asian people' would implicitly undermine the concept of 'black' as a political term for all people not considered white and who share a common experience of racism.

Opinion Survey

We all hold views about ourselves and others which help make up the picture we have of our world. In completing the survey below please express YOUR OWN VIEWS AS HONESTLY AS POSSIBLE. Your name will not be attached to this paper.

A
1.   Have you ever been abroad? . . .

2.   If you have, why did you go and to which countries?

3.   What did you like or dislike most about being there?

B.   WRITE AS MUCH AND AS FREELY AS YOU WISH ABOUT THE FOLLOWING:
1.   When I think of myself I think. . .

2.   When I think of English people I think. . .

3.   When I think of Irish people I think. . .

4.   When I think of Asian people I think. . .

5.   When I think of West Indian people I think. . .

6.   When I think of South Africa I think. . .

7.   My experience of people of another colour from my own is. . .

C.   READ EACH STATEMENT BELOW AND PUT A CIRCLE AROUND THE LETTERS THAT BEST SHOW HOW YOU FEEL:

SA — Strongly Agree

A — Agree

U — Undecided

D — Disagree

SD — Strongly Disagree

	AGREE — DISAGREE				
1. It would be good if our school had more black students.	SA	A	U	D	SD
2. Irish people are just as intelligent as English people.	SA	A	U	D	SD
3. West Indians have a good sense of rhythm.	SA	A	U	D	SD
4. Jokes about people from other cultures are just a bit of fun.	SA	A	U	D	SD

5. The slogan 'Keep Britain White' is really quite sensible.   SA   A   U   D   SD

6. Television shouldn't show films where black people are made to look like savages.   SA   A   U   D   SD

7. There isn't racism in our area.   SA   A   U   D   SD

8. It's harder for black people to get houses in Britain than for white people.   SA   A   U   D   SD

9. Immigration is making Britain overcrowded.   SA   A   U   D   SD

10. A black child born in Britain should have the same rights as a white child.   SA   A   U   D   SD

11. I wouldn't like a family of another colour to move next door.   SA   A   U   D   SD

12. Black people in Britain have as much right to getting jobs as white people.   SA   A   U   D   SD

13. People who come to Britain should behave like the British.   SA   A   U   D   SD

14. It's good to see black and white people marrying each other.   SA   A   U   D   SD

15. We need to do something in school about racist attitudes.   SA   A   U   D   SD

16. Words like *paki*, *wog*, *chink*, *gippo* are harmless really.   SA   A   U   D   SD

D.   ABOUT YOURSELF! CIRCLE YOUR ANSWER

1. Have you ever had any contact   YES   DON'T RECALL   NO
    with someone of another colour
    from your own?

2. Have you ever had a good   YES   DON'T RECALL   NO
    friend of another colour from
    your own?

3. Has any member of your   YES   DON'T RECALL   NO
    family ever had a good friend
    of another colour from his or
    her own?

4. Have you ever visited the   YES   DON'T RECALL   NO
    home of someone of another
    colour from your own?

5. Has someone of another colour   YES   DON'T RECALL   NO
    from your own ever come to
    your house for a meal or to
    play?

6. Are you male/female?   7.   What is your age?

     . . . .

Your Comments on This Questionnaire!

What did you feel, or think, while answering this questionnaire?
Please feel free to make your own comments.

6 'I Treat Them All The Same' Teacher–Pupil Talk In Multiethnic Classrooms

A.P. BIGGS and VIV EDWARDS

Introduction

There is ample evidence over 20 years that ethnic minority children in the United Kingdom are not fully recognising their potential within the educational system (Swann, 1985). A real problem exists. But a viable solution depends on how one chooses to define the problem. The underachievement of ethnic minority children has sometimes been explained, for instance, in terms of their supposed 'poor self-image' (see Milner, 1983, and Stone, 1981 for a critique of this position). On other occasions, blame has been located firmly within the family (Bullock, 1975; Hawkins, 1984). In short, minority children have been viewed not as the principal victims of an education system which has failed to cater to their needs, but as the primary cause of this failure.

There was a gradual move in the 1980s, however, towards a rather different interpretation of events. For the first time there was official recognition of the role of institutionalised racism in the underachievement of ethnic minority children (Rampton, 1981; Swann, 1985). While there can be no doubt that minority children are frequently subjected to overt acts of racism (CRE, 1988), awareness has also grown of the ways in which traditional structures and attitudes in education are inappropriate for culturally diverse populations and place many children at a serious disadvantage. Many teachers remain unaware that their behaviour may be discriminatory in effect, if not in intent. Yet the importance of recognising and remediating examples of institutionalised racism is critical if we are serious about providing equality of opportunity for all the children in our schools.

Language is an important aspect of this behaviour. The present paper describes research undertaken in British primary schools in an attempt

82

to identify patterns of language behaviour which may place ethnic minority children at a disadvantage.

Cross-cultural Communication in the Classroom

The recognition that language is central to the processes of education has been duly acknowledged in British schools at least since the Bullock Report (1975) made its authoritative statement on the matter. The report's well-known catchphrase—'language across the curriculum'— captures the essence of its most important recommendations. Teachers were encouraged to explore the possibility that language is the most powerful instrument of learning and that this is so not only in subjects like English and Modern Languages, but in other areas of the school curriculum.

The Swann Report (1985) on the education of ethnic minority children also addresses various language-related issues (e.g. bilingualism, the teaching of minority languages). It remains strangely silent, however, on one aspect of language behaviour which has emerged in recent years as potentially important in the explanation of the underachievement of minority children. A substantial body of research points to the misunderstandings which can occur when pupils and teachers encode their messages in culturally different ways.

It is possible to identify a number of different ways in which the language background of a given group of children may impinge on classroom performance. For example, discourse styles can vary greatly from one cultural group to another. Michaels & Collins (1984), for instance, describe how two distinct discourse styles—one typically black, the other typically white—can be discerned during 'sharing time', a daily classroom activity where children are invited to describe an object or give a narrative account of some past event. White children tend to use a 'topic-centred' style in which a single clearly identified topic is developed in a linear manner. Black children tend to prefer a 'topic-associating' style made up of a series of implicitly linked topics. The children's teacher related easily to the topic-centred style which she expanded through comments and questions. When children adopted a topic-associating style, however, the teacher could not discern the underlying theme nor predict where the talk was going.

Research undertaken by Gumperz and his associates points to still further mechanisms which contribute to cross-cultural misunderstanding. Gumperz (1982) and Gumperz, Jupp & Roberts (1979), for instance, examine prosodic features (such as intonation, pitch and tempo) which are critical in determining the meaning of utterances in context. These studies indicate that concepts such as the 'openings' and 'closings' of conversations are particularly susceptible to cross-cultural misinterpretation. One such example is the way in which Indians are likely to raise their voices slightly at the end of an utterance, whereas British English speakers lower their voices. In practice, this often means that Indian speakers of English start to speak before their conversational partner has finished. Negative stereotyping from both sides is likely to result.

The Present Study

The foregoing research points convincingly to a wide range of ways in which ethnic minority pupils may be disadvantaged in western urban classrooms. We know that different cultural groups have different expectations about the learning process. We know that discourse styles vary considerably between different cultural groups. We know that different language patterns carry different meanings for different groups of speakers.

Although the focus for the present paper is on ethnicity and education, there is also evidence of differences between male and female speakers which have a bearing on education. It has been shown on many occasions, for instance, that boys tend to monopolise teacher attention; they talk more, ask more questions and therefore demand more teacher time (Coates, 1986; Graddol & Swann, 1989). It seemed to us that it would be interesting to explore whether similar classroom dynamics might come into play as a result of differences in discourse style associated with ethnicity. Do black children make fewer or more demands than white children? Do they receive more or less attention than their white peers? Are there any qualitative differences in the kinds of interaction which take place between, on the one hand, teachers and black pupils and, on the other hand, teachers and white pupils? Underpinning the data collection and analysis was the basic premise that communication is a two-way process where all participants carry responsibility. In this, our study departs from many other models which define success in communication as conformity to the patterns and expectations of the dominant group (Singh et al., 1988).

The particular group of children who formed the main focus for the study came from households whose members originated from Mirpur province in Pakistan. This group was chosen purely on practical grounds: Panjabi speakers are the largest linguistic minority in the area where we had good access to schools. The children who took part in the project were all aged between five and six years of age and were in their first year of full-time school.

At the beginning of the 1989 academic year, one of the present writers (Netta Biggs) spent a period of several months taking part in and observing classes which had been selected for the study. During this initial period, the main objective was to familiarise both teachers and pupils with the researcher so that she became a 'part of the furniture' of the classroom. In this way, we hoped to minimise the possible effects that the presence of a stranger in the classroom might have on the behaviour of both teacher and of pupils during our actual data collection. Participant observation helped us fine-tune the project in various other ways. Whilst in the classroom, it was possible to identify a range of situations in which pupils and teachers interact in the primary classroom (group discussion, reading to the teacher, small group teaching, etc.), and possible loci for differences in conversational style, as a prerequisite for the second stage of the project. During this second stage, five teachers (all female) and 81 children participated in the study, with two of the teachers working with the same group of children on separate school days.

It soon became apparent that we needed to narrow the focus. There is so much going on in the classroom—peer group interaction as well as teacher–child interaction. We could make the focus the individual child and how he or she spent the day; or the teacher and how the teacher distributed her time between the various different children. We decided, partly for reasons of time and partly because of the critical role which the teacher plays in determining the nature of interaction in the classroom, to focus on the teacher. How did the teacher spend her time? How often did she speak to different children in the class? How long were the interactions? What was the nature of the interaction, and so on. We attached a radio microphone to each of the five teachers and videotaped them teaching for the equivalent of an entire school day. The data thus collected enabled us to build up detailed profiles of the kinds of interaction which took place in these classrooms, and to make comparisons between ethnic groups across the different situations.

Analysis

The response variables

Classroom observation led us to believe that there might well be differences not only in terms of the total number of interactions between teachers and pupils but also in terms of the kinds of interaction which took place. We therefore established some 12 different response variables: comments, social exchanges, directives, questions, task-setting, boundary setting, praise, blame, non-verbal behaviour, interactions lasting less than 30 seconds, interactions lasting more than 30 seconds and the total number of interactions.

Comments were defined as reflective statements, talk which focuses on something other than the task in hand:

Pupil: Miss, my house.
Teacher: That's your house. I wouldn't like to live there! Do you know why? Why I wouldn't like to live there? . . . Why wouldn't I like to live in your house?
Pupil: It hasn't got a garden.
Teacher: It hasn't got a garden? Well alright. What happens when it rains? It's got no roof on it!

It was felt important to distinguish *comments* of this kind from what Tizard & Hughes (1984) and others have described as talk pertaining to classroom 'business'. It is widely held that, while children learn most effectively through extended talk which contains an element of reflection, most classroom talk consists of answers to teachers' closed questions. It therefore seemed useful to ask to what extent children were engaged in 'why' talk which compelled them to think beyond the teachers' immediate queries.

Social talk has much in common with *comments* in that both give rise to open-ended interactions. However, social talk is aimed specifically at developing interpersonal interaction in the classroom:

Teacher: (noticing the child's purse): My little girl has got a purse like that. It's a good idea isn't it?
Pupil: Has she got a skipping rope?
Teacher: No
Pupil: Doesn't she?
Teacher: She only has a purse. Where did you get yours then?
Pupil: I got it for Christmas.
Teacher: For Christmas? With a hoop and a skipping rope?

Such talk establishes mutual trust and respect between pupil and teacher and a friendly non-threatening atmosphere in which to work.

Comments and *social talk* stand in opposition to four other categories employed in the analysis: *directives*, *questions*, *task setting* and *boundary setting*. *Directives* were included in the analysis as an indication of teacher style (authoritative versus co-operative):

Teacher: I don't want a line here. Now you know what to do. Look! Will you please try and write the numbers down the right way round. You wrote them there! You can look at them there! I don't want to find any the wrong way round!

Questions have similarly been identified in the literature as an important feature of classroom interaction, particularly in relation to whether they are closed questions which elicit a short, factual response:

Pupil: Miss?
Teacher: Yes?
Pupil: When we've finished this can we go and play?

Teacher: We're going out for the break in a moment

or open questions which lead children to think more widely about the matter in hand. In the present corpus, only closed questions were classified as questions; questions which invited a more reflective response were categorised as comments.

Task-setting, a measure of whether interactions were about the task immediately at hand was another element in the analysis. The following teacher statement, for instance, focuses specifically on the activity which is being set for the class as a whole:

Teacher: Now first of all we're going to do sounds and I'm going to talk to all of you. So new children, although you're not going to do the first sounds we're going to talk about, you can listen and then I'll come to your sound when I've talked to the other children.

The importance of quantifying task-orientated talk lies, of course, in the indication which this gives of the extent to which an individual teacher encourages an exploratory approach, or whether they are primarily interested in getting the business of the classroom accomplished.

Boundary-setting is another aspect of the talk associated with classroom organisation. Two main kinds of boundary setting can be discerned in our data, both of which herald a new activity. The first concerns teacher or pupil talk which establishes that a new, and different, activity is to be pursued:

Pupil: Miss, what should I do next?
Teacher: Have you finished your writing?
Pupil: Yes
Teacher: You may choose

The second concerns talk or general behaviour which leads to intervention by the teacher:

Teacher: Sh! Sh! Shush a minute, please! Will you sit down and stop pinching people's things! You're getting very naughty!

In considering the ethnic dimension of teacher–pupil interactions, it was clearly important to explore teacher expressions of praise and blame, since this was an area in which there is enormous potential for discriminating between different groups of children.

Praise was defined as focusing on the positive aspects of the pupil's contribution to the classroom:

Teacher: That's a beautiful tiger. Who said you couldn't draw tigers? That's lovely! You're going to draw me nine!

Blame, in contrast, was considered to be the focusing on the negative aspects of the pupil's contribution:

Teacher: Now what are you writing? And why are you sitting here? This is your place!

In comparing responses towards children of different ethnicity, both praise and blame are indications of whether the child's contribution is valued by the teacher with wide-ranging implications for subsequent pupil behaviour.

Non-verbal approaches, defined as 'interaction initiated by non-verbal means,' were also considered a potentially important locus for cultural difference. The majority of ethnic minority children included in the present study were of South Asian origin. Although some writers take issue with this position, there is a widespread stereotype that Asian children, and especially the girls, are very passive in class (cf. Brah & Minhas, 1988). The decision to include non-verbal behaviour in the analysis allowed us to look objectively at this issue.

Finally, three measures of a purely quantificational nature were also included: what was the *total* number of interactions initiated either by teachers or pupils; how many lasted *more than 30 seconds* and how many were *less than 30 seconds*. Since most classroom interactions are relatively short, it was felt to be important to look not only at the overall number of interactions but at their relative length.

The explanatory variables

We also considered some eight different explanatory variables: time; teacher; ethnicity; the interaction of teacher and ethnicity; gender; the interaction of teacher and gender; the interaction of ethnicity and gender; and the interaction of teacher, gender and ethnicity.

The population of classrooms inevitably varies not only from one day to the next, but also within the same day. Children are ill, or leave early for appointments with doctors or dentists; they are also sometimes withdrawn for extra help or special activities. It was therefore necessary to introduce a three level time factor: those who were present for the equivalent of a whole day's recording (level one; approximately 240 minutes); those who missed half a morning or half an afternoon's session (level two, approximately 180 minutes) and those who were present for a half day session (level three, approximately 120 minutes). It was clearly very likely that the length of time children were actually observed would have an effect on the quantity of interactions and so this variable was considered first.

It was important next to look at teacher effect. Although the children in the study belonged to four different classes, they were taught by five different teachers representing a range of ages and experience, each of whom had their own distinctive approach to classroom management.

The main focus of concern, however, was the possible effect of ethnicity on classroom discourse. Ethnicity has often proved notoriously difficult to define and the present study has encountered various problems in this area. The largest minority group in the classes which we studied were Panjabi speakers, most of whom (20 children in all) were Moslems from the Mirpur district of Pakistan. However, there were also five Sikh children from the Indian Panjab and a Moslem boy from Bangladesh. In addition, there were three children of South Asian origin who came from Malaysia. Finally, there was one Afro-Caribbean girl, two mixed race girls and a Chinese boy.

Given these small sample sizes, there were compelling statistical reasons for treating ethnicity as a simple dichotomy: white and non-white. However, there are also other more objective considerations which support this decision. The background and experience of these various groups of children is certainly very different. The lack of clarity on the part of various teachers in the sample, however, supports the view that many teachers are extremely unclear about ethnicity and often make a simple white/non-white classification.

Several of the teachers were unaware, for instance, that it is possible to discern from children's names whether they are Muslim or Sikh. One teacher who needed to allow Muslim children to go early to prepare a special assembly demonstrated that she did not know which children in her class were Sikh and which were Muslim. In a follow-up visit to the school to verify the ethnicity of participating children, we were informed that all pupils from the Asian sub-continent in the classes we had studied were Mirpuri Pakistanis, yet a rapid perusal of their names showed that several were clearly either Sikh or Hindu. Another teacher was unable to decide on the ethnicity of a child in her class who was quite clearly of South Asian origin but whose name was European. The fact that children's cultural, religious and linguistic backgrounds are often very different is arguably less important than the fact that many teachers fail to perceive these differences.

Another important explanatory variable which needed to be taken into account was gender. Of the 81 children who took part, there were 42 boys and 39 girls. Our own informal observation, supported by various other studies of classroom interaction (cf. Graddol & Swann, 1989), led us to believe that there might be important differences in teachers' treatment of girls and boys.

In addition to time, teacher, ethnicity and gender, we also considered various interactions, namely teacher and ethnicity; teacher and gender; ethnicity and gender; and teacher, ethnicity and gender.

Because of widespread assumptions that, for example, Muslim and Sikh children are more passive and make fewer demands of teachers than do their white peers (cf. Brah & Minhas, 1988), it was decided to undertake two separate analyses. The first looked at interactions initiated by the teacher, the second at interactions initiated by the pupil.

Standard statistical techniques were used to do the analyses. The aim was to determine the extent to which a number of response variables (comments, social talk, directives, questions, task-setting, boundary setting, non-verbal behaviour, praise, blame, interactions lasting less than 30 seconds, interactions lasting more than 30 seconds, and total number of interactions) were related to a series of explanatory variables (time, teacher, ethnicity, the interaction of ethnicity and teacher, gender, the interaction of gender and teacher; the interaction of gender and ethnicity and the interaction of teacher, ethnicity and gender). Linear regression methods generalised to deal with quantitative variables such as gender, were used. All the statistical calculations were carried out using SAS GLIM (SAS Institute, 1988), a computer package suitable for analysing data with this type of structure.

Results

Our starting position was that communication is a two-way process for which both sides must take responsibility. It was therefore decided to do a two-tier analysis, examining both those interactions which were initiated by the teacher and those which were initiated by the pupils. We turn our attention to the analysis of teacher-initiated interactions.

Teacher-initiated interactions

Different children had spent differing amounts of time in the classroom during the recording period: some had been absent for some of the day; others had been withdrawn for varying activities. It was therefore to be expected that time would have a statistically significant effect on a wide range of response variables (questions, praise, interactions less than 30 seconds; interactions more than 30 seconds and task setting).

Far more striking, however, were the differences in the interactional styles of the five teachers who took part in the study. Some teachers made far greater use of non-verbal cues, comments, directions and questions than others; there were also differences in their use of praise, blame, boundary-setting behaviour. The sheer quantity of teacher talk was another variable which differed greatly from one classroom to another. There was large variation from one teacher to the next both in the total number of interactions, and in the number of interactions lasting less than 30 seconds. The only areas in which there was some convergence in teacher behaviour were task-setting and the number of interactions lasting more than 30 seconds (see Table 2).

Of main concern for the present study, however, is that even when

Table 1 The effect of time on teacher-initiated interactions.

	F value	Pr > F
Comment	2.16	0.1459
Directive	1.97	0.1646
Question	5.26	0.0245
Non-verbal	0.01	0.9198
Praise	5.20	0.0252
Blame	0.25	0.6214
Less	4.37	0.0399
More	6.97	0.0100
Task	5.11	0.0265
Boundary	2.49	0.1185
Social	3.09	0.0829
Total	3.86	0.0530

F values on 1 and 72 df.

Table 2 The effect of teacher on teacher-initiated interactions.

	F value	Pr > F
Comment	3.74	0.0078
Directive	10.99	0.0001
Question	16.56	0.0001
Non-verbal	3.33	0.0143
Praise	4.84	0.0015
Blame	6.91	0.0001
Less	13.17	0.0001
More	2.41	0.0561
Task	2.00	0.1023
Boundary	15.77	0.0001
Social	6.10	0.0002
Total	8.52	0.0001

F values on 4 and 72 df.

adjustments were made for the effects of time and teacher, ethnicity proved to be statistically significant in relationships with three separate explanatory variables, namely interactions lasting more than 30 seconds (significant at the 5% level), task setting (significant at the 1% level) and the total number of interactions (significant at the 4% level) (see Table 3).

These findings are of interest on several fronts. It is certainly a matter of concern that the teachers in the sample interacted more frequently with white children than with black. We need to be quite clear, however, that the differences in patterns of interaction do not simply relate to the

Table 3 The effect of ethnicity on teacher-initiated interactions.

	F value	Pr > F
Comment	4.13	0.0456
Directive	2.30	0.1331
Question	2.47	0.1203
Non-verbal	2.26	0.1365
Praise	1.00	0.3193
Blame	1.41	0.2383
Less	3.31	0.0726
More	4.10	0.0463
Task	6.97	0.0100
Boundary	0.91	0.3430
Social	0.04	0.8373
Total	4.25	0.0426

F values on 1 and 72 df.

overall number of interactions. There are also important differences in the *kinds* of interactions which take place. Teachers have significantly fewer extended exchanges with black children than with white. They also spend less time with them discussing the particular task which has been set.

It should be pointed out, however, that significant differences in two out of three variables (total and task-setting) occurred when the number of observations was high. There were far fewer examples of social interactions, praise, blame or boundary-setting in the corpus as a whole, and it may well be the case that other statistically significant differences would have emerged if the data base had been larger. There is room for a great deal more work to explore issues such as these.

As predicted, gender also has a significant effect on the pattern of interactions in the classrooms we observed. Teachers tended to initiate fewer interactions overall with girls—black and white—than with boys (significant at the 5% level). Girls were consistently given fewer directions (significant at the 2% level). In four cases out of five, girls were reprimanded less than the boys (significant at the 3% level). In short, girls take up less teacher time than boys (see Table 4).

Again, more data might well have yielded further significant differences in teacher behaviour in different kinds of interaction.

Pupil initiated responses

We had suspected that there would be marked differences in the patterns of interaction initiated by pupils which corresponded to those which we established for teacher-initiated interactions. However, the

Table 4 The effect of gender on teacher-initiated interactions.

	F value	Pr > F
Comment	0.48	0.4904
Directive	5.91	0.0173
Question	1.35	0.2494
Non-verbal	0.17	0.6852
Praise	0.02	0.8767
Blame	5.08	0.0270
Less	3.58	0.0623
More	2.39	0.1261
Task	2.74	0.1017
Boundary	3.20	0.0776
Social	0.17	0.6831
Total	3.84	0.0534

F values on 1 and 72 df.

only two explanatory variables which proved to have a statistically significant effect on the response variables were time and teacher. Time was highly significant in the case of task-setting, questions, praise, interactions lasting less than 30 seconds, interactions lasting more than 30 seconds and the total number of interactions. It was significant at the 5% level in boundary setting (see Table 5).

Children behaved in markedly different ways towards the different teachers. There were highly significant differences in the number of non-verbal approaches, in the number of interactions lasting more than 30 seconds and in the amount of social talk initiated by the children with

Table 5 The effect of time on pupil-initiated interactions.

	F value	Pr > F
Comment	5.21	0.0252
Directive	0.40	0.5292
Question	6.44	0.0131
Non-verbal	2.91	0.0918
Praise	4.72	0.0329
Blame	0.47	0.4963
Less	8.17	0.0055
More	5.98	0.0167
Task	8.10	0.0056
Boundary	2.55	0.1142
Social	1.68	0.1991
Total	7.50	0.0076

F values on 1 and 72 df.

the five teachers in the sample. Teachers were also found to have a significant effect on interactions lasting more than 30 seconds (4%) and the total number of interactions (see Table 6). Personality differences are, of course, centrally important in facilitating or hindering interaction. It may also be the case that different management styles on the part of teachers encourage different patterns of reaction on the part of children. There is, however, no clear pattern of cause and effect in our data that would allow us to say that a certain pattern of teacher behaviour gives rise to a certain pattern of pupil response.

Contrary to what we might have expected, none of the other explanatory variables—including ethnicity and gender—were found to have a statistically significant effect on the response variables. This finding is of importance for a number of reasons. In the model which we proposed earlier, it was suggested that communication was a two-way process, in which both parties must take responsibility for the outcomes. This interpretation was argued to be more realistic than the pathological framework sometimes associated with interactional analysis, which deems any departure from the norms associated with the dominant group to be in some way deficient. While not wishing to attribute responsibility for conversational outcomes to either party, we anticipated that differences in the number and kind of interactions initiated by both the teachers and the children might well exert an important influence on discourse patterns in the classroom.

The finding, however, that neither gender nor ethnicity have a significant effect on pupil-initiated interactions would suggest that the model which we originally proposed fails to explain our classroom data. Alternative explanations are clearly required. For if there are no

Table 6 The effect of teacher on pupil-initiated interactions.

	F value	Pr > F
Comment	0.89	0.4757
Directive	0.83	0.5112
Question	1.40	0.2416
Non-verbal	9.73	0.0001
Praise	16.32	0.0001
Blame	1.65	0.1699
Less	1.22	0.3087
More	3.65	0.0088
Task	2.56	0.0447
Boundary	0.18	0.9494
Social	4.33	0.0032
Total	2.51	0.0482

F values on 4 and 72 df.

differences in the patterns of interaction initiated by the children and yet significant differences in patterns of interaction initiated by teachers it no longer seems reasonable to attribute responsibility for observable differences to both parties. The fact that different amounts of time and different kinds of interaction are associated with different groups of children must surely be recognised as the responsibility of the teacher alone.

The qualitative data

Our interpretation of the effect of gender is supported by a growing body of published material. The position on ethnicity is less clear-cut. On the one hand, stereotypes of ethnic minority children and particularly of the passive Asian girl, abound; on the other hand, some attempts have been made in recent years to dispel this myth of passivity (cf. Brah & Minhas, 1988). Our study is, however, the first, to our knowledge, which has been able to quantify patterns of behaviour towards girls and boys of different ethnicity. It is also the first to attempt to identify the *kinds* of interaction which are the main loci for different patterns of teacher behaviour. The question remains, however, as to why teachers should behave differently towards children on the grounds of ethnicity and gender.

Although we had anticipated that both these explanatory variables might affect discourse patterns, it should be stressed that the differences which we quantified were relatively subtle. There was no way in which, for instance, we were confident in our role as classroom observers of what the final outcome of the analysis would be. None the less, it was possible to demonstrate the effects of ethnicity and gender across the sample and we have a responsibility to consider the role of stereotyping and racism in this process.

Information gathered as part of a triangulation exercise (see Edwards & Biggs, 1991) gives some interesting leads in this direction. In a workshop on cross-cultural communication for language support teachers,[1] many of whom came from ethnic minority communities, participants emphasised their belief that teachers often make approaches to ethnic minority children which can be interpreted as hostile, offensive or insensitive; that the ethnic minority child is often overlooked, misunderstood, or fails to get reasonable attention from the teacher; that the approaches made to the teacher by ethnic minority children are often misinterpreted or ignored; that teachers fail to realise that ethnic minority children sometimes hold back for cultural reasons; that comments made by teachers indicate a lack of understanding of the perspective of parents and the home in relation to ethnic minority children.

The teachers also expressed a strong feeling that, through words, teachers possess, and often exercise, the power to downgrade the home culture of the ethnic minority child. This is accomplished along a continuum consisting of two extremes, one of which is overtly racist, the other covert and expressed as concern for the academic welfare of the ethnic minority child. One thus finds teachers freely commenting on the dietary habits of the ethnic minority child ('What did you eat last night?'), where the context makes it obvious that the teacher is not merely expressing an unbiased interest; and also on the language used by the child and his or her relatives at home ('Why can't they speak English to him/her at home?'), where the systematic obliteration of any traces of the home language is seen as the panacea for the child's supposed problems at school.

The observations of language support teachers were, in turn, very much confirmed by our own observations of the classroom. Various classroom incidents pointed to a negative and ill-informed view of ethnic minority children. The following vignettes illustrate the kind of situations which arose:

> The school is celebrating Eid and Muslim children have been asked to prepare something for assembly five minutes before the other children. The teacher demonstrates that she doesn't know which of the Asian children are Muslims and is unaware that you can tell from the children's names whether they are Muslim or Sikh, and so on.

> Mohammed has hit a boy who was seriously provoking him. The teacher ignores the instigator and reproaches Mohammed with 'Mohammed, it's Eid today and Eid is a day for being nice to each other. Why are you being so horrid?'

> Another teacher explains the fact that a particular Asian boy sits separately from the other children in terms of disruptive behaviour, although we see no signs of this behaviour at any time we are in the class. She admits with a very bitter edge to her voice that he has 'ruined her year' and is observed to act very distantly towards him.

> The same teacher consistently reproaches an Asian girl for copying ideas from her peers, though this is based on assumption rather than any kind of systematic observation. The little girl starts crying. In discussing this with the teacher after the event, it emerges that the child's mother has a history of psychiatric illness, that the child was sent back to Pakistan on her own and has returned relatively recently to live with a stepmother. When we suggested that this might explain the fact that 'she's always crying', the teacher replied, 'I never thought of that'.

We do not wish in any way to suggest that all the teachers in the sample behaved in ways which, at best, might be considered insensitive. The level of awareness of cultural and linguistic diversity and the sensitivity shown to individual children varied between teachers. However, it is also true that even those teachers we considered to be both more sensitive and aware were found to behave in subtly different ways towards ethnic minority children on the basis of the quantitative analysis. We clearly need to look critically and in depth at the effects of our socialisation on the stereotypes which we may unconsciously hold and the wider role of what has come to be known as institutionalised racism (Rampton, 1981).

Conclusions

On the level of methodology, the project has raised a number of issues which we suspect are by no means unique to the work we have been doing. We have been faced with the very real tension between trust and what might be perceived to be betrayal. On the one hand, teachers have been generous enough to open up their classrooms and expose themselves to scrutiny. On the other hand, it is very likely that they will not be able to handle the observations we might want to make about the way they sometimes behave towards minority children. The obvious solution is only to embark on research with teachers where triangulation is more formally part and parcel of the agreement. But this often raises a host of other problems. Teachers who were prepared to take part under these conditions would almost certainly be those who were already engaging in good practice. Those who felt insecure would be very likely to hold back.

An action research project of this kind needs to be a long-term project because only a long-term project could ensure the mutual trust and support which you would need to make it work. But this raises problems for the teachers and the researchers. Teachers already feel under siege from the multiple demands which are being made on them and the researchers know that they are much more likely to get funding for a short-term low budget project than for a more costly long-term one. There seems to us no easy solution.

The sharp contrast between teacher to (ethnic) child initiations and (ethnic) child to teacher initiations which emerges from our data has far-reaching implications both for the further exploration of discourse patterns and for strategies to promote equality of opportunity in education. We believe that we have identified an area of considerable importance which should be explored in much greater depth. What might be the effect of larger samples? Would we be able to discern more subtle ethnic effects? Or might we be able to identify a relationship between different styles of classroom management and different discourse patterns? With more conversational data, might it be possible to refine the response variables? Whatever the findings of further more in-depth study, there can be no doubt of the urgent need to sensitise teachers to the ways in which they interact in subtly different ways with different groups of pupils and to the implications of these patterns of behaviour for different educational outcomes.

Acknowledgements

The research reported in this article was undertaken as part of a research project on 'Style in the Inter-Ethnic Classroom' funded by the Economic and Social Research Council (award no. X204 25 2007). Thanks to David Corson and Courtnay Cazden for their comments on an earlier version of this article.

Notes

1. During the 1980s, educational provision for children acquiring English as an additional language moved from separate classes and specialist centres into mainstream schooling. Teachers previously designated 'English as a Second Language (ESL)' teachers have now assumed a different role, working collaboratively with class teachers, and are known as 'language support teachers'.

References

Brah, A. and Minhas, R. (1988) Structural racism or cultural difference: Schooling for Asian girls. In M. Woodhouse and A. McGrath (eds) *Family, School and Society*. London: Hodder and Stoughton.

Bullock, Sir A. (1975) *A Language for Life*. London: HMSO.

Coates, J. (1986) *Men, Women and Language*. London: Longman.

Commission for Racial Equality (CRE) (1988) *Learning in Terror*. London: HMSO.

Edwards, V. and Biggs, A.P. (1991) Study of Style in the Inter-Ethnic Classroom. End of Project report No. X204 25 2007. Swindon: Economic and Social Research Council.

Graddol, D. and Swann, J. (1989) *Gender Voices*. Oxford: Blackwell.

Gumperz, J. (1982) *Discourse Strategies*. Cambridge: Cambridge University Press.

Gumperz, J., Jupp, T. and Roberts, C. (1979) *Crosstalk*. London: NCILT.

Heath, S. (1983) *Ways With Words*. Cambridge: Cambridge University Press.

Hawkins, E. (1984) *Awareness of Language*. Cambridge: Cambridge University Press.

Michaels, S. and Collins, J. (1984) Oral discourse style: Classroom interaction and the acquisition of literacy. In D. Tannen (ed.) *Coherence in Written and Spoken Discourse*. Norwood, NJ: Ablex.

Milner, D. (1983) *Children and Race: Ten Years On*. London: Ward Lock Educational.

Rampton, A. (1981) *West Indian Children in Our Schools* (Interim Report of the Committee of Inquiry into the Education of Children from Ethnic Minority Groups). London: HMSO.

SAS Institute (1988) *SAS/STAT Guide for Personal Computers, Version 6.03.* Cary, North Carolina: SAS Institute Inc.

Singh, R., Lele, J. and Martohardjono, G. (1988) Communication in a multilingual society: Some missed opportunities. *Language and Society* 17(1), 43–59.

Stone, M. (1981) *The Education of the Black Child in Britain: The Myth of Multicultural Education.* London: Fontana.

Swann, Lord (1985) *Education for All.* London: HMSO.

Tizard, B. and Hughes, M. (1984) *Young Children Learning.* London: Fontana.

7 Reading as a Social Process in a Middle School Classroom

DAVID BLOOME

The primary purpose of this article is to explore the nature of reading as a social process in urban, middle school classrooms. Of special concern is how reading as a social and cultural process mediates students' interaction with and interpretation of printed text.

A second purpose is to document part of the experience of students in urban, middle school classrooms. Documentation is important for at least two reasons. First, too frequently the history of nonmajority groups within society's institutions is lost or distorted. Second, given the contemporary concern and political rhetoric with education, it is important to have grounded descriptions of what actually occurs in classrooms so that political debate and policy-making can be properly informed.

The chapter is organized into three sections. In the first, recent research concerned with building a theory of reading as a social process is briefly discussed (see Bloome & Green, 1982b, 1984, for extended discussions of related research). The research is primarily based in anthropology, sociolinguistics, the sociology of education, and the ethnography of communication. In the second section, findings from an ethnographic study of reading in an eighth-grade classroom is presented. The findings are part of a series of studies on reading and writing as social processes in urban, middle school classrooms (see also Bloome, 1983a, 1983b, 1984a, 1984b; Bloome & Argumedo, 1983; Bloome & Golden, 1982; Bloome & Green, 1982a). Finally, in the third section, the implications of the findings for building a theory of reading as a social process are discussed.

Underlying the discussion in this chapter is a view of reading and literacy development as the process of becoming a member of a community based on written language. A community may be broadly defined (such as a profession or ethnic group) or narrowly defined (such as a family or classroom). Regardless, the community sets standards and determines appropriate ways of constituting written language events, i.e., ways of interacting with and interpreting text. Almost by definition, then, reading is a social process—a means to participate in and establish a community or social group. In this article, I am especially concerned with the social relationships among those people actually participating in a reading event. Less emphasized are those literary and psychological issues studies concerned with the social relationships between author and reader.

Research on Reading as a Social Process

Recent research concerned with reading as a social process can, for heuristic purposes, be divided into three groups. A first group of studies views reading as a cognitive-linguistic process embedded in a social-communicative context. The social-communicative context influences the nature of reading as a cognitive-linguistic process. A second group of studies is primarily concerned with the social uses of reading. Reading and writing are viewed as manifestations and reflections of the culture in which the children's day-to-day activities are embedded. Reading and writing, like sewing, working on cars, playing baseball, dating, and going to church, are viewed as manifestations of a culture. The description of reading and writing is the further description of people's culture. Among the questions asked by these studies are: What are the roles of reading in society? How, where, and when do people read? For what purposes? What counts as reading? How does what counts as reading differ across situations? How are reading activities interpersonally organized? The third group of studies is primarily concerned with literacy as a sociocognitive process. Both learning to read and reading itself are viewed as part of a society's enculturation process. Through reading, children not only learn culturally appropriate information, activities, values, and interpersonal relationships, they also learn culturally appropriate ways of thinking about the world, ways of problem solving, and other cognitive processes. Among the questions asked by these studies are: How does literacy learning influence how one views the world? How does literacy learning influence thought, problem solving, and other cognitive processes?

Reading as embedded in a social/communicative context

In order to participate in classroom reading events, students need to gain access to those events. Gaining access requires more than being present (although as McDermott, 1976, has shown, being present is itself a social accomplishment). Gaining access to classroom reading events involves gaining opportunities to interact with text or language in ways appropriate to school-based reading development.

On one hand, gaining access is a matter of communicative competence.

Students need to know how to gain the floor, hold the floor, demonstrate group membership, and engage in communicative behavior appropriate to the situation. However, gaining access can also be a matter of cross-cultural interaction between school culture and students' home culture. For example, Michaels (1981) has described how access to literacy learning situations can be denied because of students' culturally based narrative styles. However, the issue is not only whether or not students gain access to literacy learning opportunities, it is also the kinds of literacy learning opportunities students receive. Collins (1981) has described how the distribution of literacy learning tasks may be related to students' culturally based prosodic style during oral reading. That is, the distribution of different kinds of literacy learning tasks rather than being based on developmental needs may be based on the manifestation of students' home culture within the classroom.

In addition to gaining access, students need to appropriately display their reading behavior. For example, students who have read and understood a text but do not raise their hands in response to a teacher's question may not be viewed as having read the text. Cross-cultural differences between students and teachers may result (a) in some students not appropriately displaying reading knowledge (e.g., Gumperz & Tannen, 1979), and (b) in teachers misevaluating student reading knowledge (e.g., Gumperz & Tannen, 1979; Scollon & Scollon, 1982). For example, if a student answers a set of comprehension questions in terms of his/her own experience and background knowledge, the student may get answers that disagree with the answers designated as correct by the textbook or teacher(e.g., Bloome, 1983b). Yet, in terms of the student's background knowledge and experience the answers may be sensible. There is a potential in such situations for the student to be misevaluated. Part of what many students need to learn in school is not to answer questions in terms of their own background knowledge and experience but rather in terms of the text and the background knowledge and experience assumed by the text (Bloome, 1982; Scollon & Scollon, 1982).

The social uses of literacy

What counts as reading and writing may vary across situations. The expectations for what reading and writing will look like, the social meanings of reading and writing, and the purposes for which people read and write vary across situations. For example, reading prayers in a church looks different and is done for a different purpose than reading an insurance contract at Sears.

Researchers have explored the range and social meanings of literacy activities across communities (e.g., Heath, 1982, 1983; Scheiffelin & Cochran-Smith, 1984; Scollon & Scollon, 1984; Reder & Green, in press); within a community (e.g., Anderson & Stokes, 1984; Jacob, 1984; Taylor,

1983; Taylor & Dorsey-Gaines, 1982); across classroom and home cultures (e.g., Bloome & Green, 1982a; Bloome, 1984a; Cook-Gumperz, Gumperz & Simons, 1981; Heath, 1982; Gilmore, 1981; Hymes, 1981; Philips, 1983); and within classrooms (e.g., Au, 1980; Griffin, 1977; Bloome, 1982). The findings of these studies have suggested five constructs that are important for building a theory of reading as a social process.

(1) The interpersonal organizations and meanings that people have for reading and writing activities are consistent with and extensions of the cultural organizations and meanings of narrative events and other communicative, interpersonal events within their community.

(2) The social meaning of reading evolves from how reading affects interpersonal relationships.

(3) Across settings (e.g., across communities, institutions, school and nonschool settings, classrooms), there is a great deal of variety in the nature of literacy activities. However, the evaluation of literacy behavior—that is, the determination of what counts as reading or writing—tends to be both ethnocentric and situation specific. For example, in classrooms reading is typically viewed as what happens during reading groups with the basal readers. However, during school, students may engage in many other activities that involve the use of written language. But because these literacy events are not part of the formally recognized literacy curriculum they may not be counted by the teacher or the students as 'reading'.

(4) The social status given to reading ability and to engagement in reading activities depends (a) on the nature and organization of the reading activity, and (b) on the people assigning status. For example, Gilmore (1981) described how the peer literacy activities of a group of urban, black, adolescent women were often overlooked as literacy activities by teachers and were viewed as low- and even negative-status activities. However, among the adolescent women, proficiency in the peer literacy activities was accorded high status.

(5) Literacy learning and practice, as promulgated through classroom instruction, are neither based upon nor necessarily related to, in general, the reading and writing activities that actually occur outside of school at home or at work (Heath, 1983; Hendrix, 1981; Kirsch & Guthrie, 1983). Yet, it is primarily through the evaluation of school reading and writing that students gain academic status that may be translated into job and career opportunities. The connection between school literacy practice and jobs may have more to do with students acquiring social status and the dominant culture's ways of organizing talk and information (which is not to state that any one way of organizing talk or information is either more efficient or productive than another). That is, students learn—or perhaps, more

accurately put, are taught—how and where to 'fit' into the dominant culture which, in general, controls job and career opportunities (cf. Heath, 1983).

Reading as a sociocognitive process

To describe reading as a sociocognitive process suggests that reading involves both social and cognitive processes. However, as used here, the description of reading as a sociocognitive process means not only do social and cognitive factors affect reading behavior, but that reading itself is simultaneously a process of socialization, enculturation, and cognition. In brief, learning to read involves the learning of culturally bound ways of thinking (including problem solving, inferencing, and conceptualizing), which is, in part, a consequence of and an influence on the socialization of interpersonal relationships. In other words, as used here, the term *sociocognitive* refers not to a combination of separate social and cognitive processes but rather to a unitary set of processes whose nature is simultaneously social and cognitive.

It is difficult to discuss the cognitive effects of literacy learning without discussing schooling. After all, most literacy learners attend or have attended schools. Further, in schools students spend a great deal of time learning specific ways to interact with written language. Thus, schooling is viewed as not only fostering cognitive development but as fostering certain kinds of cognitive development and processes (Goody & Watt, 1968; Olson, 1977; Vygotsky, 1962).

Scribner & Cole (1977, 1981) were able to explore literacy learning and practice outside of schooling among the Vai in Liberia. Their findings suggested that the effects of literacy learning and practice on the acquisition of cognitive processes depended on the kinds of literacy activities in which people engage and the kinds of cognitive processes inherent in those literacy practices. When the range of functions and complexity of literacy activities is limited, then the cognitive skills fostered by literacy activity will also be limited.

Building on the research of Scribner & Cole (1977, 1981), questions can be asked about the cumulative effect of the kinds of literacy practices fostered by schools. If different literacy practices tend to foster different cognitive skills, then literacy curricula can be viewed as part of the means for transmitting culturally bound ways of thinking about the world and engaging the world. As such, reading and writing events become culturally bound ways of mediating reality.

Reading as a Social Process in an Eighth-grade Classroom

During the 1981–1982 school year and following summer, an ethnographic study of adolescent reading was conducted both in and out of school. The research setting was an urban middle school (grades 6–8) that served a predominately black, working-class community.

Data collection and analysis followed a type-case analysis framework. First, a general ethnographic study of classrooms, school and community was conducted (cf. Spradley, 1980). Second, based on the general ethnographic study, specific classroom events—especially recurrent gate-keeping events involving reading—were identified and videotaped. The microanalysis of the videotapes was based on recent work in the analysis of classroom face-to-face interaction, especially recent work within sociolinguistic ethnography (cf. Green & Wallat, 1981; Cook-Gumperz et al., 1981; Erickson & Shultz, 1981). Microanalysis provided a means for extracting models of social, interpersonal behavior within recurrent reading events. These models provided insights into the nature of reading—as it naturally occurred—within and across classrooms and across instructional and noninstructional settings.

Three sets of related findings have previously been reported: (a) classroom reading as text reproduction (Bloome, 1983a, 1984a), (b) classroom reading as procedural display (Bloome & Argumedo, 1983), and (c) differences in reading across instructional and noninstructional settings (Bloome, 1984a; Bloome & Green, 1982a). These findings are briefly reviewed in the next section and provide a starting place for further findings and discussion.

Text reproduction, procedural display, and reading across instructional and noninstructional settings

In the classrooms studied, reading events were typified by text reproduction. Text reproduction manifested itself in many ways including the oral rendition of printed directions and printed text, the copying of assignments written on the blackboard, the copying of reading exercises from a textbook, and the repetition of phrases and texts designated as correct by the teacher. The occurrence and dominance of text reproduction was not an explicit goal of instruction in either classroom. Rather, text reproduction was, in general, invisible and only revealed through the microanalysis of direct reading instruction events. In part, text reproduction was tied to the kinds of tasks students were asked to perform, in part to teacher–student interaction, and in part to student responses to classroom assignments independent of teachers and/or task demands.

Text reproduction also manifested itself as a kind of classroom language. For example, if during reading instruction a student knew the answer to a teacher question, it was, in general, not appropriate to respond in one's own way of speaking. Responses, in general, needed to be put into a 'book-language' form. That is, responses had to be elaborated and decontextualized. An obvious case in which book language was demanded of students was when teachers asked students to put their correct answer in the form of a 'complete sentence'.

A number of institutional constraints in the school fostered text reproduction. First, a limited supply of textbooks meant that students did not have their own texts to take home. It was often necessary throughout their K–12 experience to copy text in order to use it later. Second, the reading programs mandated for use in K-8 required copying, the repetition of phrases and written text, and extended amounts of oral rendition without subsequent reference to the meaning of the text. Further, given that skill work was completed separate from meaningful reading, there was neither purpose nor incentive for either students or teacher to engage in anything more than text reproduction. Fourth, the experience of many students in grades K–5 (and, perhaps, even earlier than kindergarten) often focused on copying as writing and oral rendition as reading (Bloome, 1984). Thus, the middle school students might expect—even demand—that tasks presented to them be interpreted in terms of text reproduction (see also Doyle, 1983).

Text reproduction was, in part, related to procedural display, that is, the display by teacher and students to each other of a set of academic and/or interactional procedures that themselves counted as the accomplishment of a lesson. Procedural display might not necessarily be related to the acquisition of academic content or to learning cognitive strategies. Simply put, procedural display occurred when teachers and students were primarily concerned with displaying to each other that they were 'getting the lesson done'; whatever academic learning occurred was, at best, secondary or accidental. Procedural display can be compared to a group of actors who have memorized their parts and who enact the play for each other's benefit without necessarily knowing what happens in the play or what it means.

Procedural display was a dominant feature of direct reading instruction in the classrooms studied despite what appeared to be important differences in classroom climate and academic content. For example, in a sixth-grade classroom studied, reading skills were emphasized with little student discussion. There were few opportunities for personal expression. In an eighth-grade classroom in the same school, the explicit focus was on literature and literary analysis (e.g., plot, characterization, theme) with explicit instructional emphases on student discussion and the expression of personal reaction to literature. However, given that procedural display and text reproduction were dominant features of both classrooms, questions can be raised as to whether explicit differences between the classrooms were actually substantive differences.

Both outside of and in classrooms, students engaged in noninstructional reading and writing activities. In classrooms, noninstructional literacy activities consisted of covertly reading a book (e.g., a comic book, magazine, or paperback book) and writing, reading, and passing notes. While both instructional and noninstructional literacy events involved the public display of procedures, noninstructional literacy events were characterized by the expression of personal feelings and relationships and by group text production. Moreover, while instructional literacy behavior was associated with social status (e.g., whether one was in the top or bottom group), noninstructional literacy behavior was not.

Neither text reproduction, procedural display, nor the differences described between instructional and noninstructional activities are psychological constructs or descriptions. They are not descriptions of learning processes. Rather, they are descriptions of social and communicative processes. They are partial answers to the question 'What is happening within a specific set of literacy events among people? And between people and texts?'

Overview of the lesson

The following lesson involved patterns of teacher–student–text interaction that were recurrent across analogous lessons in the eighth-grade class as well as across analogous lessons in other classes within the school. The lesson focused on a short story called 'The Saint'. Previously, parts of the story had been read aloud during class time. Students had also been given class time to read the story silently, and they had been assigned to read the story for homework. In preparation for discussion, students had been assigned the task of identifying words that they did not know in the story.

The lesson began with vocabulary. The teacher asked students which words they did not know. Students provided words. Using the dictionary and teacher explanation, vocabulary words were reviewed.

Following the vocabulary segment, the teacher lead a discussion on characterization focusing on one of the main protagonists. The discussion of characterization overlapped the vocabulary segment since many of the vocabulary words were descriptors of the protagonist.

Finally, the teacher assigned an essay. Students were to write on one of two questions. Each question was directly related to the day's discussion of vocabulary and character.

In the sections that follow, a detailed description is provided of the target students who were the focus of the videotape analysis, of the story, of the teacher–student discussion, and of what the students wrote.

The students

A group of eight students was the focus of intensive ethnographic study, and in particular, emphasis was placed upon the male students.

The group was chosen primarily for logistical reasons—the angle of the camera, placement of electrical outlets, windows, desks, permission slips received from every member of the group, etc. The teacher considered the group academically higher than other groups in the classroom (although there were individuals outside of the group who were considered academically equal to the group). Ethnographic interviews were conducted only with the male students. Thus, there is less background data on the female students.

The Four Female Students. Tina and Fran always sat together at one end of the group. They frequently passed notes back and forth. They tended to remove themselves from peer activities not initiated within the group and/or having to do with the rest of the class. They rarely volunteered to answer teacher questions or to pass out books, etc.

Linda sometimes sat with Tina and Fran and sometimes sat with Betty at the other end of the table. Like Tina and Fran, Linda rarely volunteered to answer teacher requests. Unlike Tina and Fran, Linda would participate in peer events (e.g., note passing) that were initiated by students outside the group. Linda was also more likely to talk with the male students. Tina and Fran limited their interaction with male students to Mark and Louis (which might have more to do with the fact that Mark and Louis were the class leaders rather than simply the fact that Tina and Fran always sat next to Mark and Louis).

Betty always sat at the opposite end of the group from Fran and Tina. Occasionally, Betty would sit outside of the group. Like Linda, Betty participated in peer events whether initiated inside or outside the group. Betty and Linda would readily interact with any of the male students in the group as well as with students outside of the group.

All four female students were considered by the teacher as 'among the better students in the class.' They always had notebooks, paper, pencils, pens, etc. When the teacher made seatwork assignments, the four would be among the first to actually begin the seatwork (this was especially true of Tina and Fran).

The Four Male Students. Mark was recognized as the leader of the class. He was good looking, tall, well built, athletic, gregarious, and desired by nearly every female student in the eighth grade. He was liked by both teachers and students. Teachers could count on Mark to comply with their requests, if not the first time, then certainly the second time. Yet, Mark was not a teacher's pet; he would talk during class, pass notes, fool around, etc. However, he seemed to be able to 'fool around' within acceptable guidelines, knowing when to stop and when to be serious about school work. Except on rare occasions, Mark had a notebook, paper, and a pencil.

Though not as athletic, tall, nor as good looking, Louis was also viewed as a class leader. He played sports earnestly—if not excellently. He was viewed as the male class intellectual. Unlike Mark, Louis would respond to teacher questions. Furthermore, when the teacher wanted a correct answer, Louis was likely to be asked. Like Mark, Louis usually had a notebook and paper. Unlike Mark, Louis would have several pencils which he would lend to other students.

Bob came to the class about midyear. He spent the first several weeks quietly reading a book about Martin Luther King, Jr., during lunch and when there was time for peer interaction. Because of his reading, he was viewed by students as 'smart,' although when asked about his reading he stated that he needed something to do until he got to know the other students. Bob usually had a notebook, but frequently he needed a pencil or needed to sharpen a pencil. Unlike Mark or Louis, Bob was not viewed as a class leader. He was more an observer of peer events than a participant. Most important to note about Bob was his religious background. His family belonged to a fundamentalist Baptist sect. They spent nearly every evening and all day Sunday either in church or doing church-related activity. When not involved in church activity, Bob usually had responsibilities around his house (e.g., take care of siblings). Of the eight students in the group, Bob and Ray were bussed to school from a predominately black, lower working-class neighborhood. Other students came from nearby neighborhoods that had larger lots, bigger houses, and more trees, and they were generally considered to be middle class or upper working class.

Ray had been held back a year. His parents predicted that he would not finish high school, although Ray stated that he was determined to finish high school no matter how many years it took. Ray viewed himself as 'slower' than other students, but he also insisted that, given enough time, he 'could get it.' Like Bob, Ray was not viewed as a class leader. However, he played sports and was viewed as one of the insiders. Ray primarily interacted with Louis, Linda, Betty, and Bob, though he would freely interact with other students in the class. Ray usually had paper and pencil for class work.

Though the eight students formed a group, on a day-to-day basis the group usually consisted of at least one other student; that is, one of the eight would usually be absent, Betty would decide to sit with other friends, or one of the eight would come to class late. When there was an opening in the group, another student would typically occupy that seat. Sometimes the newcomer would be a close friend of one of the eight, or else it might be a student wanting to get friendly with one of the female students; it might also be a student wanting to become part of the group. The teacher usually overlooked isolated changes in the seating plan until there was a disruption. At times, the teacher tried to reform a student by assigning that child with the group. With the exception of friends who were invited to sit with the group, others who sat with the group were ignored and isolated.

What the students read

For the lesson, students read 'The Saint' by V.S. Pritchett. Students began the story with a brief introduction by the teacher, and this was followed by whole-class round-robin reading. When the class eventually became disorderly, the round-robin reading was ended and students were told to read silently in class and to finish the story at home.

The story was about a 17-year-old boy and his loss of religion. He belonged to a religious sect that taught that misery, pain, discomfort, and lack of money were illusions, since God would not allow his children to suffer. Suffering was the result of 'letting in error' or sin. The boy's family was visited by Timberlake, one of the sect's hierarchy from out of town. At first, the boy's doubts regarding the sect's dogma were alleviated by Timberlake's visit. The boy was extremely impressed by Timberlake's demeanor. However, after a boating accident in which Timberlake fell in the river and made a fool of himself trying to ignore the cold and discomfort, the boy realized that his doubts about the sect's dogma were well-founded.

The content of the story could be viewed as closely related to the students, especially Bob. About half of the students regularly attended church on Sundays, and almost all had had religious training. Most participated in church social activities (e.g., church basketball leagues, barbeques). During the spring, summer, and fall, the neighborhoods that served the school were regularly solicited by Jehovah Witnesses and other sects. There was a big billboard two blocks from the school proclaiming 'Believe in the Lord and Thou will be saved.' In brief, students frequently came into contact with a broad range of church-related activities.

Teacher–student discussion

Teacher–student interaction provided a framework for interpreting and interacting with text. As mentioned earlier, previous microethnographic analysis of teacher–student–text interaction in the eighth-grade class (as well as in other classes) suggested that text reproduction and procedural display were part of the framework for student–text interaction. The following description suggested that, in conjunction with procedural display and text reproduction, the framework for interaction with text provided through teacher–student interaction could be characterized as cataloging. *Cataloging* is the listing of parts that count as the whole (which is not to say that all of the parts of the whole are listed but rather that what parts are listed do count as the whole). Cataloging differs from analysis. *Analysis* is a process of segmenting a whole into parts in order to gain insight into the nature of the whole. With cataloging, the goal is the display of a list. The whole disappears, or rather, the whole becomes the list. As is true of any catalog—e.g., the Sears catalog, a telephone book—the listing does not necessarily reflect nor is related to the nature of the whole from which it comes. A telephone book provides no information about the nature of the society or social organization of the people listed. Similarly, a catalog of vocabulary words provides little information about the nature of the story or what that story might mean to students. Yet, in the following lesson, it was the catalog of vocabulary words that provided the basis upon which students responded to the text.

The teacher–student discussion began with vocabulary. The teacher had asked students to finish reading the story at home and to make a list of vocabulary words. As shown in the transcript, either no one had made a list or no one was willing to admit to making a list.

01	T:	WHO'S DONE THAT [MADE A VOCABULARY LIST] PLEASE
02		WHO HAS A LIST OF WORDS THAT THEY NEED HELP WITH
03		YOU MEAN I CAN THROW ANY ONE OF THOSE WORDS OUT AND YOU'LL KNOW THE MEANING
04		AND YOU'LL JUMP RIGHT UP AND YEAH THAT'S IT
05	Ss:	Yup . . . uh huh
06	T:	OK
07	Ss:	no . . . no
08	T:	AH
09	Ss:	I know . . no . . yup
10	T:	ROBERT
11	R:	I wasn't here yesterday
12	T:	ALL RIGHT
13		RHONDA
14		(UNDECIPHERABLE COMMENT)
15	R:	(undecipherable comment)
16	Ss:	(loud background talking)

Students began talking with each other. One student interrupted, stating that someone from the previous class had left a book on the desk. The interruption and the disruptive talking provided an opportunity for students to scan through the text and find vocabulary words. In addition, the disruption provided an excuse for both the teacher and students since they were unable to continue, because no student could (or, perhaps, would) appropriately fill the slot created by the teacher.

The importance of noting that no one had apparently prepared a vocabulary list is that it seemed to make no difference. The lesson continued as if students had had the lists. Students raised their hands and identified vocabulary words based on scanning the pages for unfamiliar words. On one hand, this could be explained as procedural display, completing a lesson merely for the sake of completing it. It could also be explained as a refusal by the teacher to acknowledge that students did not complete the assignment. Publicly acknowledging that the students had not completed the lesson might have forced the teacher to become punitive, resulting in friction between teacher and students. More positively, continuing with the lesson could be seen as an effort to teach vocabulary and vocabulary skills. At the same time, continuing with the lesson provided one way to discuss the story and provided students with knowledge about the story.

Rodney helped to continue the lesson by raising his hand and offering a vocabulary word for discussion. Once a word was offered, the teacher established an instructional pattern: (a) the word was located in the text; (b) someone was assigned to look up the word in the dictionary; (c) the portion of the text containing the vocabulary word was read while the dictionary was being searched; (d) the dictionary definition was read and related to the use of the word in the story; and (e) the teacher elaborated on the definition, relating the vocabulary word to student experience.

However, the surface-level description of the instructional pattern does not fully describe what occurred. As mentioned earlier, text reproduction is a part of the teacher–student–text interaction. For example, consider the following transcript segment in which the teacher read from the book in order to provide a semantic context for one of the vocabulary words.

42	T:	SINCE THAT HE SAID
43		HAS
44		HE HAD A PINK SQUARE HEAD
45		AND VERY SMALL EARS AND ONE OF THOSE TORPID ENAMELED SMILES WHICH WERE
46		SAID BY ENEMIES TO BE TO COMMON IN OUR SECT
47		OK
48		THINK ABOUT TEETH
49		WHAT ARE THEY MADE OF
50	S:	enamel
51	T:	OK

52	s:	ivory
53	ss:	ivory
54	ss:	(background talking)
55	s:	rhonda your mother

Reading the text surrounding the vocabulary words (enamel and torpid) did not provide any insights into the meaning of the vocabulary words. The text, for the students, was impenetrable, especially since the teacher read the text in a 'flat' prosodic style. (As shown later in the teacher–student discussion of Mr. Timberlake's character, what the students remembered was 'small ears.') What reading the text seemed to do was to establish the dominance of text reproduction as a definition of problem solving and of interacting with text.

Also feeding into the dominance of text reproduction as a definition of problem solving and interaction with text was the time taken and effort made to locate the vocabulary words in the text.

26	T:	ALL RIGHT RODNEY AGAIN
27	r:	torpid on page 29
28	T:	ALL RIGHT ON PAGE 29 WOULD YOU COUNT
29		PUT US IN THE RIGHT PLACE WHAT PARAGRAPH
30	r:	last one
31		at the bottom of the page
32	T:	LAST PARAGRAPH
33	r:	it's the second sentence from the bottom
34	T:	SECOND SENTENCE
35		ENAMELED SMILE
36	r:	and torpid
37	T:	ALL RIGHT

Students spent a great deal of time attempting to find the right page, paragraph, and line. Many students were still trying to locate the right spot after the text had been read by the teacher. That is, it was not clear from the teacher–student interaction whether the teacher wanted the class to find the right spot. She made the location public, and, at other times when asked by a student, repeated the location. However, the teacher read the text before most of the students had had a chance to find the right spot (e.g., lines 42–46) and then moved on away from the text (e.g., lines 47–55).

Text reproduction also manifested itself in the rendition of dictionary definitions. Students read aloud the dictionary definition. The vocabulary and syntactic structures of the dictionary definitions made them nearly impenetrable for students. The hesitating and broken prosodic manner in which the definitions were read by students made the text even more impenetrable.

56	**T:**	ALL RIGHT
57		MICHAEL HAS FOUND THE WORD IN THE DIC-TIONARY
58		RODNEY
59		HE WILL GIVE US THE DEFINITION IT GIVES
60		AND THEN HE'LL FIND WHICH ONE FITS YOUR SENTENCE
61		OK
62	**M:**	number one
63		tempora temporary loss of
64		number one
65		number one
66		has lost most of power
67		power of
68		convention or failure
69		in functioning in functioning
70		oration
71		number 2
72		lacking in energy or vigor
73		vigor
74	**T:**	OK

Even though the dictionary definition had been read (lines 62–73) and the vocabulary words had twice been placed in the context of the surrounding text, students were unable to determine what the words meant. They did not respond to the teacher's request for a definition. Instead, students began a disruption (line 85):

83		OK NOW HOW WAS THE WORD TORPID USED
84		HOW WAS THE WORD TORPID USED
85	**ss:**	(background talking)

The teacher responded to the disruption by extending the slot she created for the students. That is, she provided additional opportunity for students to respond and gave them additional information that they could use to respond (lines 86–93):

86	**T:**	ALL RIGHT
87		SHOW
88		HOW HE SMILED
89		HI HOW YOU DOING

```
 90       THAT KIND OF THING
 91       OR DID IT COME JUST NORMAL
 92       A JUST KIND OF A
 93       (Teacher models an expressionless smile)
 94  ss:  (undecipherable comments and background talking)
 95  T:   ALL RIGHT A LACK OF WHAT
 96       LACK OF WHAT
 97  s:   lack of expression
```

The students, or rather at least one student, responded to the teacher's dramatization of a torpid smile and her prompting of student response (lines 93–97). However, the teacher was unable to build in the student response (lines 98–102), and finally, the teacher filled in the slot she created by once again telling students what the word meant by dramatizing it (lines 103–112).

```
 98  T:   LACK OF FEELING
 99       LACK OF EXPRESSION
100       LACK OF
101       LACK OF FEELING
102       ALL RIGHT AND
          (extended pause)
103  T:   SO A TORPID SMILE
104       LATICIA
105       WOULD BE A SMILE THAT DIDN'T HAVE MUCH
            FEELING
106       ONE THAT WE MIGHT OF AUTOMATICALLY WITH-
            OUT THINKING OR WITHOUT GIVING IT A LOT
            OF UMPH
107       A LOT OF VIGOR
108       ALL RIGHT
109       IT WAS JUST THERE
110       HI HOW ARE YOU
111       YOU KNOW THAT ISN'T ONE THAT HAS A LOT OF
            ENERGY OR A LOT OF FEELING BEHIND IT
112       ONE THAT YOU'RE NOT SURE OF
```

The interaction between the teacher and the students can be characterized as procedural display. The teacher was attempting to get the procedures of the lesson publicly displayed. However, the students were either unable or unwilling to display their part of the interactional procedure of the lesson. That they were probably more unable than unwilling to help in the procedural display is shown in the next transcript segment. The teacher attempted to solicit on-task student response by creating slots that could be answered without necessarily knowing the content. That is, the only knowledge needed was that of conversational routines. One did not need to know the meaning of torpid in order to correctly answer the question in line 113.

113 **T:**   IF SOMEONE HAD A TORPID SMILE WOULD YOU
              SAY THEY WERE A GENUINE PERSON
114 **Ss:** no

However, the teacher made a conversational error. She created an expectation that students could appropriately respond to questions on the basis of conversational routines. When she asked 'is genuine real?' (line 115), she crossed student expectations created in the previous question–answer interaction. Students expected to be able to answer the question appropriately by responding to only the form and prosody of the teacher's question—not the content. The teacher acknowledged that she violated conversational expectations (lines 117–120) and reestablished the expectation that student responses to questions could be based on conversational knowledge only (lines 121–127):

115 **T:**   IS GENUINE REAL
116 **Ss:** no
117 **T:**   AH
118   OK
119   MAYBE I MISUSED THE WORD
120   OH I DON'T MEAN THAT THIS DID
121   BUT WOULD BE A PERSON THAT YOU WOULD
              FEEL THAT
122   HIS FEELINGS COULD ALWAYS BE TRUSTED
123   THAT HE'S GIVE YOU HIS OR HER GENUINE
              FEELINGS
124   THEIR REAL FEELINGS
125 **Ss:** no
126 **T:**   NO
127   SO IN THAT WAY THAT WOULDN'T BE GENUINE

Finally, the class moved on to another word, and the pattern of text reproduction and procedural display reoccurred.

Although the vocabulary segment helped establish a cataloging framework for interacting and interpreting text, cataloging was easier to see both in the teacher–student discussion of the story itself and through comparison with other lessons.

In discussing 'The Saint' the teacher chose 'character' as the explicit frame and set the task:

202	ON THE BOARD ARE THREE THINGS THAT HAVE TO DO WITH MR. TIMBERLAKE
203	APPEARANCE PERSONALITY AND INFLUENCE ON THE BOY
204	NOW
205	THE AUTHOR TELLS YOU WHAT MR. TIMBERLAKE LOOKS LIKE
206	HE
207	HE GIVES SOME VERY DESCRIPTIVE
208	DESCRIPTION OF MR. TIMBERLAKE
209	HE EVEN TELLS US A BIT ABOUT HIS PERSONALITY
210	BUT WHEN YOU COME TO THE INFLUENCE ON THE BOY
211	EVERYBODY HAS TO READ BETWEEN THE LINES
212	BECAUSE THE AUTHOR DOESN'T TELL YOU WHAT INFLUENCE HE HAS ON THE BOY
213	BUT HE KIND OF GIVES YOU A HINT TOWARD IT
214	THIS IS THE KIND OF INFLUENCE HE HAD
215	ALL RIGHT LET'S START WITH THE APPEARANCE
216	AHH
217	LET'S FIND WHAT MR. TIMBERLAKE LOOKS LIKE
218	ALL RIGHT IN YOUR BOOK YOU MAY
219	I DON'T KNOW
220	SOMEONE HAVE AN IDEA
221	SOMEONE REMEMBER FROM WHAT THEY READ

The teacher outlined the broader communicative task framework, providing an overview of the teacher–student tasks to come (describing appearance, personality and influence; lines 201–214). Implicitly, teacher–student discussion of appearance involved cataloging based primarily on the previous vocabulary discussion. That is, students used the previous vocabulary discussion as the primary source of information for responding to teacher questions.

222	**T:**	RODNEY
223		YOU HAD ONE HE HAD A TORPID WHAT [Lines 223–226 are based on lines 42–114 during the vocabulary segment]
224	**r:**	a smile
225	**T:**	ALL RIGHT
226		HE HAD A TORPID ENAMELED SMILE
227		ALL RIGHT, WHAT ELSE DID HE HAVE
228		ANYTHING ELSE

229   YES
230 r: small ears ['Small ears' comes from the teacher's oral
         rendition of the text during the vocabulary segment.]
231 T: SMALL EARS
232   LAWRENCE SAID THAT
233 s: enameled smile
234 T: GOT THAT
235   YOU ARE JUST REINFORCING THAT I UNDER-
         STAND THAT HE HAD A SMALL ['Small head' and
         student's reading in line 238 derived from lines 44–45
         during the vocabulary segment.]
237   WHAT ELSE DID HE HAVE
238 s: a head as small as a (undecipherable)

The prompts that the teacher used to solicit student response were directly taken from the vocabulary discussion. Students completed the teacher's sentence, and the class built a catalog about Timberlake's appearance. But the catalog was a vacuous list. Students were providing items for the sake of creating a list, but the items themselves, either individually or as a group, had no significance. The items were merely repetitions of the previous discussion (including repetitions of the text read during the previous discussion) or descriptions read directly from the text without interpretation. For example, consider the following interaction.

253   MARK
254 m: i don't know the word
255   it says his eyes sparkled
256 T: SHH
257   ALL RIGHT HIS EYES WHAT
258 m: his eyes sparkled with (undecipherable)
259 T: VERY GOOD
260   ANYONE ELSE FIND SOMETHING ELSE ABOUT
         HIS APPEARANCE

A descriptor about Timberlake's appearance needed to be said and listed. Mark did not understand the description he read, and the teacher's response suggested that he did not need to understand it, merely list it. Interestingly, Mark was reading a description of another character, not Timberlake. Similar interactions occurred through the discussion of character.

The teacher might assume that in publicly cataloging items about Timberlake's appearance, students were doing more than merely cataloging. However, from the student perspective, what seemed to count was merely having an item about appearance to display that had not already been listed. For example, consider the following interaction which seems similar to the street game of one-upmanship.

240 **T:** RUTH HAS FOUND ONE THAT YOU MIGHT NOT HAVE THOUGHT OF
241 **r:** (undecipherable)
242 **s1:** I just said that
243 **s2:** I said that
244 **T:** IT DOESN'T MATTER WHO FOUND IT FIRST OR LAST
245　 WE JUST WANT IT
　　　 (background talking and laughing)
246 **ss:** shhh
247 **s:** hey I found one

The listing or cataloging of items is a communicative framework for interacting and interpreting text. As a framework it is imposed through teacher–student–text interaction. That is, teacher–student interaction mediates how students interpret what they are about and what it means.

Cataloging is a school phenomenon (as well as, perhaps, a phenomenon of other situations) that can also mediate other nonreading experience that students have. It may be part of the ways of thinking about experience fostered through school culture—or, at least, school culture as manifested in some low-track, urban middle school classrooms. (Given the hypothesis-generating nature of the study, it was not possible to specify the extent to which cataloging exists across classrooms. Preliminary review of videotapes from three other urban, middle school classrooms—both low-track and heterogeneously grouped—shows the recurrence of cataloging across the classrooms.) For example, cataloging becomes a framework for mediating the students' experience of a field trip they took to Chuck E. Cheese's pizza restaurant and video game parlor.

The field trip is described in detail for two purposes. First, it provided a comparative perspective for understanding cataloging. And second, it raised another issue about the classroom or school frame that mediates student experience and student interaction and interpretation of text. The second issue was the passivity or alienating nature of the mediating classroom frame.

The trip to Chuck E. Cheese's had been suggested by a student. The teacher told the student that if the students could find out all the information needed, make the appropriate arrangements, and set rules and organization for the trip, then the class could go on the trip. There was general agreement among the students to do so. Rachel, who suggested the trip, took leadership in making the agreements, but the discussion of the arrangements involved nearly the whole class. These discussions took place during lunch (which was eaten in the classroom). The arrangements made by the students included how much each student would pay, how many pizzas were needed, how many game tokens each student would receive, when the trip would take place, how long the trip would be, and who would share each pizza. Students also collected permission slips and money for the field trip. In order to make the trip financially feasible, another class had to be invited. The second class was told what arrangements they needed to make (e.g., figuring out who would share each pizza).

On the bus ride to Chuck E. Cheese's, antagonism was expressed toward the second class. According to the teacher, the antagonism was based on the tracking of students. The second class was recognized as a higher section, and their higher academic status was resented.

At Chuck E. Cheese's students followed the organization they set. Students moved through Chuck E. Cheese's in groups, waiting for or playing a video game. Several students would cluster at a video game to watch another student perform.

Several students seemed to be experts at specific video games. For example, Ray used only two tokens and played Pac-Man for nearly two hours. When he went to eat his pizza, he left his game to Neil, who kept the game going until Ray returned. Students shared strategies for being successful with the video games and traded stories about people they knew who were really good at the video games. A few of the girls, for example, Linda and Theodora, did not spend much time at the video games but played skee-ball and collected tickets that could be used for prizes. The collection of tickets was both an individual and group enterprise. That is, although each person collected his/her own tickets, the group shared tickets to enable individuals to get desired prizes.

The trip to Chuck E. Cheese's showed students as doers, capable of organization. As opposed to most school situations where the school prescribes and students follow, students prescribed the activity.

After returning from the field trip, students sat in their usual classroom seats. Class discussion focused on improvements they would make at Chuck E. Cheese's. Student responses were primarily lists of the additional video games they would like. Students were interested in listing improvements and additional video games. Students tried to 'top' each other's list.

Like the discussion of 'The Saint,' the class discussion of going to Chuck E. Cheese's primarily involved cataloging. Also like the discussion of 'The Saint,' the purpose of cataloging was the display of the catalog. Unlike the discussion of 'The Saint,' students were eager to participate in discussing Chuck E. Cheese's. They volunteered for rather than avoided turns. However, a distinction must be made between enthusiastic or interested participation and participation related to student experience. Although interesting to students, the classroom tasks and discussion about the field trip had little to do with the actual experience of students at Chuck E. Cheese's. The only complaining done by students on the field trip concerned the second class, not getting sausage on their pizza when they had ordered it, and other students (typically, complaints by the female students about the male students who either gave too little attention or the wrong kind of attention). There was no discussion of needed improvements. Further, the class discussion moved students away from how active they had been in 'doing' the event. That is, they had organized the event, they had created the social context and organization, and while at Chuck E. Cheese, they had taken control. The discussion tasks were outside of the experiences they had had at Chuck E. Cheese and frame the event as if the students had merely been passive consumers and/or followers.

Similarly with 'The Saint,' the discussion framed students as passive respondents to text that was unrelated to their experiences (with few trivial exceptions such as the teacher's dramatization of vocabulary words). As mentioned earlier, almost all of the students were or had been intensely involved with religious enterprises (e.g., Sunday school), and a handful belonged to religious sects that were similar to the religious sect described in 'The Saint.' In neither the discussion of the trip to Chuck E. Cheese's nor 'The Saint' were the mediating frames established through teacher–student interaction grounded in student experience.

What students wrote

Part of the lesson on 'The Saint' and part of the field-trip 'lesson' involved writing essay responses to teacher questions. Student writing is discussed here as a dimension of student reading. That is, the writing was one reflection of student reading. The following writing samples are not presented in order to discuss student writing ability per se but only as it affected or reflected student reading.

The two topics/questions the teacher wrote on the blackboard about 'The Saint' were:

(1) What the boy thought of Mr. Timberlake before and after the boating incident.
(2) Tell what influence Mr. T. had on the boy's loss of religion.

The following samples of student writing come from the eight previously described students. Tina's essay is omitted because she declined to allow it to be reproduced. However, the content and nature of her essay was consistent with the general comments made about the essays. (In the samples, an asterisk (*) refers to a cross-out.)

(1)

Betty XXXXX
Section XX
May 11, 1982

    What The Boy Thought of
Mr. Timberlake's * befor
********* He fight like
it was not his fight at first
But after That he Taught
it was his

(2)

Fran XXXXXX

The man had made no
influence on the boy he had
just gave up and the man
did have infeucence at him again
he wanted to have the clothes and
money and afther values.

(3)

Ray
Minnis
Sec. 14
May 11–1982

(Ray turned in a blank paper with just the
heading shown above.)

(4)

Mark XXXXXX
Sec XX
May 11, 1982

Your thoughts:

(1) What the boy thought of Mr. T. before
and after the boating incident.
(2) Tell what influence Mr. T. had
on the boy's loss of Religion.

(5)

Louis XXXXX
Sec. XX
May 11, 1982

Reading

By the way Mr. Timberlake handled himself, the boy's
doubts were edivible of him. The boy was impressed
because Timberlake was a retired merchant captain.

After

(6)

Linda XXXXX
May 11, 1982

Your Thoughts

1.) What the boy thought of Mr. T. before
and after the boating *** incident. He
thought he was really religious.

2.) Tell what influence Mr. T. had on
the boy's loss of religion. His behavior
and the way he acted towards him.

(7)

Bob
XXXXXXX
5–11–82
Sec XX

1. The boy thought of Mr. T. ar an important
man like a Movie star our something.
After Mr. T had fallen in the boy felt
imbaviert surprized and scarded
he had faith in the man and was surprized
by the wau th Man acted. startled
with amazement

As samples of writing, these essays reveal problems with grammar, mechanics, cohesion, clarity of references, organization, etc. Several students did little more than copy the essay questions (e.g., 4, 6), if even that (e.g., 3). Those students who did respond made short, one or two sentence responses (e.g., 1, 2, 5, 6, 7, 8) that were unelaborated and almost telegraphic.

There are several possible explanations for the writing products the students produced—e.g., lack of student ability and/or knowledge, failure of the academic task or other instructional factors, student engagement in procedural display and/or mock participation. However, the essays were also one source of data about student reading. After all, the students were to base their responses on what they had read and the classroom discussion of what they had read.

Much of the content of student responses was based on the class discussion. For example, Linda's comments were taken directly from the teacher's comments made during the discussion of Timberlake's personality and during the discussion of the essay questions. Fran's response was a reiteration of teacher comments and an item from the 'catalog' discussion of Mr. Timberlake's appearance. In discussing the essay question, the teacher had said to notice: 'the way the boy acted,' 'the way Mr. Timberlake handled himself,' 'Did Mr. Timberlake have an influence on the boy or did he have no influence on the boy?' The teacher's phrases, meant only as aides for students, became student written responses. In part, the reiteration could be viewed as a manifestation of text reproduction. Throughout earlier grades and when studying grammar, students copied directly from the text. The spelling tests and assignments that the students had throughout middle school (grades 6–8) called for students to write down every word dictated by the teacher. While it is not suggested that there was a direct connection between how grammar and spelling tasks were acted out and text reproduction within essay writing, there is a potential that the cumulative effect of student participation in text reproduction-type activities provided a frame for students to respond to reading tasks.

Some student written responses were unrelated to both the task and the story. For example, the content of Betty's essay, although seemingly related to the task, had nothing to do with the story. There was no fight in the story.

The content of Louis's essay and Bob's essay contained items not found in previous class discussion. Louis noted that the boy had been impressed because Mr. Timberlake had been a merchant captain. Despite the fact that the story said nothing about a merchant captain (Timberlake had been in insurance before going into religion), Louis showed that he understood the task. That is, he responded with an opinion supported by 'fact.' Bob's written response was the only one not to involve text reproduction. He described the boy's impression of Timberlake in his own words ('like a movie star') and made an appropriate before-and-after comparison.

With the exception of Bob (and to some extent Louis), student responses were vacuous. Either there was no response or the response seemed primarily based on text reproduction. Further, the text reproduced by students was not always appropriate to the task, suggesting that either students did not understand the task or they interpreted the task in other ways. Specifically, they interpreted the task in terms of the previous class discussion. That is, they pulled items out of the catalog created in the class discussion that might not have had anything to do with the task.

The effect of classroom discussion can be seen in comparing what the students wrote about an experience with what they wrote about something they had read. After returning from the field trip to Chuck E. Cheese's (pizza restaurant and video arcade), there was a class discussion about Chuck E. Cheese's. As mentioned earlier, the discussion concerned improvements that students would have liked to make to Chuck E. Cheese's. After the discussion, the teacher assigned an essay on one of two questions:

(1) If you were the designer of Chuck E. Cheese, what new things would you add?
(2) Explain how going to Chuck E. Cheese's is educational.

The student's essays were longer than the ones written on 'The Saint.' But, similar to the essays written on 'The Saint,' the content of the essays reflected the content of the class discussion. (The essays on Chuck E. Cheese contained a longer list of content items from class discussion than the essays on 'The Saint' did, which partially explains the greater length of the Chuck E. Cheese essays.) For example, each listed in Mark's essay came from the class discussion.

Mark XXXX
Sec. 14
May 13, 1982

2. If I were the designer of (C.E.C.) I would
add some more games like ms. Pac-
Man popeye pacman and pooltable.
Then I would have different Kinds of
food beside Pizza. I would Have
French Fries, and some sandwiches. That
Hippie That sings Needs a man to sing.
To

Like the class discussion, student essays were primarily lists. Those few students who attempted to answer the second question—about why the field trip was educational—wrote shorter essays and reiterated comments made by the teacher when she presented the task. For example, consider Louis' essay. He began with the 'educational' question, gave up, and attempted the 'designer' question.

Louis
XXXXXXX
Section 14
Grade 8

Not only Chuck E. Cheese is fun and entertaining,
it is educational. They show *** us the uses of comput
ers and entertainment mixed together.
If I was the designer of Chuck E. Cheese

The construction of the classroom frame for mediating experience—whether the experience was interacting with a text or going to a field trip—involved an interesting contribution from student–student interaction. As mentioned earlier, during class discussion students played one-upmanship or 'Can you top this?' In so doing they helped create lists, though the items on the list were not always related to the task (e.g., listing qualities about Timberlake that were not in the book). Also interesting is that the catalog frame provided a means for students to play 'street games.' The relationship between the classroom catalog frame and student–student interaction is almost always implied and not overt. For example, when students tried to list increasingly exaggerated improvements for Chuck E. Cheese it was less a result of creatively doing an academic task than a student–student game of 'Can you top this?' When interactional games such as 'Can you top this?' become explicit (e.g., when students incorporate direct insults into their responses), they are negatively sanctioned by the teacher. In Ray's essay on Chuck E. Cheese, the relationship between student–student interaction and the mediating classroom framework is made explicit.

Ray
XXXXXXX
Section 14
5/13/82

1. If I was the
designer of C.E.C.
I would make my
game room more
bigger and I would
add more games I
also have the little
pupetts come around
and talk to the people
and I wouldn't let
Bob come in because
he likes to tear up
**** your game like
Ms. Pac Man and
supper Cobra.

Implications

These detailed descriptions about the nature of reading events in a low-track, urban middle school classroom yielded four theoretical constructs. The theoretical constructs involved the nature of the frame concertedly constructed by teacher and students for interacting with the interpreting text. Specifically, the frame involved (a) text reproduction, (b) procedural display, (c) cataloging, and (d) a passive, 'alienated' stance toward extended text. In part, the frame was constructed through teacher–student interaction; and, in part, the frame was constructed by the tasks (both explicit and implied) presented to students.

In many ways, the frame was functional for both teacher and students, because it provided a means for getting through and displaying accomplishment of the lesson. The frame also allowed teacher and students to appropriately operate within institutional constraints. That is, school requires progress to be made—or, at least, displayed—on the prescribed curriculum. The frame allowed for display of curriculum coverage although that coverage might be to an extent 'hollow.'

Review of videotapes within the corpus of data collected on reading events in the other middle school classrooms participating in the study confirmed the validity of the theoretical constructs. That is, text reproduction, cataloging, procedural display, and a passive stance toward extended text were recurrent patterns across the classrooms. Even when classrooms differed in their overt pedagogical approach to the teaching of reading (e.g., isolated skills mastery approach vs. a broader, comprehension-based approach), the identified patterns reoccurred across classrooms (for further discussion see Bloome, 1983a, 1984a).

The findings raise additional questions. First, questions need to be asked about the extent of the recurrence of the findings across schools and classroom situations. In particular, questions need to be asked about the recurrence of the findings across schools within an urban setting, across urban and suburban schools, across magnet versus nonmagnet schools, across schools with predominately Anglo populations versus predominately black populations, and across grade levels.

Questions also need to be asked about the extent to which ways of interacting with text acquired in the classroom influence ways of interacting with text outside of the classroom. Part of the difficulty in exploring the influence of classroom-acquired frames is that literacy tasks and situations outside of the classroom may not be analogous to tasks inside the classroom.

In addition, the findings also raise questions about the nature of reading development. Specifically, to what extent can reading be viewed as a decontextualized process, extractable from the face-to-face contexts in which reading development occurs? The findings reported in this chapter suggest that reading development may not necessarily be extractable from the face-to-face contexts of its occurrence. That is, reading development should be viewed not only as a question of magnitude but also, and perhaps more importantly, as a question of direction and substance. Questions need to be asked about the directions and substance of reading development and their ties to the cumulative social and communicative agendas within which reading events occur. To respond to these questions, new conceptions of reading are necessary which are both complementary to current cognitively based definitions of reading and definitions of reading as a social process.

References

Anderson, A. and Stokes, S. (1984) Social and institutional influences on the development and practice of literacy. In H. Goelman, A. Oberg & F. Smith (eds) *Awakening to Literacy*. Exeter, NH: Heinemann Educational Books.

Au, K. (1980) Participation structures in a reading lesson with Haawaiian children. *Anthropology and Education Quarterly* 11, 91–115.

Bloome, D. (1982) *School Culture and the Future of Literacy*. Paper presented at Future of Literacy Conference, Baltimore (ERIC #ED231 899).

——(1983a) Classroom reading instruction: A socio-communicative analysis of time on task. In J. Niles (ed.) *32nd Yearbook of the National Reading Conference*. Rochester, NY: National Reading Conference.

——(1983b) Reading as a social process. In B. Hutson (ed.) *Advances in Reading/Language Research* (Vol. 2). Greenwich, CT: JAI Press.

——(1984a) A socio-communicative perspective of formal and informal classroom reading events. In J. Niles (ed.) *33rd Yearbook of the National Reading Conference*. Rochester, NY: National Reading Conference.

——(1984b) *Gaining Access to and Control of Reading and Writing Resources: K–8* (Final report submitted to National Council of Teachers of English Research Foundation). Urbana, IL: National Council of Teachers of English.

Bloome, D. and Argumedo, B. (1983) Procedural display and classroom instruction at the middle school level: Another look at academic engaged time. In T. Erb (ed.) *Middle School Research: Selected Studies*. Columbus, OH: National Middle School Association.

Bloome, D. and Goldman, C. (1982) Literacy learning, classroom processes, and race: A microanalytic study of two desegregated classrooms. *Journal of Black Studies* 13(2), 207–26.

Bloome, D. and Green, J. (1982a) *Capturing Social Contexts of Reading for Urban Junior High School Youth in Home, School and Community Settings* (Final report to the National Institute of Education). Washington, DC: United States Department of Education.

——(1982b) The social contexts of reading: A multidisciplinary perspective. In B. Hutson (ed.) *Advances in Reading/Language Research* (Vol. 1). Greenwich, CT: JAI Press.

——(1984) Directions in the sociolinguistic study of reading. In P. Pearson, R. Barr, M. Kamil and P. Mosenthal (eds) *Handbook of Research on Reading*. New York: Longman.

Bruce, B. (1981) A social interaction model of reading. *Discourse Processes* 4, 273–311.

Collins, J. (1981) Differential treatment in reading instruction. In J. Cook-Gumperz, J. Gumperz and H. Simons (eds) *School–Home Ethnography Project* (Final report to the National Institute of Education). Washington, DC: United States Department of Education.

Cook-Gumperz, J., Gumperz, J. and Simons, H. (1981) *School–Home Ethnography Project* (Final report to the National Institute of Education). Washington, DC: United States Department of Education.

Doyle, W. (1983) Academic work. *Review of Educational Research* 53(2), 159–99.

Erickson, F. and Shultz, J. (1981) When is a context? Some issues and methods in the analysis of social competence. In J. Green and C. Wallat (eds) *Ethnography and Language in Educational Settings*. Norwood, NJ: Ablex.

Gilmore, P. (1981) Shortridge school and community: Attitudes and admission to literacy. In D. Hymes (project director) *Ethnographic Monitoring of Children's Acquisition of Reading/Language Arts Skills in and out of the*

Classroom (Final report to the National Institute of Education). Washington, DC: United States Department of Education.

Goody, J. and Watt, I. (1968) The consequences of literacy. In J. Goody (ed.) *Literacy in Traditional Societies*. London: Cambridge University Press.

Green, J. and Wallat, C. (1981) Mapping instructional conversations. In J. Green and C. Wallat (eds) *Ethnography and Language in Educational Settings*. Norwood, NJ: Ablex.

Griffin, P. (1977) How and when does reading occur in the classroom? *Theory Into Practice* 16(5), 376–83.

Gumperz, J. and Tannen, D. (1979) Individual and social differences in language use. In C. Filmore *et al.* (eds) *Individual Differences in Language Ability and Language Behavior*. New York: Academic Press.

Heath, S. (1982) Questioning at home and at school: A comparative study. In G. Spindler (ed.) *The Ethnography of Schooling*. New York: Holt, Rinehart & Winston.

Heath, S. (1983) *Ways with Words*. Cambridge: Cambridge University Press.

Hendrix, R. (1981) The status and politics of writing instruction. In M. Whiteman (ed.) *Variation in Writing: Functional and Linguistic–Cultural Differences*. Hillsdale, NJ: Erlbaum.

Hymes, D. (project director) (1981) *Ethnographic Monitoring of Children's Acquisition of Reading/Language Arts Skills in and out of the Classroom* (Final report to the National Institute of Education). Washington, DC: United States Department of Education.

Jacob, E. (1984) Learning literacy through play: Puerto Rican kindergarten children. In H. Goelman, A. Oberg and F. Smith (eds) *Awakening to Literacy*. Exeter, NH: Heinemann Educational Books.

Kirsch, I. and Guthrie, J. (1983) *Reading Competencies and Practices: Reading Practices of Adults in one High Technology Company* (Technical Report #6). Newark, DE: International Reading Association.

McDermott, R. (1976) *Kids Make Sense: An Ethnographic Account of the Interactional Management of Success and Failure in one First-grade Classroom*. Doctoral dissertation, Stanford University, Stanford, CA.

Michaels, S. (1981) 'Sharing time': Children's narrative styles and differential access to literacy. *Language in Society* 10(3), 423–42.

Olson, D. (1977) The languages of instruction: On the literate bias of schooling. In R. Anderson, R. Spiro and W. Montague (eds) *Schooling and the Acquisition of Knowledge*. Hillsdale, NJ: Erlbaum.

Philips, S. (1983) *The Invisible Culture: Communication in Classroom and Community on the Warm Springs Indian Reservation*. New York: Longman.

Reder, S. and Green, K. (in press) Contrasting patterns of literacy in an Alaska fishing village. *International Journal of Sociology of Language*.

Schieffelin, B. and Cochran-Smith, M. (1984) Learning to read culturally: Literacy before schooling. In H. Goelman, A. Oberg and F. Smith (eds) *Awakening to Literacy*. Exeter, NH: Heinemann Educational Books.

Scollon, R. and Scollon, S. (1984) Cooking it up and boiling it down. In D. Tannen (ed.) *Coherence in Spoken and Written Discourse*. Norwood, NJ: Ablex.

Scribner, S. and Cole, M. (1981) *The Psychology of Literacy*. Cambridge, MA: Harvard University Press.

——(1978) Literacy without schooling: Testing for intellectual effects. *Harvard Educational Review* 48(4), 448–61.

Spradley, J. (1980) *Participant Observation*. New York: Holt, Rinehart & Winston.

Taylor, D. (1983) *Family Literacy: Young Children Learning to Read and Write.*
    Exeter, NH: Heinemann Educational Books.
Taylor, D. and Dorsey-Gaines, C. (1982) *The Cultural Context of Family Literacy.*
    Paper presented at The National Reading Conference, Clearwater, FL.
Vygotsky, L. (1962) *Thought and Language.* Cambridge, MA: MIT Press.

8 Children's Voices: Talk, Knowledge and Identity

J. MAYBIN

Introduction: The Dialogic Model

Much of the research on talk in school over the last twenty years has focused on teacher-pupil dialogue (e.g. Sinclair & Coulthard, 1975; Barnes, 1976; Edwards & Furlong, 1978; Edwards & Mercer, 1987), with a relatively small number of researchers looking at pupil-pupil talk in small groups set up by the teacher or researchers with particular learning tasks (e.g. Barnes & Todd, 1977: Phillips, 1987; Bennett & Cass, 1989). There has been considerable interest in what kinds of talk might be the most effective for helping pupils gain curriculum knowledge and understanding. Very little, however, is known about the structure of children's own undirected informal talk, or the processes of learning which it might be supporting. In this article[1] I want to look at some examples of informal talk between 10–12 year olds from various different contexts across the school day. I shall discuss the structure and function of this talk in relation to the children's negotiation and construction of knowledge and understanding.

There is plenty of theoretical justification for seeing peer group talk as an important site for learning. Vygotsky (1978, 1986) suggests that language mediates between the cognitive development of the individual on the one hand and that individual's cultural and historical environment on the other. Children's conceptual development occurs first through social interaction and dialogue before these dialogues are internalised as 'inner speech' to provide an individual resource for reflection and planning. Vygotsky goes so far as to argue that the internal processes of cognitive development can operate 'only when the child is interacting with people in his environment or with his peers' (1978: 90). If this is so, then children's conversations with each other, (as well as their talk with adults), should provide a rich site for looking at the ways in which they are constructing meanings and knowledge. From an educational point of view, it would also be useful to know more about the relationship

131

between talk and learning in children's informal, naturally occurring conversations, since much of the research has focused on more tightly structured, pre-arranged learning contexts.

In order to research children's naturally occurring talk, I would suggest that we need to move away from the transmission model of communication which characterizes talk essentially as a medium for the conveying of information, with varying degrees of effectiveness, from a speaker to a listener. Although this model is still powerful within educational discourse, it cannot begin to address the complexities of informal talk. A more useful framework is what Wells (1992) calls the dialogic model, which he sees as drawing heavily on the constructivist ideas of Piaget and Vygotsky. In this model understandings are constructed between people, through dialogue, and are shaped by the social and cultural context of the interaction. Talk is not a transparent conduit through which knowledge is passed, but an integral part of how understanding is collaboratively accomplished.

The dialogic model is also associated with the work of Volosinov and Bakhtin[2] who suggest that there is a complex chaining relationship between utterances and responses both within and across conversations. Every utterance is always also a response, implicitly or explicitly, to some previous utterance either from within the immediate conversation or from some previous occasion, and every utterance also anticipates and takes into account its own possible responses. One cannot therefore judge the meaning of any particular utterance in isolation, but only in the context of its relationships with other related utterances. As well as the dialogic relationships between utterances, Bakhtin suggests that dialogues are set up within utterances by our taking on and reproducing other people's voices either directly through speaking their words as if they were our own, or through the use of reported speech. Like Vygotsky, Bakhtin and Volosinov see language as socially and culturally formed, and therefore they argue our use of it inevitably conveys particular value judgements and commitments. As Bakhtin puts it, we learn words not from dictionaries but from people's mouths, and these words are always overpopulated with the meanings of others. They invoke particular connotations, contexts, and power relationships, and there is a struggle within any one utterance between these previous meanings and the speaker's current conversational purposes. We have no alternative but to use the words of others, but we do have some choice over whose voices we appropriate, and how we reconstruct the voices of others within our own speech. Because of the value laden nature of language this selective assimilation of the words of others, Bakhtin suggests, is part of 'the ideological becoming of a human being' (1981: 341).

The research reported here constitutes an attempt to operationalise this dialogic model, and to use it as a basis for analysing children's talk. In relation to my own data, I shall try to unpick part of the collaborative process through which meanings are constructed in informal talk. I also want to examine how children take on and reproduce the voices of others as a central part of their meaning making. I hope to show that informal talk is an important site for the construction of knowledge and understanding and that children's language practices are closely tied up with their developing identities as people and their 'ideological becoming', as they move from childhood into adolescence.

Researching the Talk

Some of the most powerful research into language in context which recognises the social constitution of its meaning comes from anthropologists working in the ethnography of communication tradition. It is they who coined the term 'language practices', to emphasise the embeddedness of language in everyday social life. Hymes argues that language should be studied 'as situated in the flux and pattern of communicative events' (1977: 5), and he shows how the different layers of context within any particular social situation contribute to the meaning of the language being used: for example, the meaning of a joke told at a party will derive from the words used, the content of the conversation in which the joke occurs, the kind of party it is, and from cultural understandings about what counts as funny, appropriate, and so on. Developing from Hymes' work, Heath's detailed accounts of literacy events and practices in specific communities illustrate how rather than acquiring abstract, disembedded skills and knowledge, children are inducted into particular social practices and culturally valued ways of taking meaning from texts, of being particular kinds of readers, and so on.

I found that Hymes and Heath's notion of language events and language practices and their practical unpicking of the contextual constitution of meaning provided me with a helpful guide to the collection and analysis of data. They show the close integration of oral and literate practices, and the complexities of language use which children have to learn in addition to its formal features. Their approach, grounded in the actions of real people in real events, complements Bakhtin's more theoretical and politically sensitive discussion of intertextual references, and Vygotsky's ideas about the social and cultural nature of dialogue and thought.

I carried out my fieldwork in two middle schools serving council estates in a new town in south-east England. Almost all of the 10–12 year old children were monolingual English speakers. Few had been born in the estate where they now lived and many had moved home

four or five times, often as a result of the break-up or reconstitution of
family units. In the first school I focused on the conversations of a ten
year old girl, Julie, described by her teachers as a fairly 'typical' average-
ability talkative child. I fixed a radio microphone on her (she carried the
transmitter in the pocket of her skirt or shorts) and recorded all her
conversations over three consecutive days from when she arrived in
school at 8.45am until she left for home at 3.00pm. The microphone
picked up everything Julie said (including, for instance, sotto voce
comments to her neighbour while the teacher was addressing the class),
and everything that was said to her, or within her hearing. I used a small
personal cassette recorder to record other children in the class and this
was also carried around by various children at break time. I made
observation notes as unobtrusively as possible from the back of the
classroom, and collected copies of texts read or written by the children
being recorded. On the third day I informally interviewed Julie, a friend
of hers called Kirsty and a number of other children about some of the
topics cropping up on the tapes.

In the second school I carried out a similar but longer study over
three weeks, focusing on two groups of friends: three girls and three
boys (including Martie and Darren who figure in the extracts below).
Each of these six wore the radio microphone in turn, and I again used
a small personal recorder to collect the talk of other children in the
class, kept observation notes, and collected copies of texts. I began to
realise that I needed more than my observation notes to understand
many of the references made in children's conversations, and after the
three weeks' recording I interviewed all of the 35 children in the class
in friendship pairs and talked with them about themes in the tapes and
about their own personal interests and relationships. As well as providing
useful background information about the different layers of context for
my other recorded talk, these interviews unexpectedly generated a rich
variety of anecdotes, accounts and explanations about quite intimate
aspects of children's lives. Two extracts from my interview with Karlie
and Nicole are discussed later in this article.

I believe my position within both schools as a friendly outsider who
didn't fit the more familiar roles of teacher, work experience student or
pupil helped keep my interactions with the children relaxed and informal,
and also meant that they were more explicit with me in their interview
accounts and explanations than they would have been with someone who
was more familiar with their circumstances. In both schools the children
appeared to trust my promise that no-one except myself would listen to
the tapes of the interviews, or those of their talk during the day. Most
of the time I was recording the children appeared to have forgotten or
become bored with the fact they were being taped.

The researching of people's private conversations does of course raise particular ethical issues, and perhaps more especially in the case of children because of the very asymmetrical relationship of power between the researcher and the researched. Fishman (1978) who studied private conversations between adult couples within their homes asked them to listen to the tapes she had collected and indicate any material which they did not want her to use (in fact, suprisingly little needed to be erased). Such procedures are not always followed with children who are often willing and vulnerable research subjects, particularly in the school context where they are in a sense held captive, and usually delighted to receive extra adult attention and a change from normal routines. In my own research it would have been impracticable to ask children to listen to the six hours of recordings which I was collecting each day, but I often, at their request, played parts of the tapes in which they figured back to them at breaktime and I tried to answer their questions about my research as fully and clearly as possible. Near the beginning of the study I played a couple of tapes of teacher-pupil dialogue to the teacher, and discussed with her how these dialogues might be supporting children's learning. I was careful not to play the tapes of talk between children or discuss their contents with anyone other than the children concerned. My contact with adults during the study was kept to a minimum. I obtained parental permission through the school for my main study and in both schools the headteachers had an interest in research and greatly supported and facilitated my work. At the end of the longer three week study I submitted a brief written report of general findings which I thought might be useful, to the head and the class teacher.

In both schools I managed to collect an extensive amount of naturally occurring talk between children from a wide variety of contexts across the school day. I shall now go on to discuss what I think are significant features in the structure and content of this talk, and to suggest some ways in which it serves to construct forms of knowledge for the children.

Collaboration and Provisionality

As I listened to the tapes and transcribed them, one of the first things that struck me was the extent to which classroom activities were not just accompanied by talk but were being actually defined and accomplished through talk.

Readings, for instance, were not only something happening between individuals and texts, but were being collaboratively accomplished between children and adults through dialogue. In the first transcript example Julie, Kirsty and Sharon have returned from a scavenging expedition in the school grounds, and Julie is drawing a snail on the card where they are going to mount their findings. Kirsty and a parent helper, Mrs Reilly, have just brought a book on snails across from the class library. At one point in the extract below Julie also has a parallel conversation with a pupil who is reading a puzzle magazine and trying to make up as many words as possible out of the word 'peanut'.

In the transcriptions which follow, interrupted speech is shown by a slant (/), simultaneous speech by a bracket ([) and incomprehensible speech by a dotted line (....).

Julie:	I'll just write 'This was drawn by bla bla bla'
Kirsty:	It's got thousands of teeth (reads) 'Its long tongue is covered with thousands of tiny teeth'. He's got thousands of teeth.
5 **Julie:**	He has, he's got thousands of teeth, that little snail has.
Sharon:	Look at its trail (teacher comes over)
Julie:	Miss it's got hundreds and. . . it's got thousands and thousands of teeth/
10 **Kirsty:**	/on its long tongue
Teacher:	It's got what?
Kirsty:	Thousands of teeth. It says here.
Mrs Reilly:	Those are tentacles. It's got four tentacles.
Julie:	Yea, teeth, teeth.
15 **Mrs Reilly:**	(reads) 'to touch, feel and smell, and it breathes through [the hole in its side. '
Julie:	[teeth
Mrs Reilly:	So there must be a hole somewhere.
Julie:	'eat' (a suggestion to the pupil with the puzzle
20	magazine)
Mrs Reilly:	We saw its eyes, didn't we? At the end of its tentacles and it can only see light and dark.
Julie:	(to puzzle magazine pupil) 'tune'
Pupil:	It can only be three letters/
25 **Julie:**	/(reads) 'or more'. Three letters or more.
Kirsty:	Miss its got a thousand- thousands of teeth on its tongue.
Sharon:	Yes, cause we went into the library. Mrs Reilly and Kirsty went into the library to look it up.
30 **Teacher:**	What's that, the snail?
Sharon:	Yea.
Pupil:	Miss, where's the sellotape?
Sharon:	And it breathes through its side.
Kirsty:	It breathes [through. . . its side
35 **Sharon:**	[it's got this little hole/
Kirsty:	/It breathes through a hole in its side.

Mrs Reilly: Mrs Smiley (their language teacher) would be interested in this.
Teacher: Where are its eyes then?
40 **Kirsty**: These little things are for feeling.

There are a number of different people who are engaged in what might be called 'reading' in this extract. Although it is only Kirsty and Mrs Reilly who read directly from the text in the library book (lines 2 and 15), Julie and Sharon are also centrally involved in relating the information in the book to the snail in front of them. Julie and Kirsty in lines 8–10 and Sharon and Kirsty in lines 34–36 collaboratively reproduce pieces of information from the text for the teacher. Although they are not decoding a text in front of them, they are also centrally involved in the reading event. This involvement is very social in nature, for instance the talk involves a lot of 'duetting' (Falk, 1980; Coates, this volume) where one girl starts an utterance and another completes it. Also, the pupils' extraction and announcement of suprising and newsworthy pieces of information to each other and the teacher is accomplishing social as well as intellectual ends. This is one particular way of engaging with the text and using it. Mrs Reilly illustrates an alternative approach and could be said to be performing a rather different kind of reading. Her approach was characteristic of the way the teachers in my recordings tended to encourage pupils to relate to science texts, and I believe that it reflects the way knowledge is constructed in teacher-pupil dialogues. She tries to get the girls to use the text as a frame for organizing how to look at the snail—to reconstruct their experience of it in the light of information from the book about its teeth, tentacles, eyes and breathing mechanism. She links direct observation with information in the text; '"it breathes through the hole in its side". . . so there must be a hole somewhere'; 'We saw its eyes, didn't we . . . and it can only see light and dark'. Thus direct empirical experience of the snail is mediated through the authority of the text. In more formal classroom talk the teacher's approach to using the text will probably be the dominant one, and it may not even be apparent that children are using rather different ways of engaging with it. In this less formal situation, however, where the power relationships between speakers are more symmetrical, their talk can provide evidence of a number of different kinds of readings, and of a more active struggle between authorized and other approaches.

The parallel, unofficial literacy event connected with the puzzle magazine represents another kind of collaborative reading which occurred frequently in my data: the attempt to intrepret instructions in order to carry out an activity. The example below also illustrates this kind of process. Julie, Kirsty and Sharon have finished with the book on snails

and are now looking back at their list for the scavenging hunt to decide
how to display their findings. Julie starts by reading out the instruction
which asked them to collect 'a small creature'.

Julie:	Ah look (reads) 'A small creature, be very careful' cause here it is. We've got to draw that, we've got to draw the snail. I've drawn. . ./
Kirsty:	/(points to a dead insect on the table) That's our small creature.
Julie:	No that's what we're doing for our small creature(points to snail)
Sharon:	He's dead, in 'e, he's dead.
Mrs Reilly:	It's a greenfly
Kirsty:	It was, but. . ./
Sharon:	/That's not our creature
Julie:	The snail is our creature.
Kirsty:	Get hold of it and glue it on.
Julie:	No, you're not meant to glue the snail on, we're meant to draw a picture of it, you. . ./
Kirsty:	/(looks at Julie's picture) Is that meant to be a snail?
Julie:	Yea
Kirsty:	I can't see its tentacles.

The interpretation of the instruction 'a small creature' here highlights
the close relationship between the social and cognitive aspects of talk. It
depends not on some kind of category criteria (e.g. can an insect count
as a 'creature'), but on the outcome of the tustle for power between
Julie and Kirsty. For Mrs Reilly the insect on the table may represent a
species which can be usefully labelled, but for the girls the task of
matching items to the list they have been given, and the business of
managing their own relationships, are closely intertwined. Interestingly,
Kirsty refers back to the authority of the library book, by using the term
'tentacles', to lend added weight to her dismissal of Julie's drawing.

In the extract above Julie's interpretation of the written instruction
(that they should use the snail and that she should draw it) seems to be
the one that will be acted on and carried forwards as the negotiated
outcome from that discussion. But the children's talk I collected is often
rather more ambiguous in terms of meaning and outcome. The next
extract illustrates how particular meanings can be challenged or changed
within the space of one brief snatch of conversation. Julie's class were
drawing a picture as part of followup work to their teacher's reading
from 'The Silver Sword', and the exchange below occurred shortly after
the teacher announced that pupils would be getting their school reports
to take home at the end of the week.

Pupil 1:	Since I started at this school I've only been to see Mr. Clayson once/
Pupil 2:	/Neither have I.
Julie:	(gasps) I've been there about ten times. . . always going to Clayson every single day. Wak wak wak because she's been a good girl! I normally go there because I say I've been involved, when I'm not. I stick up for my other friends.
Pupil 3:	I know, you're trying to get your nose in and things
Julie:	I'm not, I'm sticking up for my friends and I say that I was doing it as well.

At the opening of this conversation it might be assumed that there is a shared understanding about the significance of being sent to the headteacher: it is a fairly awesome punishment meted out for particularily naughty behaviour. Julie however undermines this meaning in a number of ways. She jokes that she goes to the head's office every day, caricatures what happens to her there (corporal punishment was not used in the school), and inverts the normal relationship between behaviour and punishment. In addition, she suggests that loyalty to one's friends should take precedence over honesty, as defined in school terms. Thus the initial meaning of being sent to the headteacher is radically subverted by Julie, who suggests that in her case punishment constitutes a martyrdom to friendship rather than a just response to bad behaviour. Julie's meaning is however itself contested by a third pupil, who claims that her actions should not be interpreted as loyalty, but as nosiness. The issue is never resolved and, as in many other conversations, a number of possible meanings are carried forwards, any of which may be drawn on in future dialogues.

Ambiguity of meaning is especially apparent in the next piece of transcript, where Julie and David are sitting together eating their sandwiches at lunchtime. I would suggest that the way Julie sets up and manages this ambiguity is an intrinsic part of her accomplishment of particular conversational purposes.

Julie:	Do you know where I live? Right if you go along Redlea the only blue door, that's where I live. The only blue door in Redlea.
David:	Only?
Julie:	Right, if you can't get through, go to my next door neighbour's, that side. . . , go through her place, jump over the fence and go down my path.
David:	Which number do you bang on?
Julie:	One three four. And if you can't get through, go

	to. . . go round to number one three two, go through the fence, over the wood. . ./
David:	/you got a bike?
Julie:	Puncture . . . got lost. I got skates. I can hold onto the back of your bike and go oooooh! (pause) Do you really go out with thingy—Ma-
David:	Who?
Julie:	Mellie
David:	No.
Julie:	What, did she chuck you? Why? (pause) Do you think Warren will mind if I move onto your table?
David:	No. It's my table, I was the first one on it, so I own it.
Julie:	You don't, the school does. What's the hottest part of the sun? What's the hottest part of the sun? (pause) Page 3!

The conversation starts off in a child's world of knocking on each other's doors after school to go out and play. Julie's question about whether David is going out with Mellie, however, retrospectively adds a different kind of meaning to her previous invitation. It seems she was not just suggesting a casual children's game, but was also tentatively exploring the possibility of a boyfriend/girlfriend relationship between herself and David. Her response to his stated ownership of the classroom table also provides mixed messages. On the one hand she quickly contradicts his assumption of dominance, 'you don't, the school does', but she follows this up immediately with a joke 'what's the hottest part of the Sun?' which relies for its humour on a pun between the sun and the *Sun* newspaper, with its regular page 3 photograph of a naked female model.

In one sense Julie is using language as a resource, drawing on both childhood and teenage discourses to negotiate her relationship with David, whose response will to some extent determine which meanings are carried forwards. But these discourses are also themselves shaping the choices of meanings available. The words 'go out with', 'chuck' and 'hot' all have specific cultural connotations, and invoke particular kinds of gender relations. Thus although language may be a resource, it is not a neutral one, but rather pushes Julie towards taking up particular positions and values. The ambiguity and provisionality of her approach allow Julie a way of trying out and testing these positions and values in relation to her own experience.

The next extract also illustrates this kind of exploration of teenage roles and concerns. In addition it shows the sensitivity of talk to context, and how different contexts can invoke very different forms of discourse.

The transcript starts in the maths class, where Julie is working out how much each of a number of customers in a cafe will have to pay for their meals. She has just added up 'Tom Ato's' bill.

Julie: Three pounds twelve I make Tom Ato. Back in a second. Miss, can I go to the toilet please?

Teacher: Yes alright.

(sound of Julie's heels as she goes down the corridor. When she enters the toilets the accoustics on the tape change abruptly, with the tiled walls making the voices echo. Carol and Nicole are already there)

Julie: Oh, hi. Where did you get your hair permed?

Nicole: (indistinct)

Julie: You're not going out with Sasha, are you?

Nicole: Yea.

Julie: Are you?

Nicole: Yea, I hope so (laughs)

Julie: You've got darker skin than me, I've got a sun tan. (pause) (to Carol) I should think so too, it's disgusting, that skirt is! Aii. . . don't! (Nicole starts tapping her feet on the tiled floor) Do you do tap dancing? (both girls start tapping their feet and singing)

Julie and Nicole: 'I just called to say I love you / And I mean it, from the bottom of my heart.'

Julie: Caught you that time, Carol- ooh! What's the matter, Carol, don't show your tits! (laughs) (to Nicole) I went like this to Carol, I says, I pulls down her top, I went phtt 'don't show your tits!' (Nicole laughs).

(Julie leaves the toilets, walks down the corridor, reenters the classroom, and sits down.)

Julie: Turn over—six plates of chips—oh I've nearly finished my book. I've got one page to do.

The conversation in the toilets seems to belong to a different world from that in the maths classroom. The vocabulary is different, the subject matter is different, and the role of the girls are different. They are no longer pupils straining to interpret the teacher's instructions and produce a neat, acceptable piece of work, but young adolescents concerned with trying out particular notions of femininity. Personal worth here is determined not by how quickly and accurately sums can be completed, but by how attractive you are to boys, and how much experience you have had in 'going out' with them. The authoritative voice is not the text book, but the pop song; the institutional authority of the school seems to fall away at the toilet door. Julie, however, makes the switch between these two different kinds of discourse without any apparent effort or hesitation.

The Taking on of Voices

In the extracts above there are a number of instances where children invoke voices carrying particular kinds of power within their conversations; textbooks, library books and popular songs are all quoted as sources of authority in different contexts. I also have examples of children quoting teachers or other adults, particularily where they are trying to win an argument or put a point more strongly. And frequently within their conversations they repeat each other's words, or their own words from a previous occasion. Sometimes, as in the first example about the snails book, it becomes difficult to ascribe exact ownership to the voice for a particular utterance. In this second part of the article I want to use Bakhtin and Volosinov's ideas about the invoking of voices within utterances to show in relation to my own data how these can explain some of the complexity of the way in which different layers of meaning are built up in children's conversations.

As I discussed earlier, Bakhtin and Volosinov see our use of other people's voices as part of the negotiation of our own ideological development, and as setting up complex dialogic relationships within and across utterances, which are an important part of meaning making.

We often reproduce other people's voices unattributed, as if they were our own and of course it is impossible to always trace when this is happening. In the example below, however, Karlie subsequently identifies the voice she has reproduced. This extract comes from my interview with Karlie and Nicole; I had just asked Nicole who else lived at her house and Karlie mentioned that Nicole's sister had recently had a baby.

Janet:	So does your sister live quite near you?	
Nicole:	She lives with us	
Karlie:	Cause ⌈ she's only quite young	
Nicole:	⌊ she's young, she's sixteen	
Janet:	Ah right	
6 **Karlie**:	She did the best thing about it though, didn't she, Nicole?	
Nicole:	She didn't tell a soul, no-one, that she was pregnant	
Karlie:	Until she was due, when she got into hospital, then she told them	
Nicole:	On Saturday night she had pains in her stomach and come the following Sunday my mum was at work and my sister come to the pub and my aunt Ella was in it and my sister went in there and said 'I've got pains in	

my stomach' so my auntie Ella went and got my mum, and took her to hospital, and my mum asked her if she was due on and she said 'No, I've just come off' and when they got her to hospital they said 'Take her to maternity'. My mum was crying!

Janet:	Your mum didn't realise she was pregnant?
Nicole:	No, and my mum slept with her when she was ill!
22 **Karlie**:	My dad said she did—Terri did the best thing about it—her sister's Terri
Nicole:	Or if she did tell, as she's so young, she weren't allowed to have him.

Karlie initially provides what appears to be her own evaluation of Terri's decision to conceal her pregnancy (line 6), but in line 22 we learn that this evaluation was originally made by her father. In reproducing or appropriating his voice, Karlie is also taking on and communicating his judgment as if it were her own. This is a particularily obvious example of how taking on someone else's voice also involves taking on a value position, but Bakhtin and Volosinov would argue that, since language is ideologically saturated, our words *always* convey value judgements, and our reproduction of the words of others must always be a political act.

In addition to taking on voices wholesale, as it were, we can frame the words we reproduce in particular ways which create a distance between our own voice and the voice we are invoking. One of the most obvious ways in which the children in my study reproduced other peoples' voices was through reported speech in their anecdotes. Apart from its force as a way of creating a context away from the here and now, the dialogue of an anecdote sets up a second conversational layer within which a particular theme can be explored in more depth. As we shall see in the examples below, anecdotes also create their own resonances and additional themes. New dialogic relationships are set up between the speaker's voice and the voices they invoke in the anecdote, and between the themes of the anecdote, and of the conversation in which it occurs (Volosinov, 1973; Bakhtin, 1986). Many of the children's anecdotes were told almost entirely through reconstructed dialogue, and I want to look at two of those now.

In the first example, Julie is talking to Kirsty while they mount their findings from the scavenging hunt. They have been discussing their anxiety about the amount of swearing on the tapes I was collecting. When Julie states firmly that 'children aren't meant to swear', Kirsty responds 'If people swear at them, they can swear back'. A few minutes later, Julie returns to the subject.

Julie:	I swore at my mum the other day because she started, she hit me

Kirsty: What did you do?

Julie: I swore at my mum, I says 'I'm packing my cases and
                         I don't care what you say' and she goes 'Ooh?' and
                         (I go) 'yea!'. I'm really cheeky to my mother

Julie's story here provides her with an opportunity to explore the question she is discussing with Kirsty in a bit more detail. Although partly agreeing with Kirsty's statement that if people swear at you then you can swear back, Julie is arguing extreme provocation in her case: her mother hit her and she felt like leaving home. In these exceptional circumstances, she seems to be suggesting, it is permissable to swear, although it is still being 'really cheeky'.

Julie's story also however has a particular resonance as one of a chain of anecdotes she tells her friends about her somewhat picaresque relationship with her mother. The theme of resisting or subverting adult authority is also a familiar one in her stories generally (like her visits to the headteacher in the example quoted earlier above). Julie's account of swearing at her mother will therefore be read by Kirsty in terms of themes around responses to adult authority, and relationships between mothers and daughters, as well as in relation to their current conversation. Julie's anecdote is thus operating simultaneously at the level of a reported dialogue between herself and her mother, and as part of the conversation with Kirsty. The theme of the reported dialogue, her relationship with her mother, and the theme of the conversation with Kirsty, when it is permissable to swear, are of course not totally unconnected. They both involve issues of power and authority, the cultural appropriateness of particular kinds of language behaviour, and the potential of oral language to contest or subvert particular power relationships.

In reporting her mother's speech, Julie is not expected by Kirsty to reproduce her mother's words exactly as she heard them. She in fact manufactures a voice for her mother, to fit in with the purpose of the story. In the next example, Darren also manufactures his own and a man's voice in an anecdote told while children are queueing in the playground, waiting to go in to lunch. There was always a lot of noise and milling about in the queue, and anecdotes told in this context need to be extremely arresting and lively in order to hold their audience. At this point, one child has just sworn at another.

Martie: I said that to a real man and he went, he went 'dick
                         head' [and I went] 'of course I am!' (laughter) And
                         he goes 'erm!' (growling and laughter)

Darren: This man called me a fucking bastard, right, I go
                         'back to you', he goes 'come here', I go 'come on,
                         then' and he's got about size 10 trainers and he chased
                         me, right, and then when he got, he catched me,

> right, like that, and he goes 'who's fucking saying?'
> And I goes 'fuck off', I says 'fuck off' and he goes,
> he goes, 'Do you want a fight?' I go 'not tonight,
> darling' and he goes 'piss off!'

Again, this anecdote opens up the possibility for constructing meanings through the relationships between the different conversation layers, and through the links these make with the themes and voices of other contexts, and with the speakers' previous conversational history. In the boys' conversations they often seem to be jostling for position, capping each other's comments with a more impressive contribution. Here, Darren's story is a response to Martie's rather abbreviated anecdote. It is more developed, the man is more frightening, and the turnaround at the end more dramatic and ingenious. As well as providing a turn in the immediate conversation, it also contributes to a recurring theme in the boys' talk concerning their toughness and canniness, which are important aspects of the way they present themselves to each other. And it echoes the concern of Julie's anecdote about how far adult authority can and should be contested.

Within the dialogue Darren, like Julie, uses reported dialogue to tell his story. But Darren doesn't just create voices for himself and the man. He also, inside the story at the point when things are getting really alarming, portrays himself as taking on a different voice ('not tonight, darling'). Darren adopts a slightly higher pitched voice at this point, portraying what could be either a woman or a homosexual man rejecting a partner's advances. The use of this voice, as in Julie's 'I'm packing my cases', invokes a particular scenario or scenarios with associated relationships. In Darren's case, calling up this particular speech genre changes the relationship between himself and the man in a way which defuses the situation through humour and signals a kind of submission which still enables him to maintain face rather more successfully than Martie did in his story. This is Darren's internal intention, as it were, within the context of the anecdote. There is also his intention as a speaker who is following and hoping to decisively cap Martie's contribution, and the manufacture of voices within Darren's anecdote also contributes towards this conversational aim. There is thus a complex nesting of different conversational contexts: from the recurring conversational theme about canniness and resisting authority and of language itself as a means of doing so, to Darren's and Martie's conversation, to the reported interchange between Martie and the man, to the scenario invoked by 'not tonight, darling'.

Volosinov (1973) explores at some length how novelists' voices enter and colour the voices of their characters, and how the perspective of a particular character can be conveyed through what is ostensibly a piece of authorial description. The interplay between an author's and a character's voice can sometimes be used to produce an ironic effect, where we hear both voices as it were simultaneously. This can also happen orally, in the use of reported speech. In the next example Geoffrey provides an ironic parody of his own voice in order to clarify a misunderstanding. Sarah also ironically assumes the concerned voice of a naive mother who thinks her daughter's bruises have come from fighting. The conversation occurs while the children are queueing in the school corridor, waiting for the coach to arrive which will take them swimming. Darren has just pretended to give Sherri a love bite.

Sherri:	(laughing) My mum thinks I've been in fights again!
Sarah:	What do your mum go? 'Who gave you a big bruise?' (laughter)
Terry:	I'll give her a double bruise, aha!
Darren:	I gave her one on the arm
	....
Geoffrey:	Oi, you could never give someone a lovebite on the arm, could you, could you? You can't!
Sherri:	You can, if you've got a T-shirt on.
Geoffrey:	Yea I mean, look, it's really exciting look, let's get down to there, next time it'll be your finger! (noise of kissing).

Both Sarah and Geoffrey frame their use of irony—'What do your mum go?' and 'Yes, I mean, look. . .', and they adopt a particular tone to convey the naivity of the person whose voice they are using. Sarah pitches the mother's voice high, as if she were addressing a young child, and Geoffrey puts on an excited, enthusiastic voice to show just how ridiculous such enthusiasm would be. He is trying to explain to Sherri that he was not asking whether it is physically possible to bite an arm, but whether it is culturally appropriate, and we are aware of Geoffrey's authorial voice mocking his own exaggerated parody. (Some features of these manufactured voices are inevitably lost in the written medium of this article).

Both Volosinov and Bakhtin, like Vygotsky, suggest that conversations are internalised to become inner dialogues. Thus individual thought processes also involve the taking on of voices which provide responses to voices heard in previous conversations, and which call up particular relationships and contexts. The last extract comes again from the interview with Karlie and Nicole. Karlie has explained that she sometimes goes to visit her Dad in prison, and I ask her what it is like doing that. Karlie answers me by representing her feelings at the prison as a kind of inner dialogue, which involves invoking her own voice as if she were talking first to herself, and then to her dad.

Karlie: It's like—it's just loads and loads of bars. So you
                 think 'What's my dad doing in here, he didn't do
                 nothing' because he got accused by chopping someone's
                 hand off so—and it weren't true, ... and you get
                 in there, and you're seeing him, and you think 'Come
                 with us, come with us, you can't stay in here cause
                 it's not true really, is it?' so you think 'You can come
                 with us now, you can get out', but it's just not true.

When I was trying to punctuate this transcribed talk with speech
marks it was difficult to make out where one voice ends and another
starts, or to identify particular audiences. Sometimes Karlie seems to be
addressing herself, sometimes her father, sometimes myself and sometimes
previous voices she has heard. It's difficult to know, for example, to
whom her final 'it's just not true' is addressed, and whether it refers to
the crime of which her father is accused or to the possibility of taking
him home with her, or to both. The fragmented nature of the dialogues
invoked in Karlie's response to my question would suggest that her talk
here is close to what Vygotsky calls 'inner speech', where dialogues we
have had and those which we might have with other people feed into
our internal thought processes. This utterance then has its own internal
business: Karlie is struggling to come to terms with her father's
imprisonment, and positioning herself in relation to the differing accounts
of his guilt which she has heard people give. She is also, at the level of
my interview conversation with her, constructing the voices in the
representation of her inner dialogue in order to convey a particular
presentation of herself to me and to Nicole.

Conclusion

I shall now try to summarize some main points about the structure
and purposes of children's informal talk, in relation to their construction
of meanings and understanding.

(1) Most of the talk is highly collaborative. Children complete each
    other's utterances, repeat something another child had just said, echo
    the voice of the teacher or of a text they have been reading, and
    frequently use reported speech in relating incidents or anecdotes.
    Meanings do not seem to be generated within one mind and then
    communicated to another through talk; rather, they are collaboratively
    and interactionally constructed between people.
(2) Talk, like writing, can create and hold a context away from the here
    and now, for example in anecdotes. The here and now is also to a
    large extent constructed and established through talk, whether it is
    negotiating and contesting ways of engaging with a text, the working

through of a relationship between children in the course of carrying out of a classroom activity, or discussing one's hair style in the school cloakroom.

(3) Social and cognitive aspects of talk are closely integrated, and utterances are multi-functional, that is, one utterance can (and usually does) serve a number of different cognitive and social purposes simultaneously. It is therefore not possible to separate out 'talk for conveying information' from 'talk for maintaining social relations', as is suggested in the Cox Report (DES, 1989) for example.

(4) The meanings and knowledge which children are jointly negotiating and constructing are provisional, and frequently contested. There is a fluidity about them which contrasts with the more clearly defined, fixed forms of knowledge circulating in the official curriculum through more formal teacher-pupil dialogue, worksheets and text-books.

(5) Associated with this provisionality, there is often an ambiguity in individual utterances; out of a range of possible meanings it is the respondent, not the speaker, who chooses a particular interpretation, which may then in its turn be reinterpreted or subverted. This ambiguity disperses the responsibility for the meaning and purposes of particular utterances between the participants in the conversation, rather than lodging it with the speaker. It can also provide a creative function for the speaker who may be 'over interpreted' and be taken to mean far more than she intended. She then has the opportunity to go along with, or refute, a meaning which is being imputed to her.

(6) Language is a resource for making meaning, but it is not a neutral one. Language choices bring with them particular values and positions, so that individuals are inducted into cultural practices. The provisionality and ambiguity of informal talk helps children to negotiate the complex relationship between individual purposes and cultural authority, and to develop their own personal identities.

(7) One of the ways in which children construct personhood, and build up the contextual layers in their talk, is through the reporting and taking on of other people's voices. The articulation of different conversational layers, the cross-cutting dialogues and the references out to other contexts and longer term themes all serve to create a particularily rich resource for negotiating and constructing meaning.

It would be theoretically inconsistent if I did not end by saying something about my own purposes in framing and reproducing children's voices within this article. Part of my motivation for the research comes from a dissatisfaction with the over-simplistic and misleading transmission model of communication which still influences so much of educational policy and the training of teachers. I have tried to show that an alternative, dialogic model is more appropriate for exploring the way children talk and learn. I am also unhappy about the widespread assumptions that some children's language use is deficient, or essentially different in quality from the language believed necessary for educational purposes. I hope that I have countered such assumptions by demonstrating something of the richness of the resource which all children have at their disposal, and the intensity and urgency of their endeavours to achieve understanding.

Notes

1. This article revises and brings together the analysis and discussion of data in Maybin, 1991 and 1993.
2. There is some controversy about whether works published under Volosinov's name were in fact written by Bakhtin. The 1973 translators of *Marxism and the Philosophy of Language* however claim that the weight of evidence supports Volosinov's authorship.

References

Bakhtin, M. (1981) Discourse in the novel. In *The Dialogic Imagination*. Austin: University of Texas Press.

Bakhtin, M. (1986) *Speech Genres and Other Late Essays* (ed. Caryl Emerson and Michael Holquist). Austin: University of Texas Press.

Barnes, D. (1976) *From Communication to Curriculum*. Harmondsworth: Penguin.

Barnes, D. and Todd, F. (1977) *Communication and Learning in Small Groups*. London: Routledge and Kegan Paul.

Bennett, N. and Cass, A. (1989) The effects of group composition on group interactive processes and pupil understanding. *British Educational Research Journal* 15 (1), 19–32.

Clark, K. and Holquist, M. (1984) *Mikhail Bakhtin*. Cambridge, MA: Harvard University Press.

DES (1989) (The Cox Report) *English for Ages 5 to 16*. London: HMSO.

Edwards, A.D. and Furlong, V.J. (1978) *The Language of Teaching*. London: Heinemann.

Edwards, D. and Mercer, N. (1987) *Common Knowledge: The Development of Understanding in the Classroom*. London: Methuen.

Falk, J. (1980) The conversational duet. *Proceedings of the 6th Annual Meeting of the Berkley Linguistics Society*, Vol. 6, 507–14.

Fishman, P. (1978) Interaction: The work women do. *Social Problems* 25 (4), 397–406.

Heath, S.B. (1983) *Ways with Words*. Cambridge: Cambridge University Press.

Hymes, D. (1977) *Foundations in Sociolinguistics: An Ethnographic Approach*. London: Tavistock.

Maybin, J. (1991) Children's informal talk and the construction of meaning. *English in Education* 25 (2), 34–49.

—— (1993) Dialogic relationships and the construction of knowledge in children's informal talk. In D. Graddol, L. Thompson and M. Byram (eds) *Language and Culture*. Clevedon: British Association for Applied Linguistics/Multilingual Matters.

Phillips, T. (1987) Beyond lip-service: Discourse development after the age of nine. In M. Mayor and A. Pugh (eds) *Language, Communication and Education*. London: Croom Helm/The Open University.

Sinclair, J. and Coulthard, R. (1975) *Towards an Analysis of Discourse: The English used by Teachers and Pupils*. London: Oxford University Press.

Volosinov, V.N. (1973) *Marxism and the Philosophy of Language*. New York: Seminar Press.

Vygotsky, L. (1978) *Mind in Society: The Development of Higher Psychological Processes (ed. M. Cole et al.)*. Cambridge: Harvard University Press.

—— (1986) *Thought and Language*. Cambridge: MA: MIT Press.

Wells, G. (1992) The centrality of talk in education. In K. Norman (ed.) *Thinking Voices: The Work of the National Oracy Project*. London: Hodder and Stoughton.

9 Gender Inequalities in Classroom Talk

JOAN SWANN AND DAVID GRADDOL

Introduction

A history of professional attitudes to classroom talk would need to draw upon a much broader history of educational fashion. The Victorian ideal in which silent children listened to a teacher's authoritative words—speaking only when required in order to demonstrate their skill at reading or their acquisition of an acceptable accent—has given way to a celebration of children's talk and its role in learning and personal development. This change in attitude has been associated with a broader educational shift; from a view of the school as a place where children are introduced to their proper place in society and encouraged to develop a proper respect for authority to a more progressive idea of the school as a location which facilitates a child's learning (rather than an adult's teaching) and personal growth.

The oracy movement is principally one which identifies talk as the major mechanism through which these progressive ideals are achieved. The *Plowden Report*, for instance, referring to psychologists such as Bruner and Luria, concluded in 1967:

> Spoken language plays a central role in learning. Through language children can transform their active questioning response to the environment into a more precise form and learn to manipulate it more economically and effectively. . . Language increasingly serves as a means of organising and controlling experience and the child's own responses to it.

Several influential educationists were, at that time, insisting upon the importance of children's participation in classroom talk and by the end of the 1960s the idea that children learn as much through talking as through doing, listening or observing had become commonplace. Through talking, children are said to make meanings their own; to work through and solve problems; to spur each other on to explicit understandings and so on. Indeed, children's talk is seen as a prerequisite to learning and the provision of learning experiences for children is, at times, no more than the provision of occasions for pupil talk. 'It is as talkers, questioners, arguers, gossips, chatterboxes, that our pupils do much of their important learning' said Harold Rosen in one of the most influential and widely read texts (Barnes *et al.*, 1971: 127). This view of classroom talk became an orthodoxy by the mid 1970s, greatly influencing the *Bullock Report*, and the 'language across the curriculum' movement.

Given this developing emphasis on talk as the key to learning, there was an understandable concern generated by analyses of classroom talk which showed how little time was in fact made available to pupils. Flanders (1970) in a study of American classrooms put forward the well known two thirds rule: two thirds of talk is taken by the teacher, one third by the pupils. Other studies have shown that not only is such restricted opportunity for pupil talk widespread in junior and secondary schools, but that Flanders' two thirds rule may underestimate the proportion of teacher talk. Educationists were shocked by the implications of such findings. By restricting opportunities for pupil talk, teachers were restricting access to learning. Douglas Barnes reported on his analysis of British secondary school lessons in the late 1960s:

> Here lies the importance of pupil participation. It is when the pupil is required to use language to grapple with new experience or to order old experience in a new way that he is most likely to find it necessary to use language differently. . . . It is the first step towards new patterns of thinking and feeling, new ways of representing reality to himself. . . . This would suggest that the low level of participation in these lessons, if they are at all typical of secondary lessons, is a matter of some educational urgency. All teachers might well contemplate the classroom implications of this (Barnes *et al.*, 1971: 61, 62).

Barnes and others have urged the use of strategies which allow pupils more opportunity to talk, such as the greater use of small groups within which pupils can talk through problems collaboratively. This, suggests Barnes, not only gives pupils space to talk, but allows them to apply oral skills which they have gained outside the school and which rarely find use within. In an analysis of the discussion of four eleven year old girls, Barnes tells us:

> During their eleven years of life they have learnt a great deal about using language for collaborative thinking, for encouraging one another, for coping with disagreement, and for rational persuasion. If these skills, which are not unusual in eleven year olds, do not appear in lessons, this is partly because of the communication patterns of classroom and school (Barnes, 1976: 30).

But more recent studies of classroom interaction have uncovered a further source of concern: talk is not only unequally distributed between teacher and pupils but also between pupils themselves. In particular, recent studies of gender divisions in the classroom have demonstrated that girls contribute far less to classroom talk than boys.

This gender inequality in talk is not a feature peculiar to schools. It is now well known that mixed sex talk amongst adults is often dominated by men, both in the sense that men talk more, and in the sense that men seem to control topics, interrupt women more than they are interrupted by women; use various aggressive tactics in order to get to speak, and so on (see Coates, 1986, and Graddol & Swann, 1989 for a review of research in this area). In other words, the inequality of talk amongst adults is not an incidental feature of women's reluctance to talk—it rather results from a complex social process which seems to endow men with greater power than women in social interaction.

The fact that social processes which occur in the classroom mirror those in the outside world will be no surprise. Schools and classrooms are not isolated from their wider social and political context. On the other hand, such findings ought still to be of serious concern to educationists since the distribution of talk is one of those aspects of classroom life supposedly mediated, if not controlled, by the teacher.

In this paper we describe two analyses we have made of classroom talk in primary classrooms. Whereas previous studies have examined transcripts and overall interactional patterns, we have been interested in the precise mechanisms which lead to boys' dominance of pupil talk. In particular, we were interested in how individual pupils get to speak in any instance, how turns at speaking are allocated and how pupils are selected or put themselves forward to speak; and what roles are played in this by different participants, including the teacher and both talkative and quieter pupils. The studies emerged from inservice work we were doing with teacher groups in various parts of the country, rather than from a preconceived experimental design. An informal approach, such as this, inevitably leads to certain gaps in the data, but gains qualitatively in naturalness and relevance.

The Two Classroom Contexts

We have analysed two sequences of talk each between a teacher and a small group of primary school children. Since we wished to examine two different styles of classroom management and pupil background, the two sequences were recorded, using a video camera, in different schools. For reasons which will become clear, the first sequence we have called *The pendulum sequence*, the second *The mining sequence*.

The Pendulum Sequence

This sequence was recorded by colleagues at the Open University for other research purposes. The recording took place in a Buckinghamshire primary school in which a class of 10–11 year olds were describing and discussing the results of experiments they had carried out with pendulums. The pupils were seated at either side of an overhead projector on which they displayed the results of their experiments. The girls sat on one side and the boys on the other, with the teacher sitting next to the girls.

The teacher's style in this lesson was relaxed and informal. Much of the sequence was taken up with a teacher-led question and answer session but the pupils seemed to 'chip in' to answer questions. They did not raise their hands nor were they often selected by name by the teacher.

The Mining Sequence

Our second sequence was recorded in a school in Co Durham. A class of 9–10 year olds had watched a television programme on coal-mining and the video-recording is of a follow-up session between the class teacher and eight pupils, four girls and four boys.

As with the 'pendulum' sequence the girls sat at one side and the boys at the other but this time the teacher stood in the middle, between the two groups, occasionally moving around to collect items for the pupils to look at as part of her lesson (e.g. a miner's lamp and other pieces of equipment). Beside the teacher was a model of a pit which she used for part of the lesson. The teacher's style was more formal than the one adopted by the teacher in the pendulum sequence. Pupils raised their hands to speak and were normally selected by the teacher by name.

In neither sequence were the participants aware of the exact nature of our research at the time of the recording (although we later discussed this with both teachers). We also did our best to minimize the intrusive effects of the camera, which was situated on the far side of the classroom. The teachers were interacting with small groups of children but the work carried out was part of their normal classwork. We made no attempt to influence the choice of topic nor the way in which this was presented by the teacher.

The Analysis

Overall analysis of pupil contributions We first made a simple quantitative analysis of both sequences to find out how much each pupil talked. This is summarised in Tables 1 and 2 below.

The tables show that despite the differences in class management style

Table 1 Contribution of individual pupils to discussion during pendulum sequence

	Total words spoken	Total turns	Total interchanges	Average words per turn	Average turns per interchange	Silent turns	Failed turns
Sarah	79	17	6	4.6	2.8	1	1
Laura	20	5	4	4	1.2	0	1
Donna	37	5	5	7.4	1	2	0
Unknown Girls	18	9	9	2.0	1	1	5
TOTAL	154	36	24	4.3	1.5	4	7
Mathew	133	23	14	5.8	1.6	7	0
Trevor	83	20	10	4.1	2.0	1	1
Peter	55	10	6	5.5	1.7	0	0
Unknown Boys	48	20	19	2.5	1.0	1	2
TOTAL	319	73	49	4.4	1.5	9	3
TOTAL	473	109	73	4.3	1.3	13	10

and pupil background, there are broad similarities in the distribution of talk in the two sequences. Looking first at the total figures for girls and boys in each table, it can be seen that in both classrooms boys talk more than girls (overall) whatever measure is taken: in terms of the number of words they utter, the number of speaking turns they take and the number of interchanges they have with the teacher. While these results are clearly not statistically significant with samples of this size it is important to note that they are in the same direction and size as as measures derived from research using larger numbers of pupils (e.g. French & French, 1984) and a wider range of classrooms (e.g. Sadker & Sadker, 1985).

The figures for 'amount of talk' also show, however, that there is variability within each group—there are some talkative girls and quiet boys. Again this is consistent with findings from research using large numbers of pupils (e.g. French & French, 1984).

It appears that even though the overall participation rates are similar in both classes, this state of affairs is arrived at through a different process in each case. At first glance, the figures suggest that in the pendulum sequence the boys verbal dominance derives from the way they 'chip in' uninvited whereas in the mining sequence, where pupils are always selected by the teacher, it appears that the boys verbal dominance must be attributed to a bias in the teacher's selection of pupils. These summary figures, however, conceal the complexity of the interaction between pupils and teacher that leads to a turn at speaking.

Table 2 Contribution of individual pupils to discussion during mining sequence

	Total words spoken	Total turns	Total interchanges	Average words per turn	Average turns per interchange	Silent turns	Failed turns
Kate	127	9	6	14.1	1.5	0	0
Lorraine	13	7	4	1.8	1.75	1	8
Anne	23	8	6	2.9	1.33	0	1
Emma	8	4	1	2.0	4.0	1	1
Girls							
TOTAL	171	28	17	6.1	1.6	2	10
Mark	47	9	8	5.2	1.12	0	1
Ian	80	23	11	3.5	2.09	1	0
John	35	5	2	7.0	2.5	0	6
Darren	101	15	7	6.7	2.0	1	0
Unknown	3	2	2	1.5	1.0	0	0
Boys							
TOTAL	266	54	30	4.9	1.8	2	7
TOTAL	437	82	48	5.3	1.7	4	17

Notes: The term *interchange* is used to describe a question and answer sequence between the teacher and a pupil. The shortest interchange may involve only one pupil turn. Many interchanges are longer than this however, involving further questioning of the pupil to elicit more information. The end of an interchange in our data is normally marked by a switch to a different pupil or to a brief exposition.

We use the term *silent turn* to describe an occasion on which no words were spoken but a response was clearly made, by means of conventional nonverbal sign such as a shrug of the shoulders or head nod. A *failed-turn* occurs when a pupil is offered a turn at speaking but produces no response.

This interaction we will refer to as the 'turn exchange mechanism'—a term widely used in the research literature on discourse analysis (see, for example Sacks *et al.*, 1974). This term draws attention to the fact that the smooth intervention and taking of the floor by one speaker (whether teacher or pupil) requires a degree of coordination and complicity between participants. Classroom discourse has been termed 'asymmetrical discourse'—talk in which one party (the teacher) has pre-allocated rights (like those of a chair at a meeting) both to talk more and to regulate the talk of others. This clear asymmetry of speaking rights should not blind us, however, to the role of the pupils themselves. The research on turn-taking in conversation and meetings has shown that the taking of a turn at speaking requires the collaboration of all parties, for example, the use of nonverbal cues by the person speaking to enable the next person to synchronize his or her entry (see Graddol *et al.*, 1987, for a fuller discussion of this mechanism). The turn exchange mechanism, therefore, consists of at least two parts: the selection by some means of the next speaker; and the exchange of cues and gestures which permit the fine timing and synchronization of the next speaker's entry. In ordinary conversation, where there is little if any delay between speakers, the synchronization problem is more important than the selection of speaker. In the classroom, where relatively long gaps are left by the teacher for a pupil to respond, it is the selection of speaker which is the more important issue in the maintenance of a smooth flow of talk.

The collaborative nature of the exchange mechanism suggests that in the pendulum sequence the boys' 'chipping in' could not be successfully and smoothly accomplished without the active support of the teacher (not merely because the teacher has rights over selection but also because she happens, in each case, to be the speaker who is yielding the floor). In the mining sequence, on the other hand, where the teacher appeared to be selecting and favouring the boys, the nature of turn exchange mechanisms suggests that this required the collaboration of the pupils. We studied the turn exchange mechanisms in both sequences in some detail.

Analysis of the Turn Exchange Mechanism in the Pendulum Sequence

We examined one portion of this lesson in detail which was chosen for several reasons. The discussion at this point had become more open, and pupil talk was less directed by the practical organisation of reporting back on experiments. In addition this was a part of the lesson in which boys seemed successfully to be chipping in and participating more than the girls. Lastly, the portion was one in which we had a full video record of the teacher's nonverbal behaviour, in particular her direction of gaze.

Gaze is perhaps the single most important nonverbal gesture involved in turn taking. A teacher may select a pupil to speak through eye contact as effectively as by calling a pupil's name. Furthermore, patterns of gaze have been shown to be important in cuing and synchronizing a new speaker's turn in conversation (see Kendon, 1967; Goodwin, 1981). In addition to its role in selecting and cuing pupils to talk, gaze also provides a basis for distinguishing between talk addressed to boys from talk addressed to girls. One of the claims about gender inequalities in classroom talk made by previous researchers is that teachers interact more with boys than with girls and pay them more attention, thus stimulating them, perhaps, to participate more in discussion. One non-linguistic way of paying someone attention is, of course, to look at them whilst speaking or listening.

Transcript 1

Teacher: If you have a pendulum (.) which we established last week
           was a weight a mass (.) suspended from a string or whatever

	(.) and watch I'm holding it with my hand so it's at rest at the moment (.) what is it that makes the pendulum swing in a downward direction for instance till it gets to there? [1]? { (.) just watch it
Mathew:	{ gravity
Teacher:	What is it Mathew? [2]
Mathew:	Gravity
Teacher:	{ Yes (.) } now we mentioned gravity when we were
Boy:	{ ( ) }
Teacher:	actually doing the experiments but we didn't discuss it too much (.) OK so it's gravity then that pulls it down (.) what causes it to go up again at the other side? [3]
Boy:	{ Force the force }
Boy:	{ The string Miss } it gets up speed going down.
Teacher:	It gets up speed going { down(.) does } anyone know the { word }
	(force) ( )
Teacher:	for it when you get up speed? [4] (.) as in a car when you press the pedal? [5]
Boy:	{ accelerate }
Boy:	{ momentum }
Teacher:	You get momentum (.) M { athew (.) } it accelerates going down
Mathew:	{ ( ) }
Teacher:	doesn't it and it's the (.) energy the force that it builds up that takes it up the other side (.) watch (.) and see if it's the same (.) right- (.) OK (.) em (.) anything else you notice about that? [6]? (.) so it's gravity what about the moon? [7] (.) that's a bit tricky isn't it? [8] (.) is
	{ there grav } ity on the moon? [9]
Boys:	{ ( ) ( ) } No it would float
Teacher:	There isn't gravity on the moon? [10] (.)
Several:	No
Mathew:	There is a certain amount
Teacher:	A certain amount Mathew? [11]
Mathew:	({) }
Boy:	{ Seven } times less
Teacher:	You reckon it's seven? [12]
Boy:	Times less than on earth
Teacher:	Yes (.) well it's a it's a difficult figure to arrive at but it is between 6 and 7

Transcript Conventions:

⌢⌢⌢⌢⌢ means gaze to boys

———— means gaze to girls

{ } overlap

(.) pause
(   ) unclear

The transcript shows that the teacher is looking much more often towards the boys. This imbalance seems to be a characteristic of the whole lesson and not just this sequence. An analysis of all parts of the video tape in which the teacher's gaze was visible showed that 60% of pupil-directed gaze was towards the boys. More important, perhaps, is the precise timing of this gaze. The teacher is more often looking towards the boys at critical points, such as when a question is to be answered. Of the 12 questions which appear in this extract, 8 are directed towards the boys and 4 towards the girls. This will have the effect of inviting or authorising a self selection from boys rather than girls.

Of the four girls' questions, two (nos. 4 and 6) occur after a last-minute switch of gaze from the boys to the girls. Another (no. 8), although we coded it as a question, seems to function more as an aside, or a comment on the activity, than as an attempt to elicit information. If boys are selected earlier when a question is formulated, then they might be expected to have longer in which to plan a response. If girls are given less notice of their (rarer) questions then they are likely to be slower to respond when finally selected. There is no indication, however, that the teacher gives them longer before giving up and turning back to the boys (4) or filling in the answer herself (6).

It does seem, then, that pupils are in some way being selected to speak in spite of the first impression of a free for all. Selection, however, does not necessarily occur at the individual level. At the most general level, a teacher's gaze behaviour may indicate points at which pupil participation is expected or authorised. More specifically, however, such encouragements or invitations to speak seem to be directed at either boys or girls as a group. Such group selections, we have observed, are more often directed to boys than girls. Within such group selection there may be selection through eye contact of a particular pupil. Such selections cannot be identified on the video, but we can note that eye contact, as a selection mechanism depends on a pupil's readiness to meet and not to avert gaze. Unlike calling a name, therefore, it is a mechanism more akin to hand-raising in that it selects from those offering to respond.

The teacher's decision to favour the boys rather than the girls is unlikely to be a conscious one. The overall bias in gaze direction, for example, may derive in part from the scanning strategies of an experienced class teacher, who will regularly monitor boys' behaviour for signs of potential misdemeanour and discipline problems. A teacher's gaze will also quickly be drawn by any movement in peripheral vision, or by sotto voce muttering. In this recorded sequence there were no signs of gross discipline problems, but in several interchanges we found the teacher's gaze drawn towards the boys by muttering, which ensured that a boy was invited to respond. A further important influence on the teacher's group selection will be the classroom layout. Here, it was the segregation of boys from girls that permitted this group selection in the first place and the sitting position of the teacher alongside the girls made a certain bias in her gaze direction almost inevitable. It is important to note, however, that the group sitting arrangements were arrived at by the teacher and pupils themselves, not by the researchers, and that classroom organisations usually reflect such things as a teacher's expectation of discipline problems, friendship patterns amongst children, and the strategic sitting of children in places where they will obtain more or less teacher attention according to their inclinations. All three factors are known to be gender sensitive.

In summary, it seems that, in spite of the first impression that boys obtained their larger number of interchanges with the teacher by chipping in, the teacher herself played an important role in determining whether a boy or a girl would respond to a question. Furthermore, one of the boys' contributions to the turn exchange mechanism was not a direct one but played upon the teacher's selection role by behaving in ways that would encourage or oblige her to pay them more gaze attention.

Analysis of the Turn Exchange Mechanism in the Mining Sequence

Our video-recording of the mining sequence was designed to allow us to test whether these observations held true in another context. As we mentioned above, the teaching style in this sequence was rather different. The interaction seemed to be (at least overtly) more directly under the teacher's control. However an analysis of verbal and non-verbal behaviour could show whether she was in fact more often selecting boys to talk, or whether the imbalance shown in Table 2 was due to the initiatives of the pupils themselves. Because the mining sequence was video-recorded for our own purposes we were able to keep the camera static, and thus obtain a much clearer picture of the teacher's and pupils' non-verbal behaviour throughout the interaction. A simple analysis of the teacher's gaze behaviour revealed that she looked towards the boys for 65% of the time (pupil directed gaze) and towards the girls for only 35% (this includes questioning and general exposition).

At each interchange beginning we noted how a pupil obtained a speaking turn (for instance whether by volunteering or following selection by the teacher) and also the direction of the teacher's gaze as she formulated her questions. By analysing interchange openings frame by frame we were also able to determine the order in which pupils' hands were raised. An example of the analysis of one interchange is given below:

Transcript 2

Teacher: How did they know that those men were
            [K J M E A]
            alive? (.) Yes
Kate: Miss they were knocking
Teacher: They were knocking . . .
            [K = Kate; J = John; M = Mark; E = Emma; A = Anne]

An interchange between teacher and Kate, showing order of hand-raising.

Note: Teacher looking at boys but can see girls. As K's hand goes up, teacher turns to look at girls. By the time boys' hands are raised, teacher has already begun to turn to girls. By the time E's hand rises, teacher's gaze is already directed towards K.

Here Kate's hand is the first raised, and draws the teacher's attention towards her. In this and other interchange openings, hands are raised very rapidly, hence the need for a frame by frame analysis to distinguish reliably the order in which they are raised. Table 3 shows the different ways a pupil may begin an interchange with the teacher.

Table 3 shows that the commonest way for a pupil to be selected to speak is after volunteering (normally with hand-raising). Of the 45 interchanges, 35 were with pupils who had volunteered. The teacher seemed very sensitive to which pupil had first raised a hand, despite the fact that hands were raised very rapidly. Of the 35 occasions on which a volunteering pupil was selected, 23 of these were 'first hands'. When the teacher was in a position to see the hands being raised, she selected a second or subsequent hand on only 7 occasions. (Furthermore, some of these selections can be 'explained': for instance, on one occasion Anne's hand was second after Ian's. But Ian had just had two interchanges with the teacher, so Anne was selected.) Although we measured only hand-raising, presumably this very rapid discrimination relies upon additional cues such as pupils' gaze and posture.

There is, however, a difference in the way girls and boys begin an interchange. Of the 28 boys' exchanges, 26 are with boys who were volunteering to speak. Of the remaining two, one is with John, the quietest boy in the class. The other is to ask Darren to give an account of a visit the teacher knows he has made to a coal mine.

Of the 17 girls' interchanges, however, almost half (eight) are cases

Table 3 How individual pupils began an exchange in the mining sequence

	A	B	C	D	E	F	G	H
	Hand raised first or most decisively	Calls out 'Miss'	sub-total of (a+b)	Hand raised (not first) out of teacher's vision	Hand raised but not first	Total volunteered (a+b+d+e)	Teacher selects when hand not raised	Overall total
Kate	5	0	5	0	1	6	0	6
Lorraine	0	0	0	0	0	0	4	4
Anne	0	0	0	1	2	3	3**	6
Emma	0	0	0	0	0	0	1	1
Total Girls	5	0	5	1	3	9	8	17
Mark	7	0	7	0	1	8	0	8
Ian	4	3*	7	1	3	11	0	11
John	1	0	1	0	0	1	1	2
Darren	6	0	6	1	0	6	1	7
Total Boys	18	3	21	1	4	26	2	28
TOTAL	23	3	26	2	7	35	10	45

*On two occasions Ian's hand was *also* raised
**On one occasion Anne's hand *had* been raised but had subsequently gone down

Notes:

Column A Shows when the pupil's hand was *first* raised. The inclusion of 'most decisively' in this category is to accommodate one interchange in which a few hands remained at 'half mast' at the end of the previous interchange.

Column B The teacher's style favoured hand-raising and, in fact, only one pupil, Ian, obtained a turn by calling 'Miss' when his hand had *not* been raised first.

Column C Shows the total number of cases in which we could say the pupil, although selected by the teacher, had borne some responsibility for the selection.

Column D Includes the two cases in which a pupil was selected whose hand was not raised first, but where the teacher was not in a position to tell which hand had been raised first.

Column E Refers to occasions on which the teacher selected a pupil whose hand was not raised first, although she had been in a position to see which was first.

Column F Totals all the occasions on which a pupil was selected to speak after volunteering.

Column G Covers cases in which the teacher selected a pupil who was not volunteering.

in which the teacher selects a pupil who is not volunteering. This figure conceals some individual differences—for instance, whereas Kate, the most talkative girl, always volunteers (and, for five out of six interchanges, gets her hand up first) two of the girls, Lorraine and Emma, are always selected whilst not volunteering. It's worth noting here that this does not mean that Lorraine and Emma (or, for that matter, John) never volunteer. Their hands are frequently in the air during the lesson, but are never raised first, or decisively enough, to gain them a turn. For instance Emma, the quietest pupil, often raises her hand and on playing the video for the first time we were puzzled as to why she was selected to speak so little. However, closer analysis of interchange openings suggested she was 'playing safe'. Emma tended to raise her hand just as the teacher's gaze turned towards the pupil she was about to select to speak. As with the teacher's ability to select the first hand (from an apparent flurry) Emma's manoeuvre must have required extreme sensitivity to the behaviour both of the teacher and other pupils. It seems to trade on the fact that the way of minimising the chances of being selected to speak in this class is to volunteer, but with careful timing. It is also worth relating these findings to Table 3, showing the (relatively) long interchanges, and the number of 'failed' turns, that occur between the teacher and John, Lorraine and Emma. Although these pupils' handraising strategies mean that they are not (with one exception) selected in open competition with the other pupils the teacher seems to be encouraging them both by initiating interchanges with them and by pushing them when they do not offer answers.

We mentioned above that the teacher looked more at the boys than the girls overall but we were also able to analyse her specific gaze behaviour in relation to interchange openings. The teacher occasionally sets out to select a particular child at the very beginning of an interchange (of the 10 'teacher selects' in Table 3 seven fall into this category). In the remaining 41 interchanges, however, the teacher's gaze focuses on the pupil she is about to select only towards the end of her opening question and, normally, only after the pupil has raised his or her hand. Of these 41 interchanges which begin with fairly open selection, 28 begin with the teacher's gaze directed at the boys and only nine with her gaze directed at the girls (two begin with the teacher looking towards a piece of equipment and two could not be reliably coded). There is no direct relationship between the group to which an interchange is initially directed and the sex of the child who eventually answers, but interchanges directed initially towards boys tend to develop differently from those initially directed towards girls. When the teacher begins an interchange looking towards the boys, her gaze normally stays with the boys' group. It may flash once rapidly towards the girls but it does not dart back and forwards. More often than not (in 19 out of 28 interchanges) it is boys who answer the opening question. If a girl answers it is normally because her hand is raised while the teacher's gaze is still on the boys, attracting attention away from the boys and towards the girls (7 out of the 9 interchanges with girls). The two remaining interchanges were from the 'teacher select' category: the teacher began by looking at the boys then seemed to change her mind and select a girl who was not volunteering. When the teacher begins an interchange by looking at the girls, however, her gaze tends to switch to the boys half-way through the opening question, or to dart about between boys and girls. (With the exception of interchanges that clearly begin as 'teacher selects', there is only one occasion on which an opening question is directed entirely towards the girls.) Sometimes a switch in the teacher's gaze seems to be motivated by a boy's hand being raised, but just as often the switch precedes any hand-raising by boys.

In summary, then, we once again find that the turn exchange mechanism in this class is one in which pupil and teacher behaviour interact. Again, there is a level of group selection by gaze direction, a process which favours boys.

Discussion

What we have shown in these analyses is that although the details of the turn exchange mechanism are very different in the two cases, there are nevertheless important similarities. First, in both classes the distribution of talk derives from a close collaboration between pupils and teacher. Second, this collaboration is one which results in boys, as a group, talking more than girls. Third, it can be argued that the underlying dynamic of turn exchange is the same in both cases—it is one in which the maxim 'first in gets the floor' holds true. This competitive dynamic, in which promptness and confidence are all important, is the same that holds true in casual conversation (Sacks *et al.*, 1974). In both classes, the teacher is able to intervene and ensure that pupils of her own choosing occasionally get to speak, but this is in a minority of interchanges. We have seen, however, that individual turn exchanges occur in a context provided by the teacher; one which systematically favours boys by giving them more gaze attention, offering them more questions and cuing them to answer earlier. Lastly we suggested that girls are also complicit in these arrangements, though this is a point not so well developed. In the pendulum sequence few attempts were made to compete with the boys. In the mining sequence we noted that Emma seemed to time her hand raising carefully to avoid being selected.

Conclusion

We began this paper by noting that the oracy movement is one which celebrates children's talk as learning experience. This well placed enthusiasm for talk should not, however, blind us to the fact that not all talk serves the function of individual or collaborative learning nor is all learning accomplished through talk. These twin observations have important implications for our findings.

What is usually argued, by more careful researchers, is that talk helps in certain kinds of learning. In the music class (and skill oriented classes), for instance, observation and doing are immeasurably more effective than small group discussion. In areas of the curriculum where children are required to grapple with complex ideas and solve problems, typical of the discovery approach to science, then small group discussion and teacher directed discussion have been found to be most effective. This then suggests that the systematic exclusion of girls from this kind of talk will be denying them an opportunity for successful learning but only in those curricula areas in which talk is particularly helpful. Hence one implication of our findings is that girls may be nudged, at an early stage of their academic careers, into topic areas in which they can succeed using other learning strategies (such as rote-learning, learning through reading, silent observation, doing and so on). Alternatively, girls' low levels of participation in such talk may encourage them to adopt alternative learning strategies which work well at elementary levels but which lead to poor achievement later in their academic careers. This is largely speculative (though the lower achievement and participation of girls in science at tertiary level is not), but it demonstrates the potential educational implications of unequal participation in classroom talk.

Not all talk, we have observed, is of the valuable learning-through-talk variety. It is a commonplace, for example, that the most talkative boys in a class are rarely the most academically successful. Indeed, the contrary is often the case. How can this be reconciled with the principles of the oracy movement?

There are two points to be taken here. The first, is that even if we accept that only certain portions of classroom talk are valuable learning contexts, and others useless chatter or noise from disruptive boys, incidental talk related to classroom management and so on, it has been shown by other researchers that it is precisely this valuable talk that girls are most excluded from. Indeed, we found in our own transcripts that questions addressed to the girls were less frequently the challenging and open variety typically addressed to the boys and more often rhetorical or yes/no questions. Second, we suggest that there is a hidden curriculum at work in classroom talk, which provides boys with an important learning experience even in the kind of talk we might want to discard as worthless.

Boys, in other words, are acquiring and practising skills in competitive public speaking: the skill and confidence to seize the floor, to control topics and develop discourse strategies which ensure the flow of talk returns to them. And what better a training ground than a classroom, where there are many competitors for scarce speaking time, and which offers the added zest of the need to subvert the attempts at management by the class teacher.

Of course, the acquisition of competitive speaking skills—necessary for participation in meetings and any occasion of public speaking—can be seen as an important educational benefit. Unbridled competition in a classroom would, however, give rise to an anarchic and unmanageable state of affairs. What we observe in the classroom is a consensus, a manageable and stable state arrived at through the combined efforts of girls, boys and class teacher.

This consensus is one where an unequal distribution of talk is seen as normal. In particular, girls seem to have learnt to expect a lower participation level than boys, and boys seem to have learned that their fair share is a larger one. These are expectations that are brought to school by all participants, since such inequalities in the distribution of talk are commonplace amongst adults. What is more, boys' gendered experiences outside of school may help them within the classroom: boys more often then girls may find themselves in possession of newsworthy items to talk about, and where their own experiences fall short of the exotic they may learn to exaggerate in order to attract attention (see French & French, 1984, for instances of this). In our own data, then, we can see that it was probably not a coincidence that, in the mining sequence, it was a boy who had once been down a mine (albeit at an open air museum) and who became a centre of attraction in the lesson dressed in traditional miner's gear. The teacher denied that the choice of topic was in any way a 'masculine' one, or one which favoured the boys, saying that pits were a part of all their experience and background. But it is interesting to observe that their experiences will again be very gendered ones—the experience of a woman in a mining community is very different from that of a man, and the lesson (and TV programme) centres inevitably on the man's work rather than the woman's. Classroom talk, then, forms part of the hidden curriculum of gender roles in many ways. We have argued that one of these consists of children learning gender appropriate roles in public talk.

We have identified, then, two distinct causes of educational concern over the results of our video analysis. One, that girls may—as a group—be given less privileged access to certain kinds of learning experience. Second, that classroom talk forms an important arena for the reproduction of gender inequalities in interactional power. In arriving at this second conclusion we can observe that the Victorian ideal that schools exist to teach pupils how to take their 'proper' position in the social order may still, in at least one respect, hold true.

References

Barnes, D. (1976) *From Communication to Curriculum*. Harmondsworth: Penguin.

Barnes, D., Britton, J., Rosen, H. and The London Association for the Teaching of English (1971) *Language, the Learner and the School: A Research Report*. Harmondsworth: Penguin.

Central Advisory Council for Education (1967) *Children and Their Primary Schools* (The Plowden Report). London: HMSO.

Coates, J. (1986) *Women, Men and Language: A Sociolinguistic Account of Sex Differences in Language*. London: Longman.

Flanders, N.A. (1970) *Analyzing Teacher Behavior*. Reading, MA: Addison-Wesley.

French, J. and French, P. (1984) Gender imbalances in the primary classroom: an interactional account. *Educational Research* 26, 127–36.

Goodwin, C. (1981) *Conversational Organization: Interaction between Speakers and Hearers*. New York: Academic Press.

Graddol, D., Cheshire, J. and Swann, J. (1987) *Describing Language*. Milton Keynes: Open University Press.

Kendon, A. (1967) Some functions of gaze direction in social interaction. *Acta Psychologica* 26, 22–63.

Sacks, H., Schegloff, E.A. and Jefferson, G. (1974) A simplest systematics for the organization of turntaking for conversation. *Language* 50, 696–735.

Sadker, M. and Sadker, D. (1985) Sexism in the schoolroom of the 80s. *Psychology Today* March 1985, pp. 54–7.

10 Unequal Voices: Gender and Assessment

JULIE FISHER

Introduction

> [Pupils should be able to] participate as speakers and listeners in a group engaged in a given task.
> (*Statement of attainment for English at Key Stage 1*, DES, 1989a: 3)

> Particular attention should be paid, by task setters, teachers and moderators alike, to the danger that oral assessment might be influenced by cultural or social bias. There are differences in the verbal and non-verbal behaviour of members of different social groups, whether defined by ethnicity, gender or social class; and consequently assessors' own expectations may vary.
> (*English for Ages 5 to 11* (the first 'Cox Report'), DES/WO, 1988, para. 8.32)

The study I am reporting here took place in a combined (first and middle) school, of which I'm the headteacher. When I carried out the study (as part of a higher degree) I also had a teaching commitment of 0.5, sharing a class of 6- to 7-year-old children with a colleague.

I had become concerned about possible social biases in the assessment of speaking and listening in young children. The second report of the National Curriculum English Working Group (the second 'Cox Report': DES, 1989) mentioned a danger of bias, and 'differences' between social groups, but gave no examples. I knew, from reading and from my own observations, that there were often gender inequalities in classroom practice—so I decided to examine these more closely. In particular, I wanted to investigate how girls' and boys' talk differed when they were engaged in a variety of problem-solving tasks, consistent with the Statements of attainment for English at Key Stage 1.

Conducting the Study

I decided to observe the same four children working collaboratively on seven tasks. Some of these required discussion alone for their outcome, others necessitated a tangible finished product, such as a drawing, a design or a model. The problems, outlined in Table 1, were all taken from the stimulus of *The Jolly Postman: or Other People's Letters* by Janet and Allan Ahlberg.

I selected two girls and two boys to work together. I eliminated children with poor oral language skills, for whom English was not the home language or who presented a strong gender stereotype. I felt it was important that the four children were amicable towards each other and displayed no overt racial or gender bias if paired or grouped together. The four children ultimately chosen were Elizabeth (English); Nadia (Pakistani—home language English); Simon (English); David (Maltese/English).

These children were video-recorded as a group taking part in tasks 1–4 and task 7. For tasks 5 and 6, the girls worked with two other girls and the boys with two other boys, so that I could also look at how these children worked in single-sex groups.

Since I wished to highlight the effect of the task on the speaking and listening contributions of the children, there seemed to be two major issues for initial investigation: the amount spoken by each child, and the precise nature of their speaking turns.

As I played the video tapes of each task, and as I began to transcribe and analyse the data, the techniques used by the boys and girls appeared to indicate the adoption of certain roles chiefly concerned with initiating ideas and responding to them. I slowly developed a classification for the children's speaking under these two headings. Table 2 shows the headings under which the turns were finally categorized, and gives examples of each category.

Each of the seven tasks was video-recorded over a period of six weeks. My role was to introduce the task to the children and then withdraw, particularly for the initial period of discussion. I had decided that in order to analyse the turn-taking patterns adequately, I would need to transcribe a brief but uniform length of tape from each task. I chose the first ten minutes of each tape (taken from the time when I left the

Table 1 The sequence and nature of each problem-solving task.

Task	Title	Skills
1	An Apology to the Three Bears	Discussion and writing
2	Getting to Grandma's House	Discussion and design
3	The Wolf-Proof House	Discussion and junk-box modelling
4	Cinderella's Coach	Discussion and construction
5/6	Reaching the Giant's Letter Box	Discussion (single-sex groups)
7	The Jolly Postman's Problem	Discussion

Table 2 Examples of turn-taking categories.

Category	Example
Initiating new ideas	. . . [they] could build a big wall so the fox can't get in grandma's house.
questioning/requesting information	what can we do about the bed?
instructing/directing	I'll bolt them. *You* fix them and I'll bolt them.
stating/comment	You never thought of that.
Responding accepting/answering	Yes, that's what I was thinking.
dismissing	It wasn't a very good idea was it. I think it was really stupid.
ignoring	No response at any stage of interaction.

group) because this constituted a reasonable transcription time and because this early interaction was without teacher intervention.

The activities were recorded with the children working in a small carpeted bay just outside the classroom. Once I had introduced the task, and left the group, I either returned to the classroom if it was an afternoon session (when I had responsibility for the class), or I turned the corner and observed from the cloakroom, out of the children's line of vision. Many of my comments on the tasks come from the fieldnotes which I took at these times, as I watched and listened from the classroom or the cloakroom.

Analysing the Pupils' Talk

Using the ten-minute transcripts of each context, I first counted the number of turns taken, and words spoken, by each child. This is shown in Table 3.

Just looking at the average amount spoken by each child (the final row in Table 3) indicated that the boys spoke, overall, far more than the girls—but there was a tremendous variation across contexts. This confirmed that it wasn't enough simply to look at the *amount* each child contributed. 'Cinderella's coach' is interesting in this respect, as Elizabeth spoke more than all the other children, yet the video and my field notes confirmed that her impact on the task and its solution had been minimal.

I began the difficult task of assigning each turn from all the transcripts to a particular category or categories. This analysis revealed the truth about Elizabeth's contribution to 'Cinderella's Coach'. Although she

Table 3 Contribution of girls and boys to mixed-group problem-solving tasks.

Context	Elizabeth		Nadia		Simon		David	
	No of words	No of turns	No of words	No of turns	No of words	No of turns	No of words	No of turns
An apology to the three bears	107	17	177	29	166	21	232	36
Getting to Grandma's house	126	14	60	8	293	21	526	27
The wolf-proof house	5	1	7	1	615	22	373	21
Cinderella's coach	336	41	69	16	240	28	274	42
The jolly postman's problem	182	21	95	18	241	20	261	22
Total number of words/turns	756	94	408	72	1555	112	1666	148
*Average no. of words/turns across contexts	151	19	82	14	311	22	333	30

*Note: these figures have been rounded to the nearest whole number.

tried to break into the discussion and take a positive role in it, the boys managed to minimise her effectiveness simply by dismissing or ignoring the majority of her efforts. This pattern was apparent, to a lesser extent, in the other tasks, and revealed a great deal about how the boys perceived the girls' contributions to group discussions.

I shall now examine, in more detail, the interaction that took place in three of the seven problems. The other tasks are written up fully elsewhere (Fisher, 1989).

Task 3: 'The Wolf-Proof House'

The group had to solve the following problem:

Can you design a wolf-proof house for Red Riding-Hood's Grandma, so that the wolf cannot get in?

I told the children that the solution should fall into three parts. First, they should discuss their ideas; second, collaborate on a design for the house, and third, make up the design using junk-box materials. They were to make one house between them. As soon as the discussion began, the boys dominated it. Of the ten-minute transcript, the boys had 988 words and forty-three turns between them, to the girls' twelve words and two turns. The boys spoke almost exclusively to each other, turning to face each other and turning their backs on the girls as their ideas flowed. As these ideas became more and more blood-thirsty, Elizabeth became visibly upset, putting her hands over her ears, but the boys did not stop.

I intervened after twenty minutes to give them the piece of paper and remind them that they were to share in the design. David immediately organized them all saying he would draw the bloodbaths and Simon would draw the robots; Elizabeth was to draw the house and Nadia the garden. Simon made sure that Elizabeth did not interfere with his robot, by saying; 'Elizabeth, you can draw the actual house, but you must let me do the front door . . .' (where the robots were to be positioned).

David then told Elizabeth where to draw the house, turned over the paper, snatched her pencil and virtually drew it for her. When I joined the group and asked them all to talk me through the design, I asked Nadia which part was hers and David explained it to me.

When they began to make the design, the children were again reminded that they must start with the house first. Simon said immediately that he was going to do his robot, and David, that he needed material for his bloodbaths. Elizabeth and Nadia started on the house together. David took notice of them only to tell Elizabeth how she should be making the windows. Simon joined in 'Yes, you do all the windows and all that and we'll do all the traps'. Elizabeth at one point objected to being told what to do and said: 'Oh good old Elizabeth, she can make a house can't she. That's what you think.' David responded: 'You're making the house Elizabeth, don't argue.'

Even when the house was finished, complete with pretty pleated curtains, the boys were not interested.

Nadia: David, are you going to see our house?
David: No, not yet.
Nadia: Please.
David: Not yet.
Nadia: Please, just for a minute.
David: I said no, not yet thank you.

When the whole project was finished, the children collected me and Simon stood in front of the model saying: 'I'll explain it, I'll explain it. Hello Miss Fisher, I'll explain it.' And he did.

Task 4: 'Cinderella's Coach'

This task posed the problem:

Can you design a coach fit to take Cinderella to the Ball?

We discussed the need for somewhere for Cinderella to sit, somewhere for the footmen to stand and somewhere to harness the horses.

The children were to use a construction kit called Bau-play which is in regular use in the classroom and which all the children in the group had used with a CDT support teacher who had worked in their class in the previous term. The children were to build one coach together, and were to begin immediately with no separate time for discussion.

I have already drawn attention to the data from this transcript, because of the unexpectedly high contribution from Elizabeth. My field-notes and the video reveal that Elizabeth was particularly excited. This became noticeable when the children, quite naturally it seemed, paired off as they began construction, so that Elizabeth was working with David, and Nadia with Simon. David is considered the class leader and is extremely popular with the girls. I think a major part of Elizabeth's verbosity stemmed from the fact that David had chosen *her* to work with, and the excitement got the better of her, e.g.

Elizabeth: David, I'll make the coach. No, I'm making the bottom.
             Please let me make it . . .
Elizabeth: David, if only we can make the coach . . .
Elizabeth: Let's make it a bit more longer.
Elizabeth: . . . David, I know, let's make it a bit more wider so it will
             be a bit bigger.
Elizabeth: Can we make it? I know, let me do it.
Elizabeth: I know a way.

I was very surprised to see the pairings because it was the first time that the group had fallen into boy/girl partnerships. However, my pleasure was quickly dispelled as I realized that the boys were organizing the construction of the coach and were using the girls to fetch, carry and hold the various parts they needed:

David: [to Elizabeth] Get them.
Simon: We need four. Where are they? Get four Nadia.
David: We'll need some bits for the window, Elizabeth.
Simon: Nadia, put one of those in there.

The interesting factor was not just that the boys had set up this situation—without any deliberate discussion or planning—but that the girls so readily accepted it.

Task 7: 'The Jolly Postman's Problem'

Having read through the whole *Jolly Postman* book again, I posed the following problem:

> If you had to organize the Jolly Postman's round, in what order would you place his deliveries? Would you give him the most pleasant or the most difficult first?

I told the children that they would have to justify each decision made, as other groups were working on the same problem and there would be a whole-class debate when their solution had been reached.

This task required only discussion and no 'making and doing'. It was immediately apparent from the girls' body language that they felt more involved. They didn't sit back in their chairs but remained on their feet, gesticulating and smiling on and off throughout the activity. David fell very quickly into the leadership role. When others tried to take the initiative, he resisted quite emphatically:

Elizabeth: Two people think the witch. Simon, which one is the hardest?
David: Right, we'll do the witch first.
Simon: Why don't we do the giant, then the witch?
David: The witch, then the giant.

David rarely encourages interaction with the other children, who accept his leadership:

Simon: I'd start with the hardest one and end up with the easiest one. I think we should put that last as David says. I would do the same.
David: Put your hands here (putting his in the middle of the table) if you think the wolf is the next hardest (they all do so).

[Elizabeth tries this later in the tape and they ignore her.]

Most of the ideas the children put forward were addressed to David and all three of the others waited for his approval or comments. David and Simon both gained support for their own ideas from each other and took little notice of the girls. Indeed, although the girls were quite involved in the discussion at all times, there was still an expectation from both the boys and the girls that the ideas to be really listened to and adopted were those of the boys. So, despite a more equal contribution in terms of turns and words, the insecurity of the girls still mirrors the lack of regard which the group appeared to have for their ideas. Girls seemed to feel the need to say something—anything—to be recognized or acknowledged:

Elizabeth: Oi, oi, or what he would do is, if there was a er, the er, thing what goes to the door, right then er, what's it called, the giant, right, then the letter box down the end, right, he could go, er . . .
David: . . . *Elizabeth!*
Simon: Ohh (putting head in hands)

At the end of the activity, David fetched a piece of paper and wrote down a list of characters to whom the deliveries were to be made, putting them in the order on which the group had decided. He then took on the role of reporter when I returned to see how the children were progressing. One particularly interesting aspect of this report-back session was Nadia's contribution. Instead of her average six words per turn, she elaborated and expanded ideas at some length and clearly found more confidence in speaking with the teacher present than as one of a peer group.

Conclusions

My study focused on the implications for assessment of gender bias in small group problem-solving activities. The size of the sample I used inevitably precludes any substantial conclusions, but the data may be seen as interesting in the light of other research on gender and language.

My findings show that in all the tasks in which the mixed group were engaged, the boys talked more than the girls. This is in line with studies of teacher-led discussions (e.g. French & French, 1984). It is important that teachers are aware this may be happening and bear it in mind when assessing children's talk. It also has implications for teacher intervention and for positive discrimination towards girls/quieter pupils. If girls continue to have lower levels of participation then their confidence and self-esteem in communicative situations may be affected and the propensity of the boys to dominate will remain unchallenged.

The issues raised in this study have subsequently become incorporated into our school policies—both for the management of problem-solving areas of the curriculum and for equal opportunities. Teachers plan for a range of tasks and a variety of groupings, and teacher assessment of oracy is made with greater understanding of the inherent 'dangers' mentioned in the Cox Report. Greater experience in teacher assessment is necessary if other such dangers are to be revealed; we shall explore and hopefully expose these in due course. This study has raised the awareness of my own staff and of other colleagues with whom the findings have been shared, that the challenge of assessment is not simply one of how to find the time, but also how to find an appropriate process.

It is now accepted that children learn as much through talking as through doing. Every child has a right to an equal voice in classroom activities. This study suggests that, if teachers do not intervene in peer discussion, the voices of the girls and no doubt quieter boys may not be heard and the assessment of their performance, may be a very unequal affair indeed.

References

Department of Education and Science/Welsh Office (DES/WO) (1989) *English for Ages 5 to 16* (The second or final 'Cox Report'). London: HMSO.

Fisher, J. (1989) Unequal voices. Dissertation for Open University MA in Education (unpublished).

French, J. and French, P. (1984) Gender imbalances in the primary classroom: An interactional account. *Educational Research* 26(2), 127–36.

11 No Gap, Lots of Overlap: Turn-taking Patterns in the Talk of Women Friends[1]

JENNIFER COATES

Introduction

This paper is intended to be a contribution to our understanding of how conversation works, more specifically, our understanding of the organisation of turn-taking; it is also meant to be a contribution to the growing literature on gender differences in language. The generalisability of accepted models of turn-taking will be examined in the light of counter-examples from all-female discourse, and the function of 'deviant' turn-taking strategies for participants in such conversations will be explored.

Turn-taking is not just a mechanical procedure for speakers, but carries social meaning and is expressive of social relationships. It is 'a jointly determined, socially constituted behaviour' (Denny, 1985) which varies both between and within cultures. The smooth turn-taking procedures invoked by Sacks, Schegloff & Jefferson (1974) (often referred to as the 'No gap, no overlap' model) have normative status in English-speaking countries, both among linguists and among members of the speech communities involved (for example, children are explicitly told to wait for their turn and that butting-in is rude). However, it is recognised that certain subgroups, such as Jewish New Yorkers (Tannen, 1984) or colleagues in less focused moments at meetings (Edelsky, 1981) favour a different 'marked' set of strategies for turn taking which are 'marked' precisely because they deviate from the expected norm. In this paper I want to argue that women engaged in single-sex talk with friends are another sub-group who use 'marked' turn-taking strategies and that they do so as a Positive Politeness strategy (Brown & Levinson 1978).

Turn-taking in Conversation

The best-known (and widely accepted) model of turn-taking in conversation is that developed by Sacks, Schegloff & Jefferson (1974, henceforth SSJ). The diagram below is a flow-chart which demonstrates the mechanism which assigns turns to participants engaged in conversation. This mechanism determines that the current speaker in conversation may select the next speaker (by asking them a question, for example, or addressing them by name), in which case the person selected must speak next. If the current speaker does not select the next speaker, then one of the other participants in the conversation can opt to speak next. If none of them does so, then the current speaker has the option of continuing to speak.

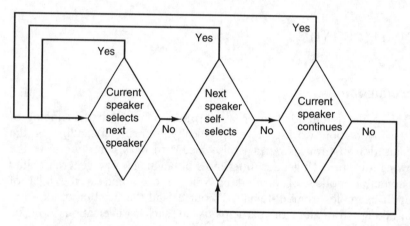

Figure 1 SSJ model of turn-taking in conversation.

The notion of 'turn' deserves closer examination. The turn-taking mechanism allows the individual to produce at least one 'turn-constructional unit', and speaker change can only meaningfully occur at a transition relevance place (TRP), that is, the end of a 'unit-type' such as a phrase or clause. In other words, in the SSJ model, the notion of 'turn' is tied to the individual speaker; turns 'belong' to individual speakers. (Note that this corresponds to folk-understanding of the operation of turn-taking: a speaker can protest 'Wait a minute—I haven't finished *my* turn'.) To take a very simple example, in an imaginary chunk of conversation consisting of four turns and involving two speakers, the model predicts that each turn will relate to one speaker, as follows:

TURN: 1 2 3 4
SPEAKER: A B A B

Many other permutations are possible,

     e.g. TURN: 1 2 3 4
     SPEAKER: A A B A

where current speaker opts to continue after Turn 1. The important
point is that one turn is co-extensive with one speaker.

The succinct 'No gap, no overlap' summary of the SSJ model (see, for
example, Moerman & Sacks, 1971) draws attention to two important claims
made by the model. 'No gap' refers to the claim that participants in
conversation interpret syntactic, semantic and prosodic clues so accurately
to predict the end of current speaker's turn that there is no perceptible gap
between the end of one turn and the beginning of the next. (As Zimmerman
& West, 1975: 117, point out, lengthy gaps between turns are symptomatic
of conversational malfunction.) The 'no overlap' claim complements this by
asserting that participants in conversation predict the end of current speaker's
turn so accurately that they start to speak just when current speaker stops
and not before. The term 'overlap' is used in contrast with 'interruption'.
Overlaps are defined as instances of speaker B over-anticipating the end
of speaker A's turn, resulting in overlap between speaker B's first words
and speaker A's last word or syllable; interruptions, on the other hand, are
violations of the current speaker's turn, specifically of their right to speak.
As Bennett (1981) points out, overlap is a descriptive term which can be
applied unproblematically to any chunk of conversation. Interruption, on
the other hand, as used by those working with the SSJ model (notably
West & Zimmerman, 1977), is an interpretative category: it evaluates a
speaker's move as a violation of participants' rights and obligations in talk.

In the next two sections, I will show that the 'no gap, no overlap'
rule does not apply to large chunks of all-female talk, and that the turn-
taking strategies deployed by women friends in conversation call into
question the theoretical status of notions such as 'speaker', 'turn' and
'floor'.

No Gap

The reason that the 'no gap' rule is problematic for all-female
conversation is not because there *are* gaps: on the contrary, all-female
talk confirms the observations of SSJ and others that the flow of
conversation is rarely interrupted by lengthy pauses. The problem is to
do with *where* there is no gap. It is axiomatic to the SSJ model of
conversation that the speaker and the turn are co-extensive; thus, the
'no gap' rule means 'no gap between turns'. In all-female talk, by
contrast, the turn is construed as potentially jointly constructed by all
participants. At its most simple, this can involve one speaker finishing
another speaker's turn (to use SSJ's terms). (In all three examples below,
the two speakers are close friends.)[2]

(1) [two friends speculate on the effect an individual's absence could have on a group]
    { **R**: they won't be so=
    { **J** :   =homogeneous

(2) [two girls talk about finding the balance between enforcing school rules and keeping people happy]
    { **Antonia**: it's a real sort of=
    { **Sarah**:   =jiggle
(Channel 4 documentary on Benenden School, March 1992)

(3) [K wonders if her neighbour can see her, because she saw him undress in his living room]
    { **K**: I mean OK I'm sure he's not =
    { **C**:   =peeping

These are all examples of a 'turn-constructional unit' which is constructed by two speakers. They are remarkable because semantically, syntactically *and prosodically*, they are identical to utterances produced by a single speaker.

The SSJ terminology now starts to fail us: are we going to call the whole of (1), (2) or (3) a 'turn'? or, if turns are tied to speakers, do we have to say that each of these examples consists of two turns? In all-female talk, the turn is not tied to the individual speaker but is jointly owned. Talk is a cooperative enterprise in a much stronger sense than is normally intended by analysts (such as Grice, 1975). The following example, from a conversation involving five friends, demonstrates that the joint construction of utterances can involve more than simply adding the final word:

(4) [Topic = child abuse]
    C: I mean in order to accept that idea you're

    { **C**:   having to.
    { **D**:   yes
    { **E**:   mhm   completely review your view of your

    E: husband

Here C and E jointly construct a complex utterance, with D adding back-channel support.

These four examples all show speaker-change occurring within a turn-constructional unit. Moreover, change occurs not just within the turn-unit, but within a phrase within that unit. In example (1), next speaker takes over during an Adjective phrase complement 'so // homogeneous'), in example (2), next speaker takes over during a Noun Phrase complement ('a real sort of // jiggle'), while in (3) and (4), next speaker takes over during a Verb Phrase, ('is not // peeping'; 'are having to // (completely) review').

Examples (1), (2), (3) and (4) each involve one turn-constructional
unit. But women do more than jointly construct *turns*. More important
is the concept of shared *floor* (see Edelsky, 1981). If we look at a more
extended version of example (3), we will see that an analysis in terms
of turns would miss the point that K and C here *jointly* hold the floor.

(5) **K**: and I thought my God
    C: yeh
    K: if I can see him
    C: he can see you
5 **K**: and I don't always just get undressed in my living room
    C: (laugh)
    K: you know I mean OK I'm sure he's not
    C: peeping
    K: peeping or anything
10 **C**: but he
    K: but it just
    C: you accidentally saw him
    K: that's right
    C: oh I don't blame you I think it needs screening trees
15   round it

Sharing the construction of talk involves sharing the construction of verb
phrases (*he's not // peeping*), sharing out subordinate and matrix clause
(*if I can see him // he can see you*), sharing in the search for appropriate
words (*but he- but it just-*) and sharing in the prosodic shape of utterances.
Most importantly, a shared floor involves speakers in the joint construction
of meaning. Where two speakers can rely on a great deal of shared
knowledge, as in the case of good friends, then two speakers can function
as a single voice. This phenomenon is known as 'the conversational
duet', a phrase coined by Jane Falk (1980) to describe the linguistic
behaviour of couples talking to a third party. As examples (4) and (5)
illustrate (and as I have demonstrated elsewhere – Coates, 1991), duetting
is also found in the talk of women friends, in talk where there is no
third party present.

As example (4) has suggested, the joint construction of talk can
involve more than two speakers. In example (6) below, three women
friends struggle to define a concept they can't name (*schadenfreude*):

(6) ⎧ **D**: it's sort of pleasure
     ⎨ **C**:   a perverse pleasure=
     ⎩ **A**:   =in their
     ⎰ **C**:   =yeah
     ⎱ **A**: downfall=

Through the construction of a shared floor, the group as a whole rather than any individual speaker arrives at a summary of the topic they have been discussing.

Lots of Overlap

The talk of women friends involves not only the construction of a shared floor, but also lots of overlapping speech. Example (4) above was edited: the full version is as follows:

(7)   **C:** I mean in order to accept that idea you're

   ⎧ **C:** having to.   ⎡completely
   ⎨ **E:**   mhm.   completely review your ⎣view of your
   ⎩ **D:**   yes

   ⎧ **C:** change ⎤ your view of your husband=
   ⎪ **E:** husband ⎦ =   =that's right
   ⎨ **B:**   =yes
   ⎩ **A:**   yeah   mhm

E's completion ('completely review your view of your husband') of the utterance begun by C ('you're having to') is overlapped by C, who echoes E's words, changing 'review' to 'change'. Moreover, it would be false to see this as an example of a floor shared by only two speakers: D, B and A play a crucial, if minor, role in this chunk of talk.

Overlapping speech is also found when co-participants ask questions or make comments while another participant is speaking (see examples 8, 9. 10 and 11 below).

(8) [5 friends discuss parents' funerals]
     B: well she lived in Brisbane ((they were at Brisbane))

   ⎧ **B:** so he's going over there = Australia so he's going to
   ⎩ **E:** what   — Australia?=

     B: the funeral

(9) [3 friends talk about Oxford student murder]
   ⎧ **R:** it was the boyfriend, yeah, she was under the
   ⎩ **T:**   has he

   ⎧ **R:** floorboards   =yeah
   ⎨ **T:** been charged? =
   ⎩ **S:**   =mhm

(10) [3 friends talk about Oxford student murder]
   ⎧ **R:** and his parents are flying over from New Zealand to
   ⎩ **S:**   oh his poor parents

     R: s- to support him

(11) [J talks about crying in school]

    { J : and I cried   not for very long [dʒ] just sort of . a few
    { V: mhm   I hate

    { J : tears   =I know and. . .
    { V: it when noone notices=

Comments are often more extensive than the brief examples given in (10) and (11), and can involve participants in an elaborate descant over the main tune. In the following example, Susan is telling a story about a couple she knows where the wife won't let the husband play his guitar.

(12) { S: she pushes him to the *abs-*
      { T: he'll probably stab her with the

      { S: she pushes him to the limit   yeah, I
      { R: =yeah grrr! (vicious noise)
      { T: bread knife one day=   she'll wake

      { S: think he will   I think he'll rebel
      { R: ='here you are Ginny' (laughs--------------)
      { T: up dead=   (laughs--------------)

This is a brief extract from a long episode where R and T embroider on S's story. Note how R and T's contributions, taken in isolation, involve no overlap: their turns are carefully coordinated to alternate in a continuous commentary on what Susan is saying.

Finally, overlapping speech is found in all-female talk when two speakers pursue a theme simultaneously. Example (13), another extract from the funeral discussion, illustrates this.

(13) { A: I've [ɒp] for many [years ((have wondered)) about
      { E: [cos that's what funerals are

      { A: my *own* mother's funeral]
      { E: for is for the relatives   ]

Simultaneous talk of this kind does not threaten comprehension, but on the contrary permits a more multi-layered development of topics.

Extensive overlap of the kind illustrated in this section cannot be accounted for by the SSJ model. Overlap involving more than the last word or syllable of current speaker's turn has to be labelled 'interruption'. In other words, all simultaneous speech except brief overlaps caused by an over-enthusiastic next speaker is seen as deviant, a violation of a speaker's right to the floor.

The following is an example of what SSJ describe as 'interruption':

(14) [College students]

      Female: How's your paper coming?
      Male: Alright I guess (#) I haven't done much in the past
              two weeks
  (1.8)

{ **Female**: yeah::: know how that ⌈can-
{ **Male**:   ⌊hey ya' got an extra cigarette?
                    [West & Zimmerman, 1977: 527)

This is labelled an interruption because speaker B begins to speak before the current speaker (A) has reached a TRP (speaker A has just begun a subordinate clause, but does not complete the Verb Phrase).

The problem for analysts is as follows:

(i)   using this (syntactic) criterion, the instances of overlapping speech in examples (7) through (13) all have to be labelled 'interruptions';
(ii) the examples in (7) through (13) are *not* interruptions in any sensible sense of this term;
(iii) however, example (14) *would* be considered an interruption by all competent members of the relevant speech community.

In order to sustain the claims made in (ii) and (iii) here, we need to find *alternative* (non-syntactic) criteria for what constitutes an interruption.

One reason that members *would* consider (14) an example of interruption is that B's move results in A stopping talking: in other words, B takes the floor from A. Overlapping talk in examples (7) through (13), on the other hand, *never* results in current speaker losing the floor.[3] Beattie (1981) has argued for a more refined definition of interruption, which depends upon the notion of 'completeness'. If the current speaker stops speaking before s/he reaches a TRP, i.e. if the turn-constructional unit is incomplete, then an interruption is said to have occurred.

Beatties's definition moves us forward and allows us to explain why example (14) is an interruption, but example (13) is not. However, neither Beattie nor SSJ will help us with examples like the following:

(15) [police called out to incident of domestic violence]
     Woman complainant: you know and all of a sudden he said 'old drunken bitch' I said 'what're you talking about' I said (.) 'we're together we gotta help each other' you know?
     Male police officer: What's your date of birth?
                                              (McElhinny, in press)

In example (15), the police officer's response does not prevent the woman who has been beaten up by her long-term partner from completing her utterance. However, what he says does not respond in any way whatsoever to what the woman complainant is saying. His topic-switching question, it seems to me, is as much a violation of current speaker's rights as B's interruption in example (14).

Bennett (1981: 176) gives a good example of this type of uncooperative move in an extract from a panel discussion shown live on public TV in

San Francisco, two weeks after a riot in the area known as Hunter's
Point. A, the panel moderator, asks B, a local black man, his views on
the job situation.

(16) **A**: now Mr B/ what is your view//
    B: well' I ha- here.../ I have here/ a list of 500 jobs/ that were/ sent
       to the area/ in Hunter's Point//
→   **A**: sent by whom?//
    B: Uh' d-.../various ((xxx))
    A: are they just posted//
    B: government/ and uh departments
    A: what I was interested in was. . .

What is particularly interesting about this example is A's move in line
4 'sent by whom'. This turn comes after B has completed a 'unit-type',
yet when Bennett played the first 4 lines of this extract to about 30
undergraduate and postgraduate students, they were unanimous in seeing
A's move as antagonistic, labelling it as 'interrupting B', 'not giving B a
chance to speak', 'cutting B off' (Bennett, 1981: 171). Surely we want
to apply the term 'interruption' to the phenomenon in conversation
where one person cuts another off, or doesn't give them a chance to
speak?

The crucial factor here is the antagonistic nature of A's move. In
other words, what seems to count for members is the *polarity* of next
speaker's move. Polarity can be defined as 'a system of positive/negative
contrastivity found in language' (Crystal 1980:274). Where two chunks
of talk occur one after the other or simultanously, chunk B will be said
to have *positive polarity* in relation to chunk A where chunk B agrees
with, confirms, repeats or extends the proposition expressed in chunk
A, or makes a point on the same topic that demonstrates shared attitudes
or beliefs. Chunk B will be said to have *negative polarity* when it denies,
disagrees with or ignores chunk A. Where next speaker's contribution
to talk has positive polarity in relation to current speaker's, it will be
seen as a cooperative move, whether or not it overlaps with current
speaker's turn (examples 7 through 13), and whether or not current
speaker gets to complete their utterance (examples 1 through 6). But
when next speaker's contribution has negative polarity in relation to
current speaker's, then it will be perceived as antagonistic, as an
interruption (examples 14 through 16).

Shared Turns and Overlapping Speech: Positive Politeness Strategies?[4]

I want to suggest that the occurrence of overlapping speech in all-
female discourse is not a deviant phenomenon, but is a way of expressing

the solidarity of female friendship. In other words, the use of turn-taking strategies which emphasise what is shared through the use of shared turns and overlapping talk is a positive politeness strategy. Brown & Levinson define positive politeness as:

> redress directed to the addressee's positive face, his (*sic*) perennial desire that his wants (or the actions/acquisitions/values resulting from them) should be thought of as desirable. Redress consists in partially satisfying that desire by communicating that one's own wants (or some of them) are in some respects similar to the addressee's wants. (Brown & Levinson, 1978: 106)

Expressions of Positive Politeness are a normal part of the the language of friends; as Brown & Levinson say: 'Positive Politeness utterances are used as a kind of metaphorical extension of intimacy' (1978: 108). One of the macro-strategies associated with Positive Politeness is 'claim common ground', and one of the ways this can be realised is by claiming a common point of view/opinions/attitudes/knowledge/empathy (see Figure 2).

When a speaker completes an utterance started by another speaker (as in examples 1 through 6), they are demonstrating common ground to a spectacular degree. In order to share in the construction of utterances, you need to share a common point of view/knowledge/opinions etc. If you did not genuinely participate in this shared world, you would not be able to say the right thing at the right time. And when two speakers who are equals say something at the same time, but what they say demonstrates a common point of view/knowledge/opinions etc., then this will be interpreted as cooperative, as a Positive Politeness move, not as competition for the floor.[5]

Shared utterance-construction and overlapping speech also carry out the other macro-strategy of Positive Politeness: 'convey that S and H are cooperators' (see Figure 2). In particular, these linguistic strategies demonstrate reciprocity (strategy 14) and they include both Speaker and Hearer in the activity (strategy 12).

Evidence that such an interpretation is accurate comes from the response of participants to their utterance being completed by another, or their turn being overlapped by another. The fuller version of example (2) below shows Antonia's acceptance of Sarah's contribution to the utterance (*yup* means *yes*).

(2a) **A**: it's a real sort of =   =yup you have to work it out/
     S: = jiggle =

Other examples earlier in this paper show the same phenomenon: participants say *yes*, *yeah* or *that's right* (examples 5, 6 and 7); they incorporate next speaker's contribution into their turn (examples 5, 6

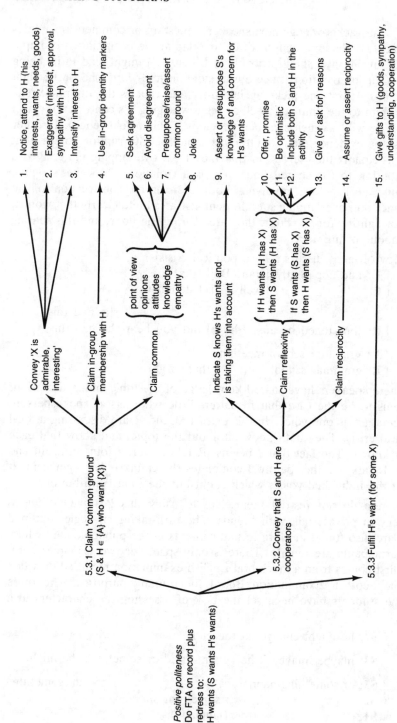

Figure 2 Positive Politeness strategies (Brown & Levinson, 1978: 107).

and 7); they acknowledge next speaker's question or comment (examples 8, 9 and 11). Cursory analysis of the overlap at the beginning of example (12) (where T says: 'he'll probably stab her. . .') might lead to its being seen as an interruption, since Susan stops in mid-word 'she pushes him to the *abs-*'), but she picks up her story and repairs the utterance 'she pushes him to the limit'), as well as acknowledging T's contribution 'yeah I think he will'), which she then develops 'I think he'll rebel'). In other words, the evidence that T's utterance is not an interruption comes from the participants themselves, in that they treat overlapping material as a contribution to the shared floor, not as a violation of speaker's rights. Example (17) below, involving both the shared construction of an utterance and overlapping speech, demonstrates quite clearly that women are not fighting for the floor: they are *sharing* the floor, and this sharing is symbolic of intimacy.

(17) [two friends discuss a local political crisis]

{ **J** : and apparently ⌈ Jane Bull ((xx))
{ **R**:   ⌊ well in fact it. felt very

{ **J** :   she had this
{ **R**: threatened because [didʒə] did you hear she had this

{ **J** : grammar school meeting=
{ **R**: grammar school   =that's right

Where speakers have shared knowledge of the topic under discussion, it seems to be the case that it matters little who acts as spokesperson; speakers act as one voice. In this extract, J and R are discussing a local political crisis. They both know all about the topic, and know that each other knows. The fact that J begins, R takes over, J joins in again and J and R talk together before J completes the chunk is not significant; it is not the individual voices which count but the joint contribution.

Women do not restrict themselves to using this Positive Politeness strategy in private talk with friends. The turn-taking strategies outlined here are also found in more formal contexts in the public domain where all participants are female. There is only space for two examples here. The first comes from a mock oral English examination recorded on video by the Scottish Examination Board for training purposes. The three female students have been set the task of assessing the characters in a play.

(18)   **S2**: he might change/ at the end/

    S3: maybe/ maybe if he gets married or something/ he might/

{ **S3**: or something happens=   =yeah, something
{ **S2**:   =something *shock*ing=
{ **S1**:   (laughs)

```
 ⎧ S3: happens=                           =dramatic/
 ⎨ S2:                        =dramatic=
 ⎩ S1:          =something=          (Wareing 1993)
```

Example (18) shows how girls as young as fifteen have already learned to speak as a single voice, and can use this skill in a public arena.

The second example is taken from interaction between young home helps and elderly clients. The inter-generational talk occurring in home help-elderly person dyads tends to be all-female because the majority of carers are female, as are most of the elderly population. Despite the asymmetry of both age and status in these dyads, Karen Atkinson (in press) has observed a significant amount of simultaneous speech in their conversations, similar in kind to that found in the talk of female friends. The following is an example from her data:

(19) [elderly client (EC) talks to home help (HH) about new gadget for arthritis]

```
1 ⎧ EC: now if my knee [b], got bad again/
  ⎩ HH:                        yeah      yeah now that'd

2 ⎧ EC:    that might be worth it/. ((your)) knee
  ⎩ HH: be lovely ((there)/       yes   yeah where

3 ⎧ EC:        you would use it on yourself/      yes/
  ⎩ HH: you can use it                yourself/ that's it, yeah/
```

This short extract illustrates the way overlapping speech is used in these interactions. Speakers perform as a single voice, saying the same thing in different words 'now that'd be lovely'/'that might be worth it', lines 2–3) and even saying the same thing at the same time 'yourself', line 3). When EC says *you would use it on yourself* in line 3, she is not trying to seize the floor from HH, but is agreeing with HH and saying the same thing in her own words.

Conclusion

In this paper I am not arguing that the turn-taking mechanism postulated by SSJ does not exist. On the contrary, it is precisely the existence of such a mechanism that allows other modes of conversational organisation to have their meaning. In other words, 'the simplest systematics for the organisation of turn-taking in conversation' described by SSJ is the base-line for speakers of English. These are the rules of turn-taking acquired first by speakers of English, and they remain as the unmarked system in our repertoire. But many speakers acquire other rules of turn-taking, expressive of particular social relationships, and 'marked' in relation to the base-line form. These alternative strategies for turn-taking frequently involve the occurrence of overlapping turns (see Goffman, 1967; Edelsky, 1981; Tannen, 1981). This pattern was also found by McDowell (1983) in his research on Kamsa ritual language, where the 'normal tendency of alternate turns at talk' (McDowell, 1983: 30) contrasts with simultaneous turn-taking in ritual settings. As he comments, because ritual language deviates from the accepted norm, the occurrence of simultaneous speech is foregrounded and signals the ritual nature of the event.

In the same way, the construction of a shared floor, where speakers jointly create text, deviates from the expected norm and marks such talk as 'friendly' or 'intimate'. All the evidence is that women friends get enormous pleasure from talking together, and that cooperative ways of talking, such as the turn-taking strategies described in this paper, are symbolic of the connection women feel with each other (see Apter, 1990; Coates, 1989, 1991, forthcoming; Gilligan, 1982; Johnson & Aries, 1983).

If we accept Brown & Levinson's claim that Britain is a Negative Politeness culture (Brown & Levinson, 1978: 250), we could argue that the unmarked (syntactically-based) turn-taking mechanism is part of the dominant, Negative Politeness, ethos. (Negative Politeness is designed to respect members' basic need not to be imposed upon. The SSJ rule, 'only one person speaks at a time', is precisely designed to respect that need.) Alternative turn-taking strategies, which facilitate *shared turns* at talk (more than one person speaking at a time, or more than one person constructing an utterance) are, by contrast, part of a Positive Politeness ethos.

Expressions of Positive Politeness are an integral part of all intimate relationships and this paper is not an attempt to claim that *only* women use the turn-taking strategies described here. Previous studies have demonstrated that, for example, Jewish New Yorkers (both male and female) (Tannen, 1984), and white middle class British friends (both male and female) (Bublitz, 1988) use similar turn-taking strategies in mixed interaction. (Diaz Martinez's, 1993, study of collaborative argument, using data obtained from dyads or triads of friends under experimental conditions, also found a significant amount of cooperative turn-construction, which he calls 'mutual completions'.)[6]

In this paper I have argued that, while acknowledging the importance of SSJ's contribution to our understanding of turn-taking, we should not ignore other, marked turn-taking strategies, used by certain groups in certain contexts to mark those relationships and those events. I have demonstrated that women friends use marked turn-taking strategies in conversation with each other, and I have argued that such strategies accomplish friendship by expressing Positive Politeness. The existence of alternative models for the organisation of turn-taking reminds us that no linguistic strategy exists in a value-free universe. In complex societies such as those of the USA and Britain, members exploit the possibilities of the turn-taking system, inter alia, to create alternative meanings. The variation we find in turn-taking practices reflects the diverse social groupings with which members of the speech community ally themselves and in which they establish their identity.

Notes

1. I'd like to thank Jenny Cheshire, Linda Thomas, Shan Wareing and Max Wheeler for their helpful comments on earlier drafts of this paper.
2. Except where otherwise acknowledged, all material quoted in this paper comes from my data-base of naturally occurring conversation in single-sex friendship groups. I would like to place on record my gratitude to all those who have participated in my research, and also to those who have generously given me material collected as part of their own research projects, to broaden my data-base: Karen Atkinson, Christine Cheepen and Shan Wareing. (Cheepen's transcripts have since been published as an Appendix to Cheepen & Monaghan, 1990.)
3. When the floor is shared, as in examples (1) through (10), the notion of 'losing' or 'gaining' the floor is not strictly applicable. There is a lack of appropriate terminology in this area but, to use a musical metaphor, women's conversation can be described as a jam session with players sometimes playing the tune, sometimes playing elaborate counterpoint, and sometimes providing backing material.
4. Much of this section of the paper was inspired by Max Wheeler's paper, 'The place of politeness principles', given at Sociolinguistics Symposium 9, Reading University, April 2–4, 1992.
5. Mary Talbot (1992) analyses a conversation in which a wife's attempts to contribute to a story about her and her husband coming through customs are labelled as interruption by her husband, rather than as contributions to a shared narrative. It seems that the conversational strategies which accomplish friendship among equals will, where participants at talk are *not* equals, be construed as moves in a power struggle.
6. Brown & Levinson argue that in complex societies, dominant groups will have Negative Politeness cultures, while dominated or oppressed groups will have Positive Politeness cultures. Since all the evidence points to the fact that men constitute a dominant group in relation to women, we could argue that women are more likely to be associated with Positive Politeness cultures and men with Negative Politeness cultures. Women's solidary turn-taking patterns provide evidence for the first of these claims, while the second claim remains to be tested (all-male conversation is still under-researched).

References

Apter, T. (1990) *Altered Loves: Mothers and Daughters During Adolescence.* London: Harvester Wheatsheaf.

Atkinson, K. (in press) *Elderly Talk.* London: Longman.

Beattie, G. (1981) Interruption in conversational interaction, and its relation to the sex and status of the interactants. *Linguistics* 19, 15–35.

Bennett, A. (1981) Interruptions and the interpretation of conversation. *Discourse Processes* 4, 171–88.

Brown, P. and Levinson, S. (1978) Universals in language usage: Politeness phenomena. In E.N. Goody (ed.) *Questions and Politeness*. Cambridge: Cambridge University Press.

Bublitz, W. (1988) *Supportive Fellow-Speakers and Cooperative Conversations*. Amsterdam: John Benjamins.

Cheepen, C. and Monaghan, J. (1990) *Spoken English: A Practical Guide*. London: Pinter Publishers.

Coates, J. (1989) Gossip revisited: Language in all-female groups. In J. Coates and D. Cameron (eds) *Women in their Speech Communities*. London: Longman.

—— (1991) Women's cooperative talk: A new kind of conversational duet? In C. Uhlig and R. Zimmermann (eds) *Proceedings of the Anglistentag 1990, Marburg*. Tubingen: Max Niemeyer Verlag.

—— forthcoming. *Women Talking to Women*. Oxford: Basil Blackwell.

Crystal, D. (1980) *A First Dictionary of Linguistics and Phonetics*. London: Andre Deutsch.

Denny, R. (1985) Marking the interaction order: The social constitution of turn exchange and speaking turns. *Language in Society* 14, 41–62.

Diaz Martinez, F. (1993) Mutual completion and collaborative argument in conversation. Unpublished paper, Dept. of Psychology, University of Lancaster.

Edelsky, C. (1981) Who's got the floor? *Language in Society* 10, 383–421.

Falk, J. (1980) The conversational duet. In *Proceedings of the 6th Annual Meeting of the Berkeley Linguistics Society* 507–14.

Gilligan, C. (1982) *In a Different Voice*. New York: Harvard University Press.

Goffman, E. (1967) *Interaction Ritual*. New York: Anchor Press.

Grice, H.P. (1975) Logic and conversation. In P. Cole and J.L. Morgan (eds) *Syntax and Semantics. Vol. 3: Speech Acts*. New York: Academic Press.

Johnson, F. and Aries, E. (1983) The talk of women friends. *Women's Studies International Forum* 6 (4), 353–61.

McDowell, J. (1983) The semiotic constitution of Kamsa ritual language. *Language in Society* 12, 23–46.

McElhinny, B. (in press) 'I don't smile much any more': Affect, gender and the discourse of Pittsburgh police officers. *Locating Power: Proceedings of the 1992 Berkeley Women and Language Conference*.

Moerman, M. and Sacks, H. (1971) On 'understanding' in the analysis of natural conversation. Paper given at the 70th Annual Meeting of the American Anthropological Association, reprinted in M. Moerman (1988) *Talking Culture: Ethnography and Conversation Analysis*. Philadelphia: University of Pennsylvania Press.

Sacks, H., Schegloff, E. and Jefferson, G. (1974) A simplest systematics for the organisation of turn-taking for conversation. *Language* 50 (4), 696–735.

Talbot, M. (1992) 'I wish you'd stop interrupting me!': Interruptions and asymmetries in speaker-rights in equal encounters. *Journal of Pragmatics* 18, 451–66.

Tannen, D. (1984) *Conversational Style: Analysing Talk among Friends*. Norwood, NJ: Ablex.

Wareing, S. (1993) Cooperative and competitive talk: The assessment of discussion at Standard Grade. Unpublished PhD thesis, University of Strathclyde.

West, C. and Zimmerman, D. (1977) Women's place in everyday talk: Reflections on parent-child interaction. *Social Problems* 24, 521–9.

Zimmerman, D. and West, C. (1975) Sex roles, interruptions and silences in conversation. In B. Thorne and N. Henley (ed) *Language and Sex: Difference and Dominance*. Rowley, MA: Newbury House.

12 Cultural Values in Samish and Australian Children's Literature: A Corpus Linguistic Approach[1]

MEERI HELLSTEN

Introduction

This paper examines literacy practices in minority education. Central to the theme of the paper is the examination of early pedagogic literature as instruments of enculturation and socialization in the context of Australian and Samish societies. The Australian Aborigines share the human rights agenda with the rest of the world's indigenous populations, among which is the indigenous group of Sami of Sapmic (Lapland). The Sami are in a linguistic and political minority in the three Scandinavian countries of Sweden, Norway and Finland. A small percentage of Sami also live in the CIS.

The analyses are based on a cross-cultural comparison of early school texts in use in Samish vernacular classes in Finnish Lapland and in classrooms of Australia. The data derive from a computer-based analysis of two corpora. The Samish corpus comprises thirteen school texts designed for 9 year old Samish children, and totals nearly 31,000 words. This corpus is compared with a similar collection of Australian texts, totalling just under 84,000 words, described in greater detail by Baker & Freebody (1989).

Children's text-books make compelling research material for investigators interested in society's portrayal of the notion of childhood. School literature differs from most other types of literature in its aim to systematically reinforce forms of cognitive and behavioural competence in its readership (Luke, 1988). Curriculum developers design school readers for the specific purpose of guiding pupils into acceptable social participation by providing models of appropriate communication skills, attitudinal evaluation and behaviour in groups (Department of Education, Queensland, 1987; Samish Board of Education, 1990). The reader is expected to readily identify with the world of the text, its characters and their activities and to make a close association between these and the world outside the classroom. Such texts incorporate certain political and social values which are expected to be readily adopted by the pupils. The normal development of the child's self-concept is thus secured by providing 'real-life' examples from mainstream society in guise of the protagonist's activities in the mundane world.

There is, however, evidence that children's text-books function in a manner different from or contrary to their designed purpose. Educational materials in Australia have been shown to provide an adult view of child culture, and offer an insight into how adults *prefer* to inform children about the world which they inhabit (Baker & Freebody, 1989). This world is often distant from the real world of the child. The world of the text-book contains animals who can speak; adults who are unable to show emotions; adults who never speak to each other; and adults who engage in seemingly desultory activities (Baker & Freebody, 1989). In brief, the Australian school texts were shown to be heavily gender and generation biased. The world portrayed is based on a fantasy which children are expected to understand and to distinguish from the real world outside the classroom. Thus children must learn to 'commute' intellectually between the two worlds of school-text fantasy and playground reality.

The fantastic content of school literature seems unique to western societies. For example, Indonesian school texts do not portray animals as participants in human conversation, but include these only as provision of food or as agricultural necessities (Nicholson, 1985). Furthermore, the stories of these texts revolve around everyday, work related events without the involvement of fantastic fairy-tale components. The messages mediated through Indonesian school-texts thus contrast with Australian texts in the way they represent the word. The contrasts suggest that Indonesian children are introduced to a more veracious version of childhood than are Australian children. Skutnabb-Kangas (1990) emphasizes the importance of spreading awareness about the potential power of education, and of working on critical evaluation of educational practices in majority societies. In a time of global research into the cultural heritage and human rights of indigenous peoples comprising what have been called 'the fourth world', and claims of linguistic and cultural 'genocide', these issues are crucial to minority populations.

Education, Power and Enculturation

Foremost on the agenda of fourth world populations has been the battle to regain their cultural heritage in the form of language and socio-political rights. However, closely related to cultural integrity is linguistic identity and the main priority of indigenous people is often the maintainance of their vernacular languages. In the past decade several language maintenance programmes have been introduced into majority society curricula around the world (Skutnabb-Kangas, 1990). Language immersion programmes are a major achievement for minority group members but do not warrant complacency. Their introduction should alert curriculum developers to the need for a critical evaluation of their function and contents. This is of especial current interest in light of the spreading threat to the minority languages of the world. Sachs (1992) estimates that more than 94% of the world's 5000 languages will die within the next fifty years. Sachs' statement makes plausible the idea that along with these dying 4700 languages will perish 94% of the world's cultures. The question arising from such grim statistics is: How is it possible? What causes the death of a language and its culture?

One of the more subtle contributions is literacy practice. Being literate in any society provides both social and political access to affluence (Lankshear & Lawler, 1989). For ethnic minority group individuals, literacy learning often means the forsaking of one's mother tongue and customs as the price for gaining knowledge in the majority society (Skutnabb-Kangas & Cummins, 1988). The various minority language maintenance programmes have attempted to combat this problem by using the vernacular for teaching the school curriculum. However, despite years of strenuous efforts, the linguistic competence of minority group speakers remains low or indeed non-functional in the mainstream community (Aikio, 1991). One of the leading causes is claimed by Aikio (1988) to be the limited opportunity to utilize the vernacular outside the classroom context. For example, the Samish language has no official rights, and hence the Samish people cannot use this vernacular as a code of communication in their everyday dealings with government agencies such as the post office.

Such socialisation processes promoting linguistic change are directly monitored by the majority culture (Skutnabb-Kangas, 1990). Aikio (1991) emphasises that this has serious effects on primary education within native families who often find it easier to transfer the majority language to the next generation rather than insisting on maintaining the indigenous minority language. Another factor contributing to the decay of indigenous language use is what Aikio (1991) calls 'the taboo'—or an attitude which reinforces a form of shame over the minority language use. Many other Samish speakers refuse to speak Samish to children, due to their indoctrinated belief that knowledge of two languages will weaken their children's competence of the majority tongue. It is in this manner that Skutnabb-Kangas (1990) (see also Fairclough, 1991 and Luke, 1988) claims that education serves to control populations. The reinforcement of power is practised through 'the instruments (i.e. language) and the ideological messages (i.e. cultural content)' (Skutnabb-Kangas 1990: 6) within the school curricula.

On the textual level, a contradictory content of the messages in the school texts and the beliefs of the home may contribute to internal conflict in the child's development of the self-concept. There are extensive reports on the learning difficulties experienced by minority group pupils which relate to the culture-adaptive problems which members of minority groups face when subjected to culturally, linguistically or socially divergent teaching materials (for example, Christie, 1989; Cummins, 1985; Harris, 1990; Lauren, 1987). The main difficulties encountered in such situations relates not so much to the cognitive aptitude, but rather to the lack of background knowledge about the topic of the text which results in poor concentration and learning difficulties. In other words, children's social and cultural background may predetermine achievement in literacy skills.

The World of the Text

It was argued by Baker & Freebody (1989) that semantic properties of the text reveal emotional and psychological aspects of child culture. In addition to depicting the emotional world, the texts also indicate the social structure of the artificial society illustrated within the stories. This paper outlines two functional aspects of texts which promote desired social norms and values. These are human behaviour (including emotional expressions, generational hierarchies and gender issues) and social structure (as evident in the culture specific activities which are carried out by the various text protagonists).

A close investigation of the characters who inhabit the worlds of the texts, reveals the kinds of human qualities that are valued in society. The characters inhabiting Australian (AR) and Samish (SR) readers' story contents are listed in Table 1 below.

The most obvious feature of the above table is that the world in children's first readers is inhabited by the immediate family and domesticated animals. However, the SR corpus has an overall higher frequency of humans compared to animals than the AR corpus. A comparison of the frequencies of all human terms in the SR and the AR corpora reveals that in the Samish texts every twenty-second word refers to a human, whereas in the Australian texts the frequency is only one per forty-three words. This can be explained by the 'human qualities'

Table 1 20 most frequently occurring words in the SR and the AR corpora referring to living creatures.

	Samish		Australian	
Rank	word	F/10000	word	F/10000
1.	eadni (**mother**)	80	mother	42
2.	áhcci (**father**)	73	children	34
3.	áddjá (**grandfather**)	55	father	32
4.	(various **reindeer** terms)	47	pig/s	29
5.	áhkku (**grandmother**)	25	cat/s	27
6.	siessá, muottá, goaski (**aunt**)	21	dog/s	27
7.	gánda, bárdni (**boy**)	20	man/s	22
8.	beana (**dog**)	19	bear/s	20
9.	oabbá (**sister**)	18	dad/s	19
10.	loddi (**bird**)	16	grandmother	19
11.	guolli (**fish**)	14	fish	18
12.	eanu, ceahci, eahki (**uncle**)	13	boy/s	17
13.	bussa (**cat**)	13	daddy/s	15
14.	gáranas (**crow**)	11	horse/s	15
15.	viellja (**brother**)	10	friend/s	15
16.	gumpe (**wolf**)	10	rabbit/s	15
17.	nieida (**girl**)	8	bird/s	15
18.	gussa (**cow**)	8	boys	12
19.	sávza (**lamb**)	7	mum/s	11
20.	heasta (**horse**)	7	kitten/s	11

allocated to animals in the AR corpus, such as verbal skills and sense of dress. While similar anthropomorphism is found in the SR corpus, there is an overall lower frequency of animal terms.

Many of the words in the SR corpus are kinship terms which extend from the immediate family, such as *aunts* and *uncles*. This finding is a reflection of the extended family network in the Samish community where contact between aunts, uncles and grandparents occurs on a more or less daily basis. Another signifier of the close interaction between families in Samish culture is the high frequency of *grandparents*. The words *grandfather* and *grandmother* are among the five most frequently occurring words referring to living things in the SR corpus, whereas the AR corpus only lists *grandmother* in this category. The occurrence of *grandparents* is a meaningful illustration of the immediate kinship structure in Samish society. The Samis commonly provide for the elder members of the family, who customarily stay living with one of their offspring's family for their final years of life. So important is this notion to Samish culture, that two of the thirteen text books in the SR corpus are named '*grandfather and the children*' (*áddjá ja mánát*).

Both the SR and the AR corpora consist of three generations: adults, grandparents, and children. The terms *mother* and *father* and indeed also *grandparents* occur at higher frequencies than do *boys* and *girls* in school texts from both cultures. The high occurrence of the world *children* in the AR corpus highlights the generational gap (Baker & Freebody, 1989). The word *child* is expressed from an adult perspective since children seldom refer to each other by this term, but instead seem to use words such as *girl/s* and *boy/s* and proper nouns. The frequencies of the latter terms in both the SR and the AR corpora are lower than of the word *child*.

Thus the texts in both the SR and the AR corpora are about parents, family members and animals which are familiar to the childhood environment in both cultures. Note here the high frequency of various *reindeer* terms in the SR corpus. The culture specific content of the Samish texts will be further elaborated on below.

Baker & Freebody (1989) suggest that the allocation of emotional descriptions to characters within the text plays a role in fostering a child's own sense of identity. Hence, affective representations demonstrate to children various possible personality traits. As was stated above, the Australian Readers entirely lack referral to adults' emotional attributes. Emotion overall is not well signalled in the AR corpus, with animals being the main characters representing the emotional world. Table 2 displays some examples of positive and negative emotional verbs and adjectives from the AR and the SR corpora.

Table 2 Frequencies of words relating to positive and negative emotions in the SR and the AR corpora.

Positive	F/10000	Negative	F/10000
Samish			
buore (**good**)	39.0	cierrut (**cry**)	8.1
suohtas (**funny**)	11.0	i liiko (**don't like**)	1.6
liikot (**like**)	9.8	morras (**grief**)	2.6
duostas (**dare**)	2.6	ballat (**fear**)	2.6
hávski (**fun**)	1.3	ahkit (**boring**)	1.9
berostit (**like**)	1.3	dolkat (**fed up**)	1.9
bohkosit (**burst out laughing**)	0.9	váillahit (**long for**)	0.6
		surges (**pitiful**)	0.6
Total	64.7		14.9
Australian			
like	71.0	sad	11.6
good	26.4	bad	8.9
fun	20.0	cry	2.3
laugh	15.2	afraid	0.8
happy	8.7	scared	0.2
love	2.9	missing	0.2
Total	144.0		24.2

Positive emotions consist of approximately 80% of all emotional words in both corpora as compared to 15% of negative emotions. The most salient of these are the contrasts in frequency of the word *love* which has a low occurrence in both corpora but more discernibly has only one instance in the SR corpus. This clause expresses the love for a family pet, which corresponds to the same affect in the AR corpus regarding animals as the target of emotional expressions. The second directional emotional verb refers to *liking* which has a ratio of 3:1 in favour of the Australian Readers. That is, half of the emotions in the AR corpus are displayed as *liking* someone or something. The SR corpus uses not only more variations of the world like (*liikot, berostan*) but also makes use of stronger emotional terms, such as *dare* (*duostat*) and the negative terms *grief* (*morras*), *boring* (*ahkit*), and *fed up* (*dolkat*). The corresponding terms in the AR corpus are the more general *sad*, *bad* and *afraid*. These words provide projections about the social environment of the two cultures. The relatively stronger negative emotional terms in the SR corpus portray the cultural reality which Samish children experience from participation in reindeer herding (the slaughtering season of reindeer) and from close contact with the elder members of the family. There are many words relating to death and dying in the SR corpus other than those denoting emotions (e.g. godda/kill, jame/die, surges/terrible) which can be seen as a natural reflection of a close Samish kinship network. Children may encounter the loss of the elder family members (i.e. grandparents) at an early age. While this realism is totally absent in the AR corpus, those negative emotional terms which are present are directed towards humans by animals, and when used by human characters the object is material rather than human (Baker & Freebody, 1989).

The portrayal of gender is also likely to be significant in a child's identity formation. A ratio of 6 to 4 male to female terms in the SR corpus corresponds to the same ratio found in the AR corpus as well as smaller text samples from others parts of the world (e.g. USA, Carroll, Davies & Richman, 1971; Canada, Luke, 1988; Indonesia, Nicholson, 1985; Singapore, Gupta & Yin, 1990). The gender division is additionally emphasized by the allocation of activities on the basis of gender as illustrated in Table 3 below.

Table 3 displays some verbs in relation to *girl/s* and *boy/s* as sentence subjects or objects. Indicated are those verbs which occur solely in connection with one gender group, that is, activities that are uniquely carried out by one gender group.

The general gender bias is also shown in the way that *girl(s)* are initiators of less activities than are *boy(s)* in both the SR and the AR corpora. This contrast is clearest in the AR corpus where *girl(s)* never occur as exclusive subjects of verb phrases. However, the Samish girls

Table 3 Verbs in relation to boy/s and girl/s as sentence subjects or objects.

	Samish		Australian	
boy/s	girl/s		boy/s	girl/s

Subject:

dahto (**want**)	fertet (**must**: aux.v)		answer	—
njuike (**jump**)	miela (**fancy**)		hurt	
dadja (**say**)	gilvu (**compete**)		shout	
daga (**let do**)	bohkosit (**burst out laughing**)		think	
leahko (**open**)	bivdimis (**chase**)		work	

Object:

dahto (**want**)	oaidnit (**look at**)		come to	hold on to
risset (**spank**)	cujuhii (**point to**)		jump with	kiss
beassat (**release**)			like	
guoddit (**carry**)			play with	
			talk to	

perform some assertive actions, for example *competing* and *killing*. The latter is a realistic illustration of village life in the SR corpus where the girls *kill* the fish which have been caught.

The cross-cultural similarities in gender bias can be illustrated by the following example from the SR corpus: while boys *let do*, girls *must*; while boys *jump*, girls *compete*; while boys *let do*, girls *fancy*; boys *look* and girls *burst out laughing*; and finally, boys *open* and girls *chase*. The unavoidable impression suggested by the above short example is that of any school yard, anywhere in the western world.

The other activity is that of the receivers, or the objects of the clause. Again, there are gender related parallels between the two corpora. In the SR texts boys are: *spanked, wanted, released* and *carried* while girls are merely *looked at* or *pointed to*. The corresponding illustration in the AR corpus is bleak, boys are: *jumped with, come to, played with* and *talked to*, whereas girls are simply *held on to* and *kissed*. In other words, boys are given not only more attention but also more demanding attention than girls in both text corpora. Thus, these brief examples illustrate the early beginning of stereotyping of sex-roles in both the Samish and the Australian cultures.

The gender bias is carried over to the adults activities in the texts of both cultures. Table 4 presents examples of verbs in clauses associated with adults in both the SR and the AR corpora.

There are similarities in the activities carried out by parents in both the Samish and Australian texts with the one exemption being the word *shout* (*bargut*) which occurs in the SR corpus. The high frequency of the word *grandparents* in the SR corpus motivated the second section in Table 4. Here a gender difference is noted in that *grandfather* is depicted

Table 4 Verbs associated with adults in the Samish and Australian corpora.

Samish		Australian
Parents:		
galget (**sort out**)		say
mannat (**go**)		have
oaidnit (**see**)		come
bargut (**shout**)		look
leigga (**play**)		
Grandparents:		
grandfather	*grandmother*	—
haviid (**hurt**)	lávlut (**sing**)	
vastidii (**answer**)	jearrat (**ask**)	
fidnet (**be busy**)	lohpidii (**promise**)	
logai (**read**)	váldit (**take**)	
Teacher:		
dádja (**say**)		say
mannat (**go**)		help
jearrat (**ask**)		write
lohkat (**read**)		read
boahta (**come**)		count
sárggut (**draw**)		weigh
muitalit (**tell**)		show

as somewhat more reserved, by mainly engaging in 'adult' type activities (reading, being busy) whereas *grandmother* engages in more verbal activities such as *singing*, *asking* and *promising*.

The activities allocated to the teacher in both cultures are similar in nature. Both cultures reinforce the authoritarian teacher role by the choice of verbs connected with intellectual activities. The generational hierarchy is thus maintained through associating *teacher/adult* with words such as *asking*, *telling*, *showing* and *helping*. Note that in neither culture does the teacher participate in leisurely activities such as *playing*, or *singing*. These are rather relegated to the home environment, where parents (and grandparents) are responsible for such behaviour.

In summary, both the Samish and Australian cultures show evidence of gender and generational divisions, through the frequencies and illustrative positions of the text characters. The protagonists are allocated tasks according to stereotypical sex role divisions which exemplify the desired normative behaviour to the reading audience.

Culture-specific Content of Texts

The Samish sample consisted of text books designed for vernacular language maintenance programmes. As stated in the above section, the curricula for minority group education is expected to reflect a desire to revive racial integrity and a dying language. The Samish text books were found to be consistent with cultural terminology promoting the distinctiveness of the Samish culture and its customs, many of which face the threat of extinction. This section displays some examples of the cultural emphasis within the SR corpus, intended to encourage the practising of Samish customs and language. Table 5 illustrates the occurrence of culture-specific terminology within the SR corpus which also promotes the enculturation of children into Samish society.

The activity most frequently described in the SR corpus is the *annual picking season of cloudberries*. Berry-picking is one of the main activities during early autumn and the manufacturing of cloudberries makes a

Table 5 Examples of culture specific terms from the Samish text corpus.

	F/10000
Activities:	
láddo (pick cloudberries)	2.93
erohus (separation of reindeer for slaughter)	0.97
cikta (patch fishnet)	0.65
Reindeer herding:	
eallu (reindeer farming life)	7.1
jeagil (lichen, reindeer feed)	2.6
muzet (dark brown reindeer)	1.6
guttii (reindeer which is producing young)	1.3
Architecture:	
goahti (home, Samish 'tepee')	8.1
lávu (tent)	7.5
loaidu (floor of goahti)	2.6
loavdda (roofing of goahti)	1.9
Food:	
luome (cloudberry)	5.2
gokebiergu (dried reindeer meat)	1.3
gumposat (bloodpudding)	0.7
Other terms:	
stálo (Samish goblin)	14.3
vuovdit (Sami of the forest)	4.5
njaveseani (women of mythological stories)	2.3
rivgu (not a Samish woman)	1.9
noaidi (shaman)	0.6

profitable form of income. The activity is reflected in the frequency of vocabulary items relating to *cloudberries* (see terms for food).

There are many terms relating to *reindeer herding life*. The realistic quality of the texts is again evident in the verb denoting the *slaughtering of reindeer* (*erohus*). The use of this term reinforces the other descriptive verbs relating to death and dying discussed earlier in this paper. Terms relating to *fishing* also occur relatively frequently in the SR corpus (e.g. *cikta/patch fishnet*).

The traditional *lávu* or *goahti* (tepee) is no longer the residence of Samish people. Rather its inclusion in recent text books is for historical education purposes. The lávu is nevertheless an identity marker for the Samis and is still occasionally in use during the summer months in the forest during reindeer herding.

The fantasy-life component which is salient in the Australian corpus is not altogether absent in the Samish school texts. Samis have a rich mythological history, which has previously been ridiculed and divested of its significance by the majority societies of the Scandinavian countries.

The recent cultural revival campaigns, however, have resulted in more mythological characters and traditional oral sagas appearing in published form, and reflected in the newer editions of teaching materials. One such example listed in Table 5 is *noaidi* or shaman believed in Samish mythology to be a chosen person with supernatural powers.

In summary, the few presented examples for culture-specific words in the SR corpus provide support for the idea that the texts provide guidelines as Samish society strives towards increased cultural integrity.

Conclusion

This study has shown how the seemingly simple story structures in children's first school readers in both Samish and Australian societies provide guidance to children of a social and cultural kind. The main contrasts in the SR and AR corpora lay in their fictional quality and cultural content. While the Australian texts contain a larger number of fictional characters and fairy-tale components, the Samish texts convey a more realistic picture of society. The Samish text books imply a serious attitude toward childhood and child culture. They portray children contributing to normal everyday activities. The Australian texts in contrast, contained a high fantasy component.

The children attending the schools in Sapmi and using the materials examined in this study face a dual form of enculturation. The attempts to assimilate children into an adult society portrayed by gender and generational inequality. The second attempts to assimilate the Sami as a minority group into the Finnish majority society. However, the dilemma in Lapland is multidimensional, as Aikio (1991) suggests. It does not seem to suffice to provide culturally relevant Samish school readers, but also to allow children to put the linguistic skills and cultural values learned from the texts into practice in the wider community. Baker & Freebody (1989) suggest this objective may be achieved by utilizing a critical approach to the study of literacy in the classroom. The teachers' role would thus consist of encouraging children to adopt an inquisitive mind about the illustrations and social norms promoted by the school text.

Note

1 This is a revised version of a paper presented at the AARE/NZARE Joint Conference 'Educational Research: Discipline and Diversity'. Deakin University, Victoria, Australia, 1992.

References

Aikio, M. (1988) *Saamelaiset Kielenvaihdon Kierteessä* (The cycle of language shift among the Sami). Helsinki: Suomalaisen Kirjallisuuden Seura.

—— (1991) The Sami language: Pressure of change and reification. *Journal of Multilingual and Multicultural Development* 12 (1 & 2), 93–103.

Baker, C. and Freebody, P. (1989) *Children's First School Books*. Oxford: Basil Blackwell.

Carrol, J.B., Davies, P. and Richman, B. (1971) *The American Heritage Word Frequency Book*. New York: Houghton Miffin Co.

Christie, F. (1991) *Beyond Bilingual Education: A Look at Some Aspects of Aboriginalization*. Unpublished paper. Darwin: Northern Territory University.

Cummins, J. (1985) *Disabling Minority Students: Power, Programs and Pedagogy*. Unpublished paper. Toronto: Ontario Institute for Education.

Department of Education (1987) *P/10 Frameworks*. Queensland.

Fairclough, N. (1989) *Language and Power*. London: Longman.

Gupta, A.F. and Lee Su Yin, A. (1989) Gender representation in English textbooks used in the Singapore primary schools. *Language and Education* 4 (1), 29–50.

Harris, S. (1989) *Alternative Aboriginal literature*. Paper presented at the Joint Australian Reading Association for The Teaching of English, Darwin, National Conference.

Lankshear, C. and Lawler, M. (1989) *Literacy, Schooling and Revolution*. London: Falmer Press.

Lauren, U. (1987) The linguistic competence of mono- and bilingual pupils in Swedish in the Finland-Swedish school. *Journal of Multilingual and Multicultural Development* 8, 83–94.

Luke, A. (1988) *Literacy, Textbooks and Ideology*. London: Falmer Press.

Nicholson, G. (1985) *A Comparison of Some Differences in Methods of Enculturation Used by Authors of Children's School Reading Books*. Unpublished Masters dissertation. NSW, Australia, University of New England.

Sachs, W. (1992) One world against many worlds. *New Internationalist* 232, 23–5.

Samish Board of Education (1990) *Annual Education Plans*. Finland: Sodankylä.

Skutnabb-Kangas, T. (1990) Language, literacy and minorities. A minority rights group report. British Library publication data UK.

Skutnabb-Kangas, T. and Cummins, J. (eds) (1988) *Minority Education: From Shame to Struggle*. Clevedon: Multilingual Matters.

13 Roles, Networks, and Values in Everyday Writing[1]

DAVID BARTON and SARAH PADMORE

In this article, we want to make sense of people's everyday writing. We will do this by investigating a particular group of adults: documenting what writing they do and finding out what value it holds for them, examining what they do if they experience problems, and seeing how writing fits into the rest of their lives.

The research reported here is just one part of a larger study in which we are building a general picture of the role of literacy in people's everyday lives in Lancaster, a small city in northwest England. As part of the study, we have carried out 20 interviews of local people. We are now carrying out more detailed case studies of a few families going about their everyday lives. We have observed how their home uses of literacy fit in with the demands of children at school, differing literacy demands at home and at work, and what people do when they identify problems of reading and writing. We are carrying out general observations of reading and writing in the local community; finding out what people read and write in shops, the post office, the hospital, and so on; and examining the 'visual environment' of advertisements, street signs, notices. Finally, we are collecting recorded data on access points for literacy: the history and use of libraries and bookshops in the city, provision of adult literacy tuition, school records, and so on. We aim to build up an overall picture of the significance of literacy in people's lives. Elsewhere, we intend to write more extensively about other aspects of literacy, about the general background of Lancaster, and about the significance of this for adult basic education. In this article, we concentrate on information from these interviews and particularly on the significance of *writing* in these people's lives.

Most studies of literacy are concerned with children and with educational settings. Only a few studies have begun to examine the role of literacy in people's lives, including adults' actual uses of reading and writing and their attitudes to the awareness of literacy. Three key studies in this area are those of Heath (1983), Street (1984), and Scribner & Cole (1981). Briefly, Heath (1983) developed close ties with three Appalachian communities in the United States over seven years and used ethnographic and sociolinguistic methods to provide detailed descriptions of people's uses of reading and writing in the home and in the community. Street (1984) studied Islamic villagers in Iran; he lived there as an anthropologist and carried out ethnographic field work. As part of this, he observed two literacies being used side by side in the community, one he terms 'commercial' and the other '*maktab*'—that of the traditional Koranic school. He documents how commercial literacy emerged out of skills developed in the traditional context of religious education. His concern is to describe different literacies rather than putting the usual emphasis on a single school-based model of literacy. Scribner and Cole (1981) have studied literacy among the Vai of West Africa, using a battery of cross-cultural psychological tests along with interviews and observations of the community. They provide detailed descriptions of forms of literacy that are learned informally and that exist outside the educational system.

There are other, smaller studies that contribute to this approach. Fingeret (1983) in the United States has studied adult literacy students and the social networks they establish, paying particular attention to different social roles people have. Moll (1989) was studying how networks act as funds of knowledge. Rockhill (1987) and Horsman (1987) have examined literacy in women's lives. Fishman (1991) has examined literacy in an Amish community. Klassen (1991) has examined the uses of literacy in bilingual communities. Similarly, Reder (1985) has worked with Inuit and Hispanic communities. Levine (1985) has studied people with low levels of literacy and the problems they have encountered in obtaining work. Taylor (1985) and Taylor & Dorsey-Gaines (1988) have used ethnographic methods to study literacy within the family. Other examples of research in the United States using ethnographic approaches are described in Schieffelin and Gilmore (1986) and in Langer (1987). Studies focusing on writing outside of educational contexts, referred to as 'nonacademic writing', include Doheny-Farina & Odell (1985), Faigley (1985), and Stotsky (1987).

Two recent studies we have carried out in Lancaster provide further background to this study. First, we examined oral history data of working-class people born around the turn of the century in northwest England, drawing together what they said about reading, writing, and education and using their words to build up a composite picture of the significance of literacy in their culture (see Barton, 1988). We have information on the extent of their literacy, what they used reading and writing for, and their attitudes and expectations related to literacy. To give one brief example of the findings: Literacy was given a moral value by them, it was a 'good thing'; what people read was often religious in nature; and there was moral censorship of what children were allowed to read. These findings can act as a starting point for examining contemporary attitudes to and beliefs about literacy. If we turn to the uses of literacy in the Lancaster community today, we find, for example, that the moral attitude toward literacy and the censorship of what children read still exists but that it seems to have a less explicit religious basis.

Second, Hamilton (1987) analyzed data from a large-scale longitudinal study of a sample of the population of Britain (the National Child Development Study), focusing on reported difficulties in reading, writing, and arithmetic. The study provides a national overview of reading and writing problems that people encounter in their everyday lives. Its breadth provides a useful context for the detailed ethnographic approach proposed here. In this study, there were far more people who expressed problems with writing than those who said they had problems with reading. This imbalance is probably not reflected in adult literacy provision: Most programs emphasize learning to read, although now often more stress is laid upon developing writing.

The Interviews

Lancaster is a city of 47,000 people, a few miles from the coast in northwest England. It was formally a mill town. The collapse of the manufacturing industry has left a legacy of unemployment. Most people who have jobs work at one of the large Victorian hospitals, at the power station, at the university, or in the retail trade. Lancaster is also an ancient market town, serving a large rural area, and is developing as a tourist centre.

The adults we interviewed were all people who had been educated locally in Lancashire, mostly in Lancaster itself, who had left school at the minimum age, 15 or 16 years. They had all left school with no qualifications, although some had since gained qualifications. Most of them had identified problems with reading and writing at some time in their adult lives and had attended the local literacy programme. Thirteen were currently attending basic education courses at the literacy program; five of them had gone on from basic education courses to other courses. Further details of the twenty people interviewed together with some indication of their levels of literacy are given in the Appendix.

Our intention when designing the interview was that it should be like an oral history interview. There were topics we wanted to cover but we also wanted to allow for the possibility of issues arising that we had not thought of beforehand. The topics to be covered came initially from our own research (such as Barton, 1988), from that of others (such as Heath, 1983), and from our experience of working in and talking to people in basic education. We added questions and dropped others after trying out the interview and going through it with participants from a research methods course.

In the end, the interview contained 160 questions, several of which had subdivisions. They were divided into groups, roughly following the sections we use to discuss the results below. We should emphasize that we did not keep rigorously to these questions in the interviews. The aim of each interview was to encourage people to talk freely about the part literacy plays in their lives. The topics were not covered in any particular order and the interview schedule was used by the interviewer to make sure that the topics we were interested in were discussed.

Each interview lasted around two hours and all but one of the interviews took place in the local adult education college, which was familiar to all the people interviewed. Everyone interviewed had met the interviewer previously, and most knew her well; she had been a teacher at the local literacy programme for the previous six years. Some people were interviewed twice. In the second interview, we were able to pick up information we had not covered in the first interview or to pursue topics we wished to know more about; we also found that the interviewees had thought more about the topics in the intervening time and, having had time to mull them over or discuss them with relatives, would arrive with further information for us. They all seemed to enjoy the interview process and welcomed the opportunity to talk about themselves and reflect on their lives with an attentive listener. No one seemed surprised at the interest we were taking in everyday details of their lives. The interviews were tape-recorded and later transcribed.

Writing

There is not a straightforward way to analyze and bring together qualitative data from 20 intensive interviews. We have analyzed our data in terms of several themes. They provide a rich way of identifying significant aspects of the context of literacy that need to be incorporated into any theory of literacy learning. The set of themes comes from the view of literacy as a social practice: Some themes were implicit in our interview questions, others came from our analysis of the interview transcripts. In this chapter, first, we document what people actually write in their everyday lives, including what, where, when, and with what they write; we situate these activities as part of *social practices*. As components of these practices, we examine particular *roles* people take and how writing varies in importance as people's roles change. We then move on to the *networks* of support in which people participate. This leads on to what *value* literacy holds for them. We will examine each of these themes in turn, documenting the role of writing in these people's lives.

Social practices

In our interviews, we obtained a great deal of information about what people write in going about their day-to-day lives. Much of the writing they reported consisted of memory aids for themselves or of messages for others, helping them to organize themselves and their households. All these categories overlap because a note on a notice board, for example, can act as a memory aid and a message at the same time. We refer to this area of writing loosely as *writing to maintain the household*, and we will deal with this first. Another general area, which we will deal with next, is *writing to maintain communication*, and a third area we observed in our data is *personal writing*.

We asked people questions about their household record keeping. One or two people ringed dates or wrote down appointments on wall calendars; one of them, Liz, wrote on a calendar in her own 'personal shorthand.' (We will use pseudonyms throughout when referring to the people we interviewed.) Five others stuck reminders straight to the wall or pinned them to a notice board. But a third of those questioned about appointments and reminders said that they never wrote any down at all.

Very few people used appointment diaries although several owned them, and two, Pat and Ruth, used out-of-date diaries for other purposes: Pat recorded how well he had done at clay pigeon shooting or made notes about his physical training courses in an old and unused diary of his daughter's, and Ruth used a childhood diary to write shopping lists until someone suggested that she was 'spoiling' it. Neil started using a diary for the first time when he went to work at a chain store, 'A diary reminds you where and what you've got to do' he remarked, but on another occasion he talked of finding his own notes difficult to make sense of, and it is not clear whether he actually did have more to remember in this job than the jobs he had had in the past.

Seven people said they had notice boards in their homes, although two were not using them—Paul's was lying in the cellar and Lesley's was lying on top of a wardrobe. Those who used them mentioned doing so for appointments, messages, lists of tasks needing doing, and the like. People's uses for notice boards varied considerably; Cath, who lives alone, had at least two notice boards. Her initial response was 'Yes, millions of them!' On her downstairs notice board, she listed domestic repairs that needed doing, 'but the bedroom one's more for pleasure' and that had more personal displays and lists of local entertainment. There were also two notice boards in Pat's household although neither had anything to do with him: one displayed things relating to his wife's work as a nurse and the other was in his daughter's bedroom: Pat remarked, 'She probably needs it more than us because she forgets things.' Rita's simply had dental and medical appointments and the occasional card from a friend, and Ruth's had great lists and timetables, mostly relating to her children's many hobbies and activities.

Pat is a good example of someone who said he led a very busy life but never felt the need to write himself reminders of dates and times. He had a full-time manual job at the local power station and a part-time evening job as a 'keep fit' instructor. He had various hobbies and interests that involved him in different clubs and organizations. He also did odd jobs for a number of elderly people in the community and had a reputation for being someone who can find out things—someone to go to if you have a problem. Although Pat was not unique in having the ability to 'keep them in me head'—good memories and literacy difficulties can go hand in hand—there were others in the interview who identified both problems with literacy and with memory. Ruth, who also led a busy life, suggested that it was so important for her to get appointments written down that she would write on anything that came to hand; it was not uncommon for her to write on a paperback book if she had one in her bag.

In some households, written messages of some sort or another were common and would be left in a set place known to family members, such as stuck to the fridge with magnets. But in other homes written messages were virtually unknown. Whether or not people left messages for each other did not appear to be indication of the amount of other writing done in the home. In addition, everyone interviewed appeared to keep writing materials in their homes. People could often identify a place in their houses where they could always find scrap paper for messages, and they said that they also had pens and pencils lying around. Each person's answer was slightly different. Often the paper was old envelopes kept in a particular drawer or scraps of paper or a memo pad kept by the telephone.

Most people made shopping lists of some sort, although they did not necessarily use them. There seem to be many ways to use a shopping list, and our informal observation of the local market and supermarket suggests, maybe surprisingly, that people do not tend to consult a shopping list while actually shopping. Julie remembers watching her mother making shopping lists as a child; this was the only writing she recalls her mother ever doing. One or two people made daily plans of 'things to do that day.' Andrea reported that she regularly wrote out shopping lists twice and suggested that she got on everyone's nerves with her perpetual list making. Her mother still criticized her for needing to make lists at all: 'Can't you remember things!'

Turning to *writing to maintain communication*, several people did some regular writing, such as writing letters to friends or relatives who do not live nearby. Rita commented that she had no need to write letters to family or friends 'because we all live local.' Liz, who had friends and relatives living away from the area, said she wished she could write letters more but did not feel able to: 'It's the spelling.' However, she did have one friend with whom she corresponded: 'Dilys makes me 'cos she knows [about Liz's literacy difficulties]. She knows and she accepts it so it's not too bad.' More common was keeping up relations with people by the regular sending of cards. Several people reported keeping a Christmas card list and/or list of people's birthdays and anniversaries. Other people also reported having corresponded with relatives at times when they lived away from Lancaster. When writing letters, 12 people said they sometimes wrote drafts or rough copies of things they were writing, which included personal letters, and only two of them mentioned letters of application for jobs. We were left with a general impression that rewriting is not an uncommon literacy activity in the home.

A third area of everyday writing we identified was *personal writing*, something people did for themselves and not for communicative purposes. We cannot get a feel of how common personal writing is in this community, and, because they were contacted via a college, the people we talked to are unlikely to be representative in this respect. Nevertheless, in this group of twenty people, we were surprised at the number who do some personal writing in their everyday lives. This took various forms, including poems, diaries, and stories. As adults, at least nine of those interviewed had written at least one poem that had nothing to do with their college work; some wrote poems or 'short pieces'; three people, Roger, Cath, and Julie, talked about writing down their thoughts; two, Lesley and Dick, had kept personal diaries for around a year.

During the period when we were interviewing, we came across two men, not included in our interviews, who composed poetry but did not write it down. One of them, an older man, had been composing poems in his head for several years, which, because he was unable to write, he had been dictating to his daughter; he came to college specifically to learn to write down his poems himself. Both men performed their poems informally in the community. These do not seem to be isolated instances.

People keep all sorts of records of themselves and their lives. Although keeping a personal diary seemed quite rare, there were people who at some point in their lives had kept a diary. Lesley had written a diary for 12 months after the birth of one of her children; Andrea and Frances had kept diaries when they were children; and Andrea was currently keeping a monthly record of her infant niece's development. Andrea's childhood diary had been a fictitious record of day-to-day life at a stables.

People had definite places for keeping personal writing, and there is a sense of secrecy about much of it. Julie saved hers in dated envelopes and put them away in a box; as a teenager, she recalls hiding secret writings in a Tampax box, a private place. Roger kept his writing in a file as well as keeping other spoken thoughts on cassettes; Dick had given his personal diary to his ex-wife and told her, 'This is for when I'm gone.' He had apologized for sounding melodramatic but was serious and trusted his wife not to open it. Andrea stored no writing apart from college work, but, in the past, when she had an office job, she sometimes used to read the thoughts and bits of conversation that she had typed on the end of spoiled letters aloud to the other women in the office before throwing them in the bin. Cath has been storing her own personal writing under her mattress since she was an 18-year-old, but she did once send a poem of her daughter's to a magazine. Finding a place to keep writing relates to other social practices to do with personal space—both mental and physical—that people have within the household; we hope to return to this in later work.

We asked people questions about where and when they wrote, and these were accepted as reasonable questions to ask. People tended to have a regular time and place for writing: Mark always did any writing he needed to do in his bedroom directly after tea; Cath always wrote letters at around 6 a.m.; Val always got her writing done right after breakfast or at night; Lynne wrote in the afternoons. People often wrote in a place and at a time when they could be by themselves, and, although several talked of needing quiet, four reported writing in the living room in the evening while other people were watching television.

People often identified a particular type of pen and special paper. Half of those questioned about paper said that it must be lined; two felt the quality of paper was important; and one, Andrea, had strong feelings about colour. Only three, Pat, Neil, and Liz, expressed no special interest in the paper they used. Most people cared about pens too and were able to describe why they had a particular preference and how different pens affected their writing; everyone had something different to say about pens.

Finally, there is a problem in trying to make generalizations about people's literacy practices, and there is a limit to the extent to which we can do this. The overall frequency of the practices we have described is hard to ascertain in most cases but we do know that Andrea, Ruth, and Cath chose to sit down and write every day; Ruth's writing was personal creative writing; the minimum that Andrea and Cath did each day was to chart the following day's activities, writing out things to be done. Another difficulty when trying to ascertain general patterns is that everyone seemed to have their own practices, something unique about the way they used writing. To give some examples, Lynne had recently written a poem for a neighbour going into hospital, to let her know that someone cared for her and was thinking of her. Paul regularly left joking messages for his partner, for example, a note saying 'empty' in the bottom of an empty tea tin. Andrea, going through a difficult period with her partner, was communicating with him almost solely through messages left around the house. Julie said she had 'pinched' bits and pieces of published poetry to put in love letters; Rita had composed a poem for the first time in her life when separated from a boyfriend and sent the poem to him in a card.

Roles

When people talked about the writing they did within the household and beyond it, it was often in terms of roles; they referred to themselves as parents, relatives, workers, neighbours, friends—each role making differing literacy demands upon them. One clear role differentiation that was apparent within the household was that between men and women. Usually this followed the common division of women writing in the personal sphere while men dealt with the official world. We had many examples of this. If we take the example of dealing with household correspondence, everyone interviewed played some part in this but in most homes, other than wholly male set-ups, letter and card writing tended to be seen as the woman's responsibility, while dealing with forms and bills was the man's.

Two factors we observed that could affect these roles were problems with literacy and employment. An example of someone with literacy problems was Dick, who left everything to do with money to his wife when they were living together. He said that this was because she was 'a good manager' while he was a 'spendthrift.' However, we noticed that, even in partnerships where the woman found all aspects of literacy easier than the man, and in cases where the man could barely read or write at all, he would still have a definite role to play in dealing with anything of a financial nature; even if, as with Neil, this amounted to was asking the bank to pay bills directly, or like Bob, who said firmly, 'I'll sort them out, who to pay, and she'll write them.'

Arranging the payment of bills was typically done by the men. This may have been connected with the man being the main breadwinner. When the woman was the main breadwinner, the roles sometimes changed, but when Bob was out of work and his wife was employed, for example, he continued to be responsible for organizing bills, even though anything involving literacy was quite difficult for him and both partners must have realized that Frances would have been quite capable of sorting the bills herself.

In Paul's male household, correspondence appeared to be similarly divided; Paul was the card sender and left bills to his partner, who provided the main income. Andrea also mentioned her lack of personal income as the reason for playing no part in bill paying. In his childhood home, Paul recalls that his father dealt with the bills: 'Well, he would leave bills that weren't paid by standing order for my mother literally to take money in the book to be paid, but I think he'd brief her very carefully on something like that.'

These literacy practices can be situated as part of broader gender roles in personal relations and relate to power in the home. Paying bills or organizing their payment is not just any household task; it would seem to represent something far more significant. To some extent, it seems to be a measure of how important such activities are perceived to be. This is true of family finances. It depends on whether they are regarded as a crucial part of negotiating with the outside world or, to use Rockhill's phrase, whether they are seen as being 'part of the housework.'

Changing roles

Roles are not static. We saw examples of how writing played a part in people's changing lives. For example, coming to college seemed to affect people's roles. It was not simply a question of people coming to college in order to change their lives deliberately. Rather, there seemed to be a complex interaction of people coming to college and, once there, discovering new possibilities for themselves, realizing from the new opportunities they came across that things could change.

We can see this best by looking at one example in detail. In Lynne's home, male and female roles were starting to change as Lynne developed her writing skills at college. When she had started there three years before, she had often asked her husband, who apparently had no difficulty himself, for help and guidance; at first, he was encouraging but, as her 'hobby' developed, he became less supportive. At first, she used to read her stories to him; but the more involved she became, the less patience he had with her writing and the 'willing ear' of the early days finally closed altogether. Rockhill has discussed this, commenting on how literacy can become a threat when the learning skills become education. Secretarial roles are encouraged, while creative writing is a threat.

Lynne expressed some sympathy with her husband's feelings and was very sensitive to the possibility of his feeling 'shut out'; she said that she rationed the amount of course work she did when he was at home and, presumably because this had caused friction in the past, avoided retiring upstairs to get on with her writing, although this was something she would have loved to have done. We can contrast this with the attitude toward other activities such as tending the garden, which Lynne also spent a lot of time doing: Gardening was seen by both partners as something that would benefit the family as a whole, whereas writing was seen as something of a threat, encroaching as it did on family activities, such as sitting down together, chatting, watching television, and threatening family members' relative status.

Lynne's husband had started asking her to deal with his correspondence, such as filling in tax returns. She said that she could hardly believe that she was now working sums out for her husband. At his request, she had started drafting letters for him to copy. It was unlikely that either of them would have dreamed of suggesting this several years earlier; so, although Lynne still tended to defer to her husband's needs and decision making, their literacy roles were changing significantly.

Another example of change in people's lives is children going to school. People's roles changed and this was often the time when they decided to go back to college as adults; also, several of the people we interviewed wanted life to be different for their children. Both Cath and Julie articulated this strongly, and it was also expressed by other people with children. Cath left school with no qualifications. She was drawn into education while bringing up her children. She made a great effort to get her children to read, choosing books for them and helping them with their homework. Her husband appeared to have played no part in this. She saw it as 'the only way out of the poverty trap for the children,' and, in fact, both her children had gone on to university education. Julie expressed herself as being desperate that her children should have the benefits of education; education had 'opened up a new world' for her, different than the one provided by her mother. She was concerned about her grandchild as she did not feel her daughter was 'doing enough with books.'

Networks

In our data, we can see clearly that social networks of support exist for people. These networks are part of everyday life whether or not people have problems. Sometimes there was support for people who identified problems. Often it was within the family. Neil, Paul, and Bob all mentioned getting help from their partners. Mark took writing problems to his sister, while Duncan relied on his parents. Liz got help from her husband and her daughter as well as from a friend who worked 40 miles away. Sometimes particular people were chosen for help; Julie's mother would approach an uncle 'because he worked in an office'—one of several examples where work skills extend into the home. When Sally got married, she found that there were many everyday tasks she could not deal with, and she turned to her mother to help her learn the new writing tasks.

These networks of support extend out into the community and include asking for help in post offices, shops, and banks. Most people we interviewed reported having seen people receiving help in the town centre, and our own observations back this up. When we asked people if they knew people in the neighbourhood who provided support, there were examples. Leslie's mother-in-law worked in a news agent's shop and was known to help customers writing greeting cards. These would be regular customers, often elderly people. She would help them choose cards, read the messages to them, and sometimes write the cards for them. To these customers, she was acting as a literacy broker. Although we did not particularly ask about skills exchanges, there were examples in which the people we interviewed helped others with literacy as a part of some other strength they had to offer. We will give two examples in which the people interviewed were used for support, even though they did not have particularly high levels of literacy. Julie said that people came to her for emotional advice and literacy:

> Neighbours, when their marriages were in trouble, they would come to me and then the forms would follow on the problem. Or filling in forms for kids for school holidays or, how to get money for free school uniform or bus passes. I was quite well known for being able to sort out that kind of thing. It's because I'm a bit of a busybody really.

While Cath, who had always painted as a hobby and had a long history of enjoying writing for writing's sake, recalled how her 'copying' was the neatest in the class when she was a child and was now quite often called upon by people in her local community to make signs or posters for them; she was also well known locally as someone to go for do-it-yourself advice. Neither of these women felt totally confident about their own literacy skills but Julie felt quite confident in handing out advice and Cath felt quite confident about her 'do-it-yourself' and her artwork.

Pat, like Julie, had become someone who people turned to for literacy help. People did not come to his house for advice, but in tea and dinner breaks at work he often assisted people with filling out forms or making sense of public service information documents. He also got information for them. He said that he was good at finding out things because there were not many stuations that he had not been through himself. Pat confronted people with their literacy difficulties. He said that it was not so much that they confided in him but his ability to tell, just by talking to people, whether they had problems. At the age of 31, Liz became a store detective despite difficulties with the writing needed for the job, and a friend gave her some help writing her reports. The friend explained that the reports were basically written to a formula, and she showed Liz how to rely on a few stock phrases and sentences. A slightly different form of support was mentioned by Val, who took phone messages for her sister who lived round the corner and had no phone; similarly Sally's mother took phone messages for her.

It is important to emphasize that often, because these networks exist, problems do not arise. People live within these networks and go about their lives without particularly identifying problems with reading and writing. Often it was when these networks were disrupted that people were confronted with problems, and this was sometimes given as a reason for coming to basic education classes. Lesley, for example, had lived near her relatives for some time outside Lancaster. She reported that several of her relatives had problems with reading and writing but that they supported each other. Her description of her life then is what Fingeret (1983) refers to as an 'interdependent' life. It was only when she moved to Lancaster itself, away from her network of relatives, even though it was a fairly short move, that Lesley felt the need to improve her reading and writing. When she moved outside of her established social network, in many ways her life turned to being more of a 'dependent' life in Fingeret's terms.

Values

When people talked about writing, everything they said was imbued with values and attitudes. They evaluated themselves and others and talked about the power of writing, its pleasure or its difficulty.

First, we can look at how they see themselves. Neil, for example, was a section manager at a branch of a food store chain and had great difficulty writing. He was sent to courses in which he trained with people who had passed all sorts of examinations. He didn't understand how he could talk and work so easily alongside these people who could produce pages and pages of writing effortlessly while he struggled to make a sentence. When discussing writing letters to the newspaper, two people, Pat and Bob, suggested it was laziness on their part that prevented them from writing such letters; Roger, on the other hand, said, 'It seems such a long, laborious task to write it out and then send it and then see if they're going to write it out,' implying the fault was in the process rather than himself. It is interesting that Bob commented, 'I must be a lazy sort of person' because his typical response to questions about writing was that he couldn't write. Like Pat, he was orally articulate and cared passionately about local and national issues.

Several people referred to 'people with problems'—meaning other people, not themselves. Val, for example, had never really thought of herself as having literacy difficulties at all; she enrolled in a basic education course in the hope that she would increase her vocabulary. In her parish work, she found she was mixing with other church people who talked in a language she could not understand; she said that all the long words they used were making her feel inadequate and this was the main reason for her joining classes. Liz reported a change over the years in her attitude to writing and, looking back, appeared surprised by her past courage in applying for jobs and dealing with problems. A few years earlier, she was apparently unconcerned by her difficulty but now even refuses to write a shopping list because she might drop it and someone might discover it.

Two out of twenty people interviewed commented that they got no pleasure whatsoever out of writing, and several others expressed negative attitudes. Neil and Bob did not get any enjoyment from writing; for them, the process was too laborious and they were frustrated by what they saw as the inadequacy of their written work. Pat wrote only out of a sense of duty: 'I feel I should, you know . . . I don't like it 'cos I'm not that good.' Liz echoed Pat's words, saying she did not enjoy writing because she could not do it. Duncan also sometimes found writing 'a pain,' when he knew what he wanted to say but could not find the words to express it. Like Pat and Sally, he preferred reading to writing. Three people felt they could express themselves better writing than speaking: Lynne, Dick, and Andrea. Dick also said he took 'comfort in writing down things instead of saying them.' This was in contrast to Andrea, who usually wrote down things in order to say them. Lynne is perhaps closer: 'I can write things down what I feel or want to say but can't say verbally because I'm embarrassed.'

Lesley and Roger definitely preferred writing to reading. Perhaps, as Pat commented, 'That's like most people—what they're good at they like, what they're not good at, they don't.' Lesley had always enjoyed writing. She was adamant that she really enjoyed writing before she was able to make any sense of reading and, in fact, still struggles with reading: 'Mmm, I'd scribble on and on. Some of it didn't make sense 'cos spellings weren't right and stuff, but I knew what it were all about— I love writing,' And Roger, who avoided reading because he found it difficult, spent a lot of his spare time recording personal thoughts and answered 'definitely' when asked if he enjoyed writing. Frances said that she enjoyed writing for herself but not for other people, and at work it worried her when she was expected to write letters.

Only four of the people questioned about writing processes, Liz, Neil, Pat, and Paul, did not mention the look of handwriting or neatness as being important to them; possibly in their cases other considerations such as spelling and self-expression simply overrode any thought of presentation. Although Neil wrote drafts and top copies, it was the content of the top copy he mentioned rather than the look of it, 'I still know it doesn't make sense to a lot . . . what other people will think. I've always known that.'

People's awareness of the value of writing was apparent when they talked about writing to the newspaper. Seven of the eight people who commented on whether they had ever written or thought of writing to the newspapers or television about anything said they had thought of it and gave examples of the kind of things they would like to write in about. Pat was angry about a local environmental issue, a meat processing business that wafts nauseous smells across the city: 'If we all wrote, we'd probably get something done,' he suggested. But in this belief he was unusual; the power to effect change through letter writing was not a belief that was typically expressed: more often, they voiced a fatalistic view of the world. Some, however, managed to discover power for themselves in writing.

Lynne was very aware of the power of writing. Recently, an item in the news about an incident in Ireland had made her furious. She felt a tremendous urge to vent her anger in a letter to a newspaper, but she didn't write it: 'You'd be scared of what you might write . . . . Once it's written down it's recorded.' Lynne said that this news item was the first thing she had ever wanted to write to the papers about: 'The first time I'd ever felt I would want to write something down and voice my own opinion.' Writing was also used as part of acts of resistance. At one time, when Andrea had an office job, she used to find she was adding paragraphs of personal writing, often commentary on things that were happening in the office, to letters she was supposed to be copying for her boss, or, if she was in a bad mood, she would express her fury in angry type print. She always threw away these writings, which she referred to as 'doodles.'

Lesley had difficulty writing; neither she nor her husband had ever written a note to school about any of her three children. The only letter she could remember writing was to complain about a family holiday because 'it weren't same as it said in brochure'; it is very unlikely that, at the time she wrote this letter, before starting basic education classes, she could actually have read what it said in the brochure herself. Since the interview, she has begun to discover the power of writing. She wrote a letter of appeal to the local education office pleading for her eldest child to be given a place at the secondary school of her choice, and she won her case. She reported that she was very pleased with the result of her letter.

Again, when we examine values, we can identify common attitudes as well as see individual ways of incorporating literacy into people's lives.

Two people expressed opposite views on the relation between writing and personal problems. One person, Dick, used writing to cope with changes in his life, involving illness, unemployment, and separation, and he kept a diary for 12 months. 'It was putting in a diary, putting on paper what I couldn't say. It was a good idea . . . but it drained me . . . mainly private thoughts.' It was the first time since leaving school that he had written anything except applications for jobs. On the other hand, another person, Rita, had the opposite reaction to the role of writing and personal problems: 'You can't read and write when you are going through a bad time.' When her husband left her and her mother died, she felt she was living on her 'nerves' and she never picked up a book or a pen.

A third person, Ruth, talked of excessive personal writing actually having contributed to a relative's mental breakdown and said she had to limit herself in her writing, not so much because she was afraid of the same thing happening to her but because she felt the family might start watching her anxiously. This contrasted interestingly with Andrea's personal use of writing when she was angry or worried; Andrea wrote down what she was going to say before an argument or tricky confrontation precisely because she was scared of what she might say. Writing provided a safety valve for her, a means of careful rehearsal; she felt safe when she wrote.

Two people, Ruth and Andrea, wrote continually, every day; Ruth sat down each evening and wrote for an hour or two, doing personal writing; she also mentioned poetry going round in her head in the middle of the night, which she would love to have jotted down but didn't because she was always too tired. Andrea made daily lists and plans and enjoyed 'rabbling on' to friends in letters.

Conclusion

We are partway through our work; nevertheless, we have something to say about writing in our local community: In a group of adults, many of whom have experienced problems with writing, there are identifiable uses of writing. Writing has a place in maintaining the household and in maintaining communication, and a proportion of them did some regular personal writing. In situating their literacy practices as part of social practices, there were clear roles with respect to literacy that people took, and these roles existed within established networks of support. People expressed attitudes about the power of writing and the relative value of writing compared with other activities. They also held strong conceptions of the nature of language and literacy and of the differences in function between spoken and written language. We intend to pursue this work, relating what we have found out about writing to other aspects of literacy and using other sources of data to build up a fuller picture of the role of literacy in people's everyday lives.

Appendix

Here we provide details of the 20 people who were interviewed, with some indication of their levels of literacy.

(1) *Cath:* aged 47, separated, two grown-up children, lives alone, works part-time, in a dairy; at time of interview was attending WEA women's group; reads broadly and writes for pleasure but asks for help with forms.

(2) *Roger:* 32, single, lives with parents; unemployed; has attended basic education classes since 1981; some difficulties with spelling and punctuation; recently started writing for pleasure at home; avoids reading.

(3) *Julie:* 45, separated, two grown-up children and one grandchild; lives alone, unemployed, attending WEA women's group at time of interview; reads broadly and writes for pleasure; sometimes turns to children for advice.

(4) *Ray:* 33, single, lives alone, works part-time as a cleaner and has attended basic education classes for a number of years; likes support when writing unless copying but is more confident about reading.

(5) *Lesley:* 34, lives with partner and three primary school age children; works part-time as a cleaner/child minder; has attended basic education classes for two years; enjoys writing but dislikes reading.

(6) *Val:* 42, single, lives with elderly relative, unemployed at time of interview but doing voluntary work for the church; has attended basic education classes for two years; reads quite broadly and quite enjoys writing.

(7) *Lynne:* 34, lives with husband and three children, works part-time (cooks, cleans, and serves in fast-food shop); attends basic education classes; enjoys both reading and writing.

(8) *Mark:* 20, single, lives with parents, works in a printers; has attended basic education for two years, now about to go to Art college; dislikes writing because he has difficulty spelling but has just started to enjoy novels.

(9) *Duncan:* 24, lives with parents (at time of interview), single, unemployed; attends basic education classes; some general writing difficulties but enjoys computer work and medical books; went to a special school.

(10) *Liz:* 39, lives with partner, two grown-up children; unemployed at time of interview and attending basic education classes; reads newspapers and novels but has some real problems with writing.

(11) *Sally:* 25, separated, lives with brother; unemployed and attending basic education classes, some writing difficulties but reads widely; came to college to take mind off physical condition—rheumatoid arthritis.

(12) *Rita:* 37, separated, lives with teenage daughter, part-time cleaner/caretaker, attends basic education classes; some writing difficulties but reads novels occasionally; came to classes for social reasons.

(13) *Pat:* 44, lives with partner and child by previous marriage; full-time manual worker; has attended basic education classes in the past; taught himself to read after leaving school, now reads broadly but avoids writing.

(14) *Neil:* 26, lives with partner and primary school child; full-time supermarket worker; attends basic education classes; can read but has real difficulties writing.

(15) *Dick:* Around 40, separated, one child; lives in room in another family's house, unemployed due to physical ailment; presently attends open college classes (ex-basic education student); reads broadly and has enjoyed writing.

(16) *Ruth:* 36, lives with partner and three children; unemployed and attends basic education classes as a step to other classes; wants to become a nurse; writes for pleasure everyday, has some writing difficulties.

(17) *Paul:* 25, lives with partner, has attended basic education classes for several years; took access courses and is now on a degree course; reads widely and enjoys writing 'short pieces' for pleasure.

(18) *Bob:* 36, lives with partner and two children; full-time builder, has attended basic education in past and has real difficulties with reading and writing but doesn't worry about them.

(19) *Frances:* 35, lives with partner and two children; full-time clerical worker, has attended basic education classes in the past; no obvious problems but doesn't read much; enjoyed creative writing at college.

(20) *Andrea:* 32, lives with partner and one child (primary school); unemployed at present, attends basic education classes; can type, enjoys reading, and loves writing; talks of herself as a compulsive writer.

Note

1. This research has been supported in part with a grant from the University Research Fund of Lancaster University awarded to David Barton and in part with a grant from the Economic and Social Research Council R000-23-1419 awarded to David Barton and Mary Hamilton. The interviews were carried out by Sarah Padmore. We are grateful to Mary Hamilton, Roz Ivanič, and Brian Street for comments on earlier drafts of this chapter.

References

Barton, D. (1988) Exploring the historical basis of contemporary literacy. *Quarterly Newsletter of the Laboratory of Comparative Human Cognition* 10(3), 70–6.

Doheny-Farina, S. and Odell, L. (1985) Ethnographic research on writing: Assumptions and methodology. In L. Odell and D. Goswami (eds) *Writing in Non-academic Settings*. New York: Guilford.

Faigley, L. (1985) Non-academic writing: The social perspective. In L. Odell and D. Goswami (eds) *Writing in Non-academic Settings*. New York: Guilford.

Fingeret, A. (1983) Social networks, independence and adult illiterates. *Adult Education Quarterly* 33(3), 133–46.

Fishman, A. (1991) Because this is who we are: Writing in the Amish Community. In D. Barton and R. Ivanič (eds) *Writing in the Community*. Newbury Park: Sage.

Hamilton, M. (1987) *Literacy, Numeracy and Adults*. London: Adult Literacy and Basic Skills Unit.

Heath, S.B. (1983) *Ways with Words*. Cambridge: Cambridge University Press.

Horsman, J. (1987) *Something in my Mind Besides the Everyday: Illiteracy in the Context of Women's Lives in Nova Scotia*. Unpublished doctoral dissertation, University of Toronto.

Klassen, C. (1991) Bilingual written language use by low-education Latin American Newcomers. In D. Barton and R. Ivanič (eds) *Writing in the Community*. Newbury Park: Sage.

Langer, J.A. (ed.) (1987) *Language, Literacy and Culture*. Norwood, NJ: Ablex.

Levine, K. (1985) *The Social Context of Literacy*. London: Routledge & Kegan Paul.

Moll, L. (1989) *Creating Zones of Learning; An Ethnographic Approach*. Paper presented at the EARLI Conference, Madrid.

Reder, S.M. (1985) *Giving Literacy Away*. Unpublished manuscript.

Rockhill, K. (1987) Literacy as threat/desire: Longing to be somebody. In J.S. Gaskill and A.T. McLaren (eds) *Women and Education: A Canadian Perspective*. Calgary: Detselig.

Scribner, S. and Cole, M. (1981) *The Psychology of Literacy*. Cambridge, MA: Harvard University Press.

Street, B. (1984) *Literacy in Theory and Practice*. Cambridge: Cambridge University Press.

Schieffelin, B. and Gilmore, P. (eds) (1986) *The Acquisition of Literacy: Ethnographic Perspectives*. Norwood, NJ: Ablex.

Stotsky, S. (1987) Writing in a political context. *Written Communication* 4, 394–410.

Taylor, D. (1985) *Family Literacy*. London: Heinemann.

Taylor, D. and Dorsey-Gaines, C. (1988) *Growing up Literate*. London: Heinemann.

Index